TOWN AND COUNTRY PLANNING IN ENGLAND AND WALES

The British Town and Country Planning machine is the most sophisticated in the world, yet its inadequacies are only too apparent to those who are familiar with its evolution and operation. During the last decade it has been in a constant state of change in an attempt to come to terms with the needs of a rapidly changing society.

This work attempts to provide a comprehensive picture of the planning system and the ways in which it is changing. An historical introduction leads into an account of the machinery of planning and the major new provisions of the 1968 Town and Country Planning Act. Special attention is then paid to the problems of land values, amenity, derelict land, planning for leisure, new and expanding towns, urban renewal and the search for an adequate means of regional planning. The book ends with an examination of some of the fundamental problems of public acceptance of, and public participation in, a democratic system of planning.

The book is aimed at the student *and* the general reader. It is not a legal text, but neither is it intended as a polemic.

J. B. CULLINGWORTH is widely known as a specialist in town planning and housing, and has published numerous books and articles in this field. He is Professor of Urban and Regional Studies and Director of the Centre for Urban and Regional Studies at the University of Birmingham.

The New Town and County Hall Series
No. 8

TOWN AND COUNTRY PLANNING IN ENGLAND AND WALES

The Changing Scene

By the same author

HOUSING AND LOCAL GOVERNMENT

in this series

HOUSING IN TRANSITION

Heinemann

HOUSING NEEDS AND PLANNING POLICY

Routledge

ENGLISH HOUSING TRENDS

Bell

A PROFILE OF GLASGOW HOUSING

Oliver & Boyd

HOUSING AND LABOUR MOBILITY

O.E.C.D.

With Valerie A. Karn

THE OWNERSHIP AND MANAGEMENT OF HOUSING IN THE NEW TOWNS

H.M.S.O.

With S. C. Orr

REGIONAL AND URBAN STUDIES

Allen & Unwin

TOWN AND COUNTRY PLANNING IN ENGLAND AND WALES

The Changing Scene

BY

J. B. CULLINGWORTH

Professor of Urban and Regional Studies
University of Birmingham

COMPLETELY REVISED
THIRD EDITION

UNIVERSITY OF TORONTO PRESS

FIRST PUBLISHED 1964
REVISED SECOND EDITION 1967
REVISED THIRD EDITION 1971
REPRINTED IN PAPERBACK 2015

PUBLISHED IN CANADA AND THE UNITED STATES
BY UNIVERSITY OF TORONTO PRESS
TORONTO AND BUFFALO 1971

ISBN 978-0-8020-1742-0 (cloth)
ISBN 978-1-4426-3960-7 (paper)
ISBN (microfiche) 0-8020-0060-6

'Planning policies depend more on political than on technical objectives; and they are always in a state of evolution. Planning is essentially a service rather than a science in its own right'.

BARONESS SHARP, former Permanent Secretary to the Ministry of Housing and Local Government*

* E. Sharp, *The Ministry of Housing and Local Government* Allen & Unwin, 1969

PREFACE

The main object of this book is to provide an outline of town and country planning and the problems with which it is faced. It attempts to strike a balance between a legal and administrative text on the one hand and a polemic on the other. The discussion is largely restricted to England and Wales, since not only are Scottish problems too large to discuss adequately within the space available, but the Scottish legal and governmental system differs significantly from that south of the Border. Within this logical self-imposed limitation there has had to be a less justifiable process of selection. Town and country planning can be regarded as covering major issues of social and economic policy – and increasingly is doing so in practice. Indeed we are now witnessing the first fumblings towards a fusion of social, economic and physical planning. It is not possible to cover the whole of this virtually indefinable territory within the covers of a modest book. Instead, there is a general discussion of the framework of planning, together with an extensive account of particular aspects which have been largely ignored in previous works. This unbalanced treatment seems justified. There is, for instance, a wealth of material on traffic planning and on new towns. Inadequate in many ways though this may be, it is far greater in volume than the writings on planning for leisure, amenity and the public acceptability of planning – all of which receive extensive treatment in this book.

Major changes have been made to a number of chapters since the 1967 edition. Only the historical sections remain intact. For the rest there has had to be an even greater selectivity, amounting at places to arbitrariness. The field has become increasingly complex and the spate of plans, studies and 'strategies' makes the chronicler's task an unenviable one. Some issues have now changed so much in character that a simple revision has been out of the question. 'Restraining urban growth' (the title of a chapter in the earlier editions) has been completely omitted. The phrase now has a quaint ring, but it is too early to provide a full account of what is replacing it. A partial attempt has been made in the largely rewritten chapter on regional planning, but a sure foothold is impossible in this quicksand of change. It was so much easier when 'planning' was concerned with the determination of land uses, but the tempo of change and the move towards adaptive and flexible policies is now rapid. Planners are increasingly talking of the unpredictability of change. Studies still pour out replete with masses of statistics, but the attempt to achieve precision is now seen as forlorn and misplaced (compare for instance the successive reduction in precision in official reports on the South-East).

Administrative changes are now proceeding at a rate simulating those of social and economic trends. Regional Economic Planning Councils and Boards, the Land Commission, the Countryside Commission, Passenger Transport Authorities, the Water Resources Board – these and a host of others (not to mention the total reorganization of local government which is under way), are recasting the machinery of government. And more are in the wind.

Where does one draw the boundaries for a book entitled *Town and Country Planning*?

This is not intended as an apologia or as a means of attempting to disarm the critics, but as a warning to the reader that this book (even more now than in earlier editions) has only a modest aim: to provide a sketch of some of the major issues, policies and administrative devices of an abstraction called 'town and country planning'.

Chapter I provides a background account of the evolution of town and country planning, the inadequacies of the embryonic instruments of the inter-war years, and the now nearly forgotten enthusiasm and confidence of the architects of post-war planning. Chapter II describes how this idealism battled against the facts of administrative and political life: a battle which is still unresolved – if it ever can be. Chapters III to V give an account of the structure of the planning machine and the general powers at its disposal. This is followed by a discussion of the most difficult – and crucial – of planning issues, that of land values. Chapter VII attempts to provide some guide to the question of amenity: a concept which the legislative draughtsmen wisely have not defined. This leads into a short discussion in Chapter VIII of derelict land and mineral workings.

In previous editions the length of Chapter IX was justified on the grounds that planning for leisure was 'a much neglected subject which unfortunately attracts little political controversy and correspondingly little action'. Much has happened – on paper at least – since that comment was written, and recent thinking, reports and legislation now figure significantly in the revised chapter.

Chapter X briefly discusses the new and expanding towns. These must be included in any book on British planning, but they have been more exhaustively treated elsewhere. The discussion of urban renewal in Chapter XI is limited to four aspects: housing, comprehensive redevelopment, planning for traffic, and clean air. In Chapter XII the trend towards regional planning is briefly analysed. The final chapter discusses the relationship between the planners and the planned in a democratic society. Again, the earlier comment that this is a neglected subject has to be revised. The 1968 Planning Act represents an extraordinarily brave attempt to democratize the planning system, with what success it is too early to even guess. The author's harsh treatment of the Skeffington Report is intended to highlight the essentially political issues which the new planning philosophy will bring to the fore.

This is the third edition of a book originally written in 1964. The second edition referred to the turmoil of change and ruefully commented that a major revision would have to await the emergence of a more settled and clearer situation. The hope for quieter times was forlorn, not to say inappropriate. Writing a book on planning is like painting the Forth Bridge: by the time the end is reached it is necessary to start again at the beginning! An attempt has been made to incorporate the changes being gradually introduced by the 1968 Planning Act, but the picture is inevitably out of focus since the 'new' system is operating side by side with the 'old' one.

At the last moment an appendix had to be written to Chapter III to incorporate the October 1969 changes in the machinery of government. As is said in that appendix, though the structure of local government is painfully slow to change, the machinery of central government can alter at a rate which defeats the chronicler who attempts to provide an up-to-date picture. Indeed, one government department – the Ministry of Land and Natural Resources – was so short-lived (April 1965 to February 1967) that it failed to gain a mention in any edition of this book. The Department of Economic Affairs (October 1964 to October 1969) was established in time to receive an appendix note in the second edition, and was abolished just too late to be deleted from the current edition.

Grateful acknowledgement is made to the many people, mostly within the planning profession, who have assisted in various ways in the writing of this book. Though anonymity must be preserved in accordance with convention, my debt is great – and, to the discerning, obvious. Thanks are due to the Controller of HM Stationery Office for permission to quote extensively from official publications. My largest debt, as always, is to my wife who has borne a large part of the social cost of this composition.

J. B. CULLINGWORTH

Centre for Urban and Regional Studies
University of Birmingham
October 1969

CONTENTS

TABLES

Chapter I

THE EVOLUTION OF TOWN AND COUNTRY PLANNING

THE PUBLIC HEALTH ORIGINS

Town and Country Planning as a task of government has developed from public health and housing policies. The nineteenth-century increase in population and, even more significant, the growth of towns led to public health problems which demanded a new role for government. Together with the growth of medical knowledge, the realization that overcrowded insanitary urban areas resulted in an economic cost (which had to be borne at least in part by the local ratepayers) and the fear of social unrest, this new urban growth eventually resulted in an appreciation of the necessity for interfering with market forces and private property rights in the interests of social well-being. The nineteenth-century Public Health legislation was directed at the creation of adequate sanitary conditions. Among the measures taken to achieve these were powers for Local Authorities to make and enforce building by-laws for controlling street widths and the height, structure and layout of buildings. Limited and defective though these powers proved to be, they represented a marked advance in social control and paved the way for more imaginative measures. The physical impact of by-law control on British towns is depressingly still very much in evidence; and it did not escape the attention of contemporary social reformers.

'. . . much good work has been done. In the ample supply of pure water, in the drainage and removal of waste matter, in the paving, lighting and cleansing of streets, and in many other such ways, probably our towns are as well served as, or even better than, those elsewhere. Moreover, by means of our much abused building bye-laws, the worst excesses of overcrowding have been restrained; a certain minimum standard of air-space, light and ventilation has been secured; while in the more modern parts of towns a fairly high degree of sanitation, of immunity from fire, and general stability of construction have been maintained, the importance of which can hardly be exaggerated. We have, indeed, in all these matters laid a good foundation and have secured many of the necessary elements for a healthy condition of life; and yet the remarkable fact remains that there are growing up around our big towns vast districts, under these very bye-laws, which for dreariness and sheer ugliness it is difficult to match anywhere, and compared with which many of the old unhealthy slums are, from the point of view of picturesqueness and beauty, infinitely more attractive'.[27]

It was on this point that public health and architecture met. The enlightened experiments at Saltaire (1853), Bournville (1878), Port Sunlight (1887) and elsewhere had provided object lessons. Ebenezer Howard and the Garden City Movement were now exerting considerable influence on contemporary thought. The National Housing Reform Council (later the National Housing and Town Planning Council) were campaigning for the introduction of town planning. Even more significant was a similar demand from local government and professional associations such as the Association of Municipal Corporations, the Royal Institute of British Architects, the Surveyors' Institute, and the Association of Municipal and County Engineers. As Ashworth has pointed out,[3] 'the support of many of these bodies was particularly important because it showed that the demand for town planning was arising not simply out of theoretical preoccupations but out of the everyday practical experience of local administration. The demand was coming in part from those who would be responsible for the execution of town planning if it were introduced.'

THE FIRST PLANNING ACT

The movement for the extension of sanitary policy into town planning was uniting diverse interests. These were nicely summarized by John Burns, the President of the Local Government Board, when he introduced the first legislation bearing the term 'town planning' – the Housing, Town Planning, Etc., Act, 1909:

'The object of the Bill is to provide a domestic condition for the people in which their physical health, their morals, their character and their whole social condition can be improved by what we hope to secure in this Bill. The Bill aims in broad outline at, and hopes to secure, the home healthy, the house beautiful, the town pleasant, the city dignified and the suburb salubrious.'[16]

The new powers provided by the Act were for the preparation of 'schemes' by local authorities for controlling the development of new housing areas. Though novel, these powers were logically a simple extension of existing ones. It is significant that this first legislative acceptance of town planning came in an Act dealing with health and housing. And, as Ashworth has pointed out, the gradual development and the accumulated experience of public health and housing measures facilitated a general acceptance of the principle of town planning. 'Housing reform had gradually been conceived in terms of larger and larger units. Torrens' Act (Artizans and Labourers Dwellings Act, 1868) had made a beginning with individual houses; Cross's Act (Artizans and Labourers Dwellings Improvement Act, 1875) had introduced an element of town planning by concerning itself with the reconstruction of insanitary areas; the framing of bye-laws in accordance with the Public Health Act of 1875 had accustomed local authorities to the imposition of at least a minimum of regulation on new building, and such a measure as the London Building Act of 1894 brought into the scope of public control the formation and widening of streets, the lines of building frontage, the extent of open space around buildings, and the height of buildings. Town planning was therefore not altogether a leap in the dark, but could be represented as a logical extension, in accordance with changing aims and conditions, of earlier legislation concerned with housing and public health.'[3] The 'changing conditions' were predominantly the rapid growth of suburban development – a factor which increased in importance in the following decades.

'In fifteen years 500,000 acres of land have been abstracted from the agricultural domain for houses, factories, workshops and railways. . . . If we go in the next fifteen years abstracting another half a million from the agricultural domain, and we go on rearing in green fields slums, in many respects, considering their situation, more squalid than those which are found in Liverpool, London and Glasgow, posterity will blame us for not taking this matter in hand in a scientific spirit. Every two and a half years there is a County of London converted into urban life from rural conditions and agricultural land. It represents an enormous amount of building land which we have no right to allow to go unregulated.'[16]

The emphasis was entirely on raising the standards of *new* development. The Act permitted local authorities (after obtaining the permission of the Local Government Board) to prepare town planning schemes with the general object of 'securing proper sanitary conditions, amenity and convenience', but only for land which was being developed or appeared likely to be developed.

Strangely it was not at all clear what town planning involved. It certainly did not include 'the remodelling of the existing town, the replanning of badly planned areas, the driving of new roads through old parts of a town – all these are beyond the scope of the new town planning powers'.[2] The Act itself provided no definition: indeed, it merely listed nineteen 'matters to be dealt with by General Provisions Prescribed by the Local Government Board'. The restricted and vague nature of this first legislation was associated in part with the lack of experience of the problems involved: Nettleford even went so far as to suggest that 'when this Act was passed, it was recognized as only a trial trip for the purpose of finding out the weak spots in local government with regard to town and estate development so that effective remedies might be later on devised'.[15]

Nevertheless the cumbersome administrative procedure devised by the Local Government Board – in order to give all interested parties 'full opportunity of considering the proposals at all stages' – might well have been intended to deter all but the most ardent of local authorities. The land taxes threatened by the 1910 Finance Act, and then the First World War added to the difficulties. It can be the occasion of no surprise that very few schemes were actually completed under the 1909 Act.

INTER-WAR LEGISLATION

The first revision of town planning legislation which took place after the first world war (the Housing and Town Planning Act of 1919) did little in practice to broaden the basis of town planning. The preparation of schemes was made obligatory on all Borough and Urban Districts having a population of 20,000 or more, but the time limit (January 1, 1926) was first extended (by the Housing Act, 1923) and finally abolished (by the Town and Country Planning Act, 1932). Some of the procedural difficulties were removed, but no change in concept appeared. Despite lip-service to the idea of town planning, the major advances made at this time were in the field of housing rather than in planning. It was the 1919 Act which began what Marion Bowley has called 'the series of experiments in State intervention to increase the supply of working-class houses'.[6] The 1919 Act accepted the principle of State subsidies for housing and thus began the nation-wide growth of council house estates. Equally significant was the entirely new standard of working-class housing provided: the three-bedroom house with kitchen, bath and garden, built at the density recommended by the Tudor Walters Report[26] of not more than twelve houses to the acre. At these new standards development could generally take place only on virgin land on the periphery of towns, and municipal estates grew alongside the private suburbs – 'the basic social products of the twentieth century', as Asa Briggs has termed them.[7]

This suburbanization was greatly accelerated by rapid developments in transportation – developments with which the young planning machine could not keep pace. The ideas of Howard and the Garden City Movement, of Geddes and of those who, like Warren and Davidge, saw town planning not just as a technique for controlling the layout and design of residential areas, but as part of a policy of national economic and social planning, were receiving increasing attention, but in practice town planning often meant little more than an extension of the old public health and housing controls.

Various attempts were made to deal with the increasing difficulties. Of particular significance were the Town and Country Planning Act of 1932, which extended planning powers to almost any type of land, whether built-up or undeveloped, and the Restriction of Ribbon Development Act, 1935, which, as its name suggests, was designed to control the spread of development along major roads. But these and similar measures were inadequate. For instance, under the 1932 Act planning schemes took about three years to prepare and pass through all their stages. Final approval had to be given by Parliament and schemes then had the force of law – as a result of which variations or amendments were not possible except by a repetition of the whole procedure. 'Interim development control' operated during the time between the passing of a resolution to prepare a scheme and its date of operation (as approved by Parliament). This enabled – but did not require – developers to apply for planning permission. If they did not obtain planning permission and the development was not in conformity with the scheme when approved the planning authority could require the owner (without compensation) to remove or alter the development. But all too often developers preferred to take a chance that no scheme would ever come into force, or that if it did no local authority would face pulling down existing buildings. The damage was therefore done before the planning authorities had a chance to intervene. Once a planning scheme was approved, on the other hand, the local authority ceased to have any planning control over individual developments. The scheme was in fact a zoning plan: land was zoned for particular uses – residential, industrial and so on – though provision could be made for limiting the number of buildings, the space around them, etc. In fact, so long as the developer did not try to introduce a non-conforming use he was fairly safe. Furthermore, most schemes in fact did little more than accept and ratify existing trends of development, since any attempt at a more radical solution would have involved the planning authority in compensation they could not afford to pay. In most cases the zones were so widely drawn as to place hardly more restriction on the developer than if there had been no scheme at all. Indeed in the half of the country covered by draft planning schemes in 1937 there was sufficient land zoned for housing to accommodate 350 million people.

ADMINISTRATIVE SHORTCOMINGS

A major weakness was, of course, the administrative structure itself. At the local level the administrative unit outside the county boroughs was the district council. Such authorities were generally small and weak. This was implicitly recognized as early as 1919, for the Act of that year permitted the establishment of joint planning committees. The 1929 Local Government Act went further, by empowering county councils to take part in planning, either by becoming constituent members of joint planning committees or by undertaking powers relinquished by district councils. A number of regional advisory plans were prepared, but these were generally ineffective and, indeed, conceived as little more than a series of suggestions for controlling future development, together with proposals for new main roads. The noteworthy characteristic of a planning scheme was its regulatory nature. It did not secure that development would take place: it merely secured that if it did take place in any particular part of the area covered by the scheme it would be controlled in certain ways. Furthermore, as the Uthwatt Report stressed, the system was 'essentially one of local planning, based on the initiative and financial resources of local bodies (whether individual local authorities or combinations of such authorities) responsible to local electorates. . . . The local authorities naturally consider questions of planning and development largely with a view to the effect they will have on the authorities' own finances and trade of the district. Proposals by landowners involving the further development of an existing urban area are not likely in practice to be refused by a local authority if the only reason against the development taking place is that from the national standpoint its proper location is elsewhere, particularly when it is remembered that the prevention of any such development might not only involve the authority in liability to pay heavy compensation but would, in addition, deprive them of substantial increases in rate income.'

The central authority – the Ministry of Health – had no effective powers of initiation and no power to grant financial assistance to local authorities. Indeed its powers were essentially regulatory and seemed to be designed to cast it in the role of a quasi-judicial body to be chiefly concerned with ensuring that local authorities did not treat property owners unfairly.

The difficulties were not, however, solely administrative. Even the most progressive authority was greatly handicapped by the inadequacies of the law relating to compensation. The compensation paid either for planning restrictions or for compulsory acquisition had to be determined in relation to the most profitable use of the land, even if it was unlikely that the land would be so developed, and without regard to the fact that the prohibition of development on one site usually resulted in the development value (which had been purchased at high cost) shifting to another site. Consequently in the words of the Uthwatt Committee, 'an examination of the Town Planning maps of some of our most important built-up areas reveals that in many cases they are little more than photographs of existing users and existing lay-outs, which, to avoid the necessity of paying compensation, become perpetuated by incorporation in a statutory scheme irrespective of their suitability or desirability'.

These problems increased as the housing boom of the 'thirties developed. 2,700,000 houses were built in England and Wales between 1930 and 1940. At the outbreak of war one-third of all the houses in England and Wales had been built since 1918. The implications for urbanization were obvious, particularly in the London area. Between 1919 and 1939 the population of Greater London rose by about ¾ million on account of natural increase but by over 1¼ million by migration.[1] This growth of the metropolis was a force which existing powers were incapable of halting, despite the large body of opinion favouring some degree of control.

THE DEPRESSED AREAS

The crux of the matter was that the problem of London was closely allied to that of the declining areas of the North and of South Wales – and both were part of the much wider problem of industrial location. In the South-East the insured employed population rose by 44 per cent between 1923 and 1934, but in the North-East it fell by 5½ per cent and in Wales by 26 per cent. In 1934 8·6 per cent of insured workers in Greater London were unemployed, but in Workington the proportion was 36·3 per cent, in Gateshead 44·2 per cent and in Jarrow 67·8 per cent. In the early stages of political action these two problems were divorced. For London various advisory committees were set up and a series of reports issued – the Royal Commission on the Local Government of Greater London (1921–3); the London and Home Counties Traffic Advisory Committee (1924); the Greater London Regional Planning Committee (1927); the Standing Conference on London Regional Planning (1937); as well as *ad hoc* committees and inquiries, e.g. on Greater

London Drainage (1935) and a Highway Development Plan (the Bressey Report, 1938). For the depressed areas attention was first concentrated on encouraging migration, on training schemes and on schemes for establishing the unemployed in smallholdings. Increasing unemployment accompanied by rising public concern (especially after hunger marches on the one hand and articles in *The Times* on the other)[23] necessitated further action. Government 'investigators' were appointed and, following their reports,[19] the Depressed Areas Bill was introduced in November 1934 – to pass (after the Lords had amended the title) as the Special Areas Act. Under the Act a Special Commissioner for England and Wales (and one for Scotland) was appointed, with very wide powers for 'the initiation, organization, prosecution and assistance of measures designed to facilitate the economic development and social improvement' of the Special Areas. The Areas were defined in the Act and included the North-East Coast, West Cumberland, industrial South Wales – and, in Scotland, the industrial area around Glasgow. By September 1938, the Commissioners had spent, or approved the spending of, nearly £21 million, of which £15 million was for the improvement of public and social services, £3 million for smallholdings and allotment schemes, and £½ million on amenity schemes such as the clearance of derelict sites. Physical and social amelioration, however, was intended to be complementary to the Commissioner's main task: the attraction of new industry. Appeals to industrialists proved inadequate; in his second report, Sir Malcolm Stewart, the Commissioner for England and Wales, concluded 'there is little prospect of the Special Areas being assisted by the spontaneous action of industrialists now located outside these Areas'. On the other hand the attempt to actively attract new industry by the development of trading estates achieved considerable success, which at least warranted the comment of the Scottish Commissioner that there had been 'sufficient progress to dispel the fallacy that the Areas are incapable of expanding their light industries'. Nevertheless there were still 300,000 unemployed in the Special Areas at the end of 1938, and though 123 factories had been opened between 1937 and 1938 in the Special Areas, 372 had been opened in the London area. Sir Malcolm Stewart concluded, in his third annual report, that 'the further expansion of industry should be controlled to secure a more evenly distributed production'. Such thinking might have been in harmony with the current increasing recognition of the need for national planning, but it called for political action of a character which would have been sensational. Furthermore, as Neville Chamberlain (then Chancellor of the Exchequer) pointed out, even if new factories were excluded from London it did not follow that they would forthwith spring up in South Wales or West Cumberland. The immediate answer of the Government was to appoint the Barlow Commission.

THE BARLOW REPORT

The Barlow Report is of significance not merely because it is an important historical landmark, but also because some of its major policy recommendations have been accepted by all post-war governments as a basis for planning policy. Only recently have these policies been questioned.

The terms of reference of the Commission were 'to inquire into the causes which have influenced the present geographical distribution of the industrial population of Great Britain and the probable direction of any change in that distribution in the future; to consider what social, economic or strategic disadvantages arise from the concentration of industries or of the industrial population in large towns or in particular areas of the country; and to report what remedial measures if any should be taken in the national interest.'

These very wide terms of reference represented, as the Commission pointed out, 'an important step forward' in contemporary thinking. Reviewing the history of town planning they noted that:

'Legislation has not yet proceeded so far as to deal with the problem of planning from a *national* standpoint; there is no duty imposed on any authority or Government Department to view the country as a whole and to consider the problems of industrial, commercial and urban growth in the light of the needs of the entire population. The appointment, therefore, of the present Commission marks an important step forward. The evils attendant on haphazard and ill-regulated town growth were first brought under observation; then similar dangers when prevalent over wider areas or regions; now the investigation is extended to Great Britain as a whole. The Causes, Probable Direction of Change and Disadvantages mentioned in the Terms of Reference are clearly not concerned with separate localities or local authorities, but with England, Scotland and Wales collectively: and the Remedial Measures to be considered are expressly required to be in the national interest.'

After reviewing the evidence, the Commission concluded that 'the disadvantages in many, if not in most of the great industrial concentrations, alike on the strategical, the social and the economic side, do constitute serious handicaps and even in some respects dangers to the nation's life and development, and we are of opinion that definite action should be taken by the Government towards remedying them'. The advantages of concentration were clear – proximity to market, reduction of transport costs and availability of a supply of suitable labour. But these, in the Commission's view, were accompanied by serious disadvantages such as heavy charges on account mainly of high site values, loss of time through street traffic congestion, and the risk of adverse effects on efficiency due to long and fatiguing journeys to work. The Commission maintained that the development of garden cities, satellite towns and trading estates could make a useful contribution towards the solution of this problem of urban congestion.

The London area, of course, presented the largest problem, not simply because of its huge size, but also because 'the trend of migration to London and the Home Counties is on so large a scale and of so serious a character that it can hardly fail to increase in the future the disadvantages already shown to exist'. The problems of London were thus in part related to the problems of the Depressed Areas:

'It is not in the national interest, economically, socially or strategically, that a quarter, or even a larger, proportion of the population of Great Britain should be concentrated within 20 to 30 miles or so of Central London. On the other hand, a policy:

(i) of balanced distribution of industry and the industrial population so far as possible throughout the different areas or regions in Great Britain;
(ii) of appropriate diversification of industries in those areas or regions;

would tend to make the best national use of the resources of the country, and at the same time would go far to secure for each region or area, through diversification of industry and variety of employment, some safeguard against severe and persistent depression, such as attacks an area dependent mainly on one industry when that industry is struck by bad times.'

Such policies could not be carried out by the existing administrative machinery: it was no part of statutory planning to check or to encourage a local or regional growth of population. Planning was essentially on a local basis; it did not, and was not intended to, influence the geographical distribution of the population as between one locality and another. The Commission unanimously agreed that the problems were national in character and required a central authority to deal with them. They argued that the activities of this authority ought to be distinct from and extend beyond those of any existing Government Department. It should be responsible for formulating a plan for dispersal from congested urban areas – determining in which areas dispersal was desirable; whether and where dispersal could be effected by developing garden cities or garden suburbs, satellite towns, trading estates or the expansion of existing small towns or regional centres. It should be given the right to inspect town-planning schemes and 'to consider, where necessary, in co-operation with the Government Departments concerned, the modification or correlation of existing or future plans in the national interest'. It should study the location of industry throughout the country with a view to anticipating cases where depression might probably occur in the future and encouraging industrial or public development before a depression actually occurred.

But though the Commission were agreed on the 'objectives of national action' and on the necessity for a central authority, they were not agreed on the powers to be given to this authority. The majority recommended that it should be a National Industrial Board consisting of a chairman and three other members appointed by the President of the Board of Trade after consultation with the Ministers of Health, Labour and Transport, and the Secretary of State for Scotland. This Board should have research, advisory and publicity functions, but also (in view of the necessity for immediate action in the London area) executive powers to regulate additional industrial building in London and the Home Counties. These 'negative powers' should be extendable by Order in Council to other areas. Finally the Board should be required to decide what additional powers it needed to carry out its functions.

Three members of the Commission (Professor J. H. Jones, Mr George W. Thomson and Sir William E. Whyte), though signing the majority report, prepared a 'Note of Reservations'. They argued that the control of industrial development in the London area was an inadequate measure to achieve the 'objectives of national action'. Such controls needed to be operated over the whole country. Furthermore, they believed that it was even more important for the Government 'to create more favourable conditions of life and work in other parts of the country and thereby weaken the inducement to seek work in or near London'. In their view the powers of the Commissioners for the Special Areas should be largely transferred to the new Board which would be given powers to enable them to offer such inducements as they thought necessary to make effective the policy of securing a better balance and a greater diversification of industry throughout the country. Regional administration was essential, and a series of Divisional Boards should be set up as an integral part of the new Authority.

A minority of the Commission (Professor Patrick Abercrombie, Mr H. H. Elvin and Mrs H. Hichens) felt unable to put their signatures to the main recommendations. They went even further in their criticisms of the inadequacy of these than the three members who signed the Note of Reservations. In their view the problems were of immediate urgency, particularly since an unprecedented amount of new factory building was under way in connection with the rearmament programme. They felt that the Majority Report seemed to imply that there was ample time for preparation and research, whereas in fact the problem was an immediate one. The urgency of the situation demanded the setting up of a powerful body with executive powers. The Board proposed by the Majority was not strong enough: what was required was a new Ministry exercising full executive powers. This Ministry would 'need to be fitted into the scheme of central and local government if it is to function properly'. It would obviously have to take over the planning functions of the Ministry of Health (and possibly some of its housing functions), as well as some of the planning powers of the Ministry of Transport. The work of the Commissioners for the Special Areas should be transferred to it – and at the same time extended to the whole country.

The differences between the three sets of recommendations were less striking than their unanimous condemnation of the existing situation and the inadequacy of both policy and machinery for dealing with it. All were agreed that a far more positive role for government was required, that control should be exercised over new factory building at least in London and the Home Counties, that dispersal from the larger urban concentrations was desirable, and that measures should be taken to anticipate regional economic depression. The differences centred largely on how such policies should be translated into terms of administrative machinery.

THE IMPACT OF WAR

The Barlow Report was published in January 1940 – some four months after the start of the Second World War. The problem which precipitated the decision to set up the Barlow Commission – that of the Depressed Areas – rapidly disappeared. The unemployed of the Depressed Areas now became a powerful national asset. A considerable share of the new factories built to provide munitions or to replace bombed factories were located in these areas. By the end of 1940 'an extraordinary scramble for factory space had developed'; and out of all this 'grew a war-time, an extempore, location of industry policy covering the country as a whole'.[13] This emergency war-time policy – paralleled in other fields, such as hospitals – not only provided some 13 million square feet of munitions factory space in the Depressed Areas which could be adapted for civilian industry after the end of the war; it also provided experience in dispersing industry and in controlling industrial location which showed the practicability (under war-time conditions at least) of such policies. The Board of Trade became a central clearing-house of information on industrial sites:

'We have collected a great deal of information regarding the relative advantages of different sites in different parts of the country, and of the facilities available there with regard to local labour supply, housing accommodation, transport facilities, electricity, gas, water, drainage and so on . . . we are now able to offer to industrialists a service of information regarding location which has never been available before.'[17]

Hence, though the Barlow Report (to use a phrase of Dame Alix Meynell) 'lay inanimate in the iron lung of war', it seemed that the conditions for the acceptance of its views on the control of industrial location were becoming very propitious: there is nothing better than successful experience for demonstrating the practicability of a policy.

The war thus provided a great stimulus to the extension of town and country planning into the sphere of industrial location. And this was not the only stimulus it provided. The destruction wrought by bombing transformed 'the rebuilding of Britain' from a socially desirable but somewhat visionary and vague ideal into a matter of practical and defined necessity. Nor was this all: the very fact that rebuilding was clearly going to take place on a large scale provided an unprecedented opportunity for comprehensive planning of the bombed areas and a stimulus to overall town planning. In Exeter: 'to rebuild the city in the old lines . . . would be a dreadful mistake. It would be an exact repetition of what happened in the rebuilding of London after the Fire – and the results, in regret at lost opportunity, will be the same. While, therefore, the arrangements for rebuilding to the new plan should proceed with all possible speed, some patience and discipline will be necessary if the new-built city is to be a city that is really renewed.'[22] In Hull: 'there is now both the opportunity and the necessity for an overhaul of the urban structure before undertaking this second refounding of the great Port on the Humber. Due consideration, however urgent the desire to get back to working conditions, must be given to every aspect of town existence.'[12] The note was one of optimism of being able to tackle problems which were of long standing. In the Metropolis: 'London was ripe for reconstruction before the war; obsolescence, bad and unsuitable housing, inchoate communities, uncorrelated road systems, industrial congestion, a low level of urban design, inequality in the distribution of open spaces, increasing congestion of dismal journeys to work – all these and more clamoured for improvement before the enemy's efforts to smash us by air attack stiffened our resistance and intensified our zeal for reconstruction.'[9]

This was the social climate of the war and early post-war years. There was an enthusiasm and a determination to undertake social reconstruction on a scale hitherto considered utopian. The catalyst was, of course, the war itself. At one and the same time war occasions a mass support for the way of life which is being fought for and a critical appraisal of the inadequacies of that way of life. Modern total warfare demands the unification of national effort and a breaking down of social barriers and differences. It 'presupposes and imposes a great increase in social discipline; moreover, this discipline is only tolerable if – and only if – social inequalities are not intolerable'.[25] On no occasion was this more true than in the Second World War. A new and better Britain was to be built. The feeling was one of intense optimism and confidence. Not only would the war be won: it would be followed by a similar campaign against the forces of want. That there was much that was inadequate, even intolerable, in pre-war Britain had been generally accepted. What was new was the belief that the problems could be tackled in the same way as a military operation. What supreme confidence was evidenced by the setting up in 1941 of committees to consider post-war reconstruction problems – the Uthwatt Committee on Compensation and Betterment, the Scott Committee on Land Utilization in Rural Areas, and the Beveridge Committee on Social Insurance and Allied Services. Perhaps it was Beveridge who most clearly summed up the spirit of the time – and the philosophy which was to underlie post-war social policy:

'The Plan for Social Security is put forward as part of a general programme of social policy. It is one part only of an attack upon five great evils: upon the physical Want with which it is directly concerned, upon Disease which often causes Want and brings many other troubles in its train, upon Ignorance which no democracy can afford among its citizens, upon the Squalor which arises mainly through haphazard distribution of industry and population, and upon Idleness which destroys wealth and corrupts men, whether they are well fed or not, when they are idle. In seeking security not merely against physical want, but against all these evils in all their forms, and in showing that security can be combined with freedom and enterprise and responsibility of the individual for his own life, the British community and those who in other lands have inherited the British tradition, have a vital service to render to human progress.'[5]

It was within this framework of a newly acquired confidence to tackle long-standing social and economic problems that post-war town and country planning policy was conceived. No longer was this to be restricted to town planning 'schemes' or regulatory measures. There was now the same breadth in official thinking as had permeated the Barlow Report. The attack on Squalor was conceived as part of a comprehensive series of plans for social amelioration. To quote the 1944 White Paper *The Control of Land Use*:

'Provision for the right use of land, in accordance with a considered policy, is an essential requirement of the Government's programme of post-war reconstruction. New houses, whether of permanent or emergency construction; the new layout of areas devastated by enemy action or blighted by reason of age or bad living conditions; the new schools which will be required under the Education Bill now before Parliament; the balanced distribution of industry which the Government's recently published proposals for maintaining active employment envisage; the requirements of sound nutrition and of a healthy and well-balanced agriculture; the preservation of land for national parks and forests, and the assurance to the people of enjoyment of the sea and countryside in times of leisure; a new and safer highway system better adapted to modern industrial and other needs; the proper provision of airfields – all these related parts of a single reconstruction programme involve the use of land, and it is essential that their various claims on land should be so harmonized as to ensure for the people of this country the greatest possible measure of individual well-being and national prosperity.'

THE NEW PLANNING MACHINERY

This broad historical approach must now give way to a series of discussions on particular issues – administration, planning powers and policies, the problem of land values, and so on. Before embarking upon this, however, it is useful to provide a brief outline of the new planning machinery. This will provide a general background which will be detailed and brought up to date in later chapters.

The pre-war machinery of planning was defective in several ways. It was optional on local authorities; planning powers were essentially regulatory and restrictive; such planning as was achieved was purely local in character; the central government had no effective powers of initiative, or of co-ordinating local plans; and the 'compensation bogey' – with which local authorities had to cope without any Exchequer assistance – bedevilled the efforts of all who attempted to make the cumbersome planning machinery work.

By 1942, 73 per cent of the land in England and 36 per cent of the land in Wales had become subject to 'interim development control', but only 5 per cent of England and 1 per cent of Wales was actually subject to operative schemes; and there were several important towns and cities as well as some large country districts for which not even the preliminary stages of a planning scheme had been taken. Administration was highly fragmented and was essentially a matter for the lower tier authorities: in 1944 there were over 1,400 planning authorities. Some attempt to solve the problems to which this gave rise was made by the (voluntary) grouping of planning authorities in joint committees for formulating schemes over wide areas, but, though an improvement, this was not sufficiently effective.

The new conception of town and country planning underlined the inadequacies. It was generally (and perhaps uncritically) accepted that the growth of the large cities should be restricted. Regional plans for London, Lancashire, the Clyde Valley and South Wales all stressed the necessity of large-scale overspill to new and expanded towns. Government pronouncements echoed the enthusiasm which permeated these plans. Large cities were no longer to be allowed to continue their unchecked sprawl over the countryside. The explosive forces generated by the desire for better living and working conditions would no longer run riot. Suburban dormitories were a thing of the past. Overspill would be steered into new and expanded towns which could provide the conditions people wanted – without the disadvantages inherent in satellite suburban development. When the problems of reconstructing blitzed areas, redeveloping blighted areas, securing a 'proper distribution' of industry, developing national parks, and so on, are added to the list, there was a clear need for a new and more positive role for the central government, a transfer of powers from the smaller to the larger local authorities, a considerable extension of these powers and – most difficult of all – a solution to the compensation-betterment problem.

The necessary machinery was provided in the main by the Town and Country Planning Acts, the Distribution of Industry Acts, the National Parks and Access to the Countryside Act, the New Towns Act and the Town Development Act.

The 1947 Town and Country Planning Act brought almost all development under control by making it subject to planning permission. But planning was to be no longer merely a regulative function.

Development plans were to be prepared for every area in the country. These were to outline the way in which each area was to be developed or, where desirable, preserved. In accordance with the wider concepts of planning, powers were transferred from district councils to county councils. The smallest planning units thereby became the counties and the county boroughs. Co-ordination of local plans was to be effected by the new Ministry of Town and Country Planning. Development rights in land and the associated development values were nationalized. All owners were thus placed in the position of owning only the existing (1947) use rights and values in their land. Compensation for development rights was to be paid 'once and for all' out of a national fund, and developers were to pay a 'development charge' amounting to 100 per cent of the increase in the value of land resulting from the development. The 'compensation bogey' was thus at last to be completely abolished: henceforth development would take place according to 'good planning principles'.

Responsibility for securing a 'proper distribution of industry' was given to the Board of Trade. New industrial projects (above a minimum size) would require the Board's certification that the development would be consistent with the proper distribution of industry. More positively, the Board was given powers to attract industries to Development Areas by loans and grants, and by the erection of factories.

New Towns were to be developed by *ad hoc* development corporations financed by the Treasury. Somewhat later (in 1952) new powers were provided for the planned expansion of towns by local authorities. The designation of national parks and 'Areas of Outstanding National Beauty' was entrusted to a new National Parks Commission, and local authorities were given wider powers for securing public access to the countryside. A Nature Conservancy was set up to provide scientific advice on the conservation and control of natural flora and fauna, and to establish and manage nature reserves. New powers were granted for preserving amenity, trees, historic buildings and ancient monuments. Later greater controls were introduced over river and air pollution, litter and noise. Indeed, the flow of legislation has been unceasing.

It would, however, be misleading even in a brief sketch to give an impression of continued progress. Certainly there have been some remarkable achievements (which the social commentator tends to forget in his analysis of shortcomings and needed reforms), but many of the problems for which this wealth of legislation was designed have themselves changed in character and become more difficult. Experience of dealing with industrial location, urban growth, amenity and so on, has shown that they present far greater problems than was originally anticipated. Above all, instead of having to plan for a static or slowly growing population, the planners have had to wrestle with the problem created by an unexpected population increase – one which on current indications will result by the end of the century in a total England and Wales population of 63 million and a Great Britain population of around 70 million.*

* Population projections are published each year in the Registrar Generals' Quarterly Returns. Annual revisions can make a huge difference as is illustrated in the table below.

Base year of projection	*Projected population for England and Wales*			
	Over approx. 20 years		*Over approx. 40 years*	
	Year	*Million*	*Year*	*Million*
1955	1975	46·4	1995	46·3
1958	1978	49·0	1998	52·0
1961	1981	52·1	2001	58·3
1965	1981	54·3	2001	66·4
1966	1981	53·5	2001	64·8
1967	1981	53·0	2001	62·9

These projections demonstrate one of the difficulties of long-term planning.

REFERENCES AND FURTHER READING

1 Abercrombie, P., *Greater London Plan*, HMSO, 1945.
2 Aldridge, H. R., *The Case of Town Planning*, National Housing and Town Planning Council, 1915.
3 Ashworth, W., *The Genesis of Modern British Town Planning*, Routledge, 1954.
4 Barlow Report, *Report of the Royal Commission on the Distribution of the Industrial Population*, Cmd. 6153, HMSO, 1940.
5 Beveridge Report, *Social Insurance and Allied Services*, Cmd. 6404, HMSO, 1942.
6 Bowley, M., *Housing and the State 1919–1944*, Allen & Unwin, 1945.
7 Briggs, A., *History of Birmingham*, Vol. 2, Oxford University Press, 1952.
8 Davison, R. C., *British Unemployment Policy: The Modern Phase Since 1930*, Longmans Green, 1938.
9 Forshaw, J. H. and Abercrombie, P., *County of London Plan*, Macmillan, 1943.
10 Geddes, P., *Cities in Evolution*, London, 1915.
11 Howard, E., *Garden Cities of Tomorrow*, edited by F. J. Osborn, Faber, 1946.
12 Lutyens, E. and Abercrombie, P., *A Plan for Kingston upon Hull*, A. Brown & Sons, 1945.
13 Meynell, A., 'Location of Industry', *Public Administration*, Vol. 37, Spring 1959.
14 Mowat, C. L., *Britain Between the Wars, 1918–1940*, Methuen, 1955.
15 Nettleford, J. S., *Practical Town Planning*, St Catherine Press, London, 1914.
16 Parliamentary Debates on the Housing, Town Planning, Etc. Bill, *H.C. Debates*, Vol. 188, May 1908.
17 Parliamentary Debates on the Distribution of Industry Bill, *H.C. Debates*, Vol. 409, March 1945.
18 Political and Economic Planning, *Location of Industry*, PEP, 1939.
19 *Reports of Investigations into the Industrial Conditions in Certain Depressed Areas*, Cmd. 4728, HMSO, 1934.

20 *Reports of the Commissioner for the Special Areas* (*England and Wales*), HMSO, 1935–8.

21 *Reports of the Commissioner for the Special Areas in Scotland*, HMSO, 1935–8.

22 Sharp, T., *Exeter Phoenix*, Architectural Press, 1946.

23 The Times, 'Places without a Future', *The Times*, March 20, 21 and 22, 1934.

24 Titmuss, R. M., *Problems of Social Policy*, HMSO and Longmans, 1950.

25 Titmuss, R. M., 'War and Social Policy', *Essays on 'The Welfare State'*, Allen & Unwin, 1958.

26 Tudor Walters Report, *Report of the Committee on Questions of Building Construction in Connection with the Provision of Dwellings for the Working Classes*, Cd. 9191, HMSO, 1918.

27 Unwin, R., *Town Planning in Practice: An Introduction to the Art of Designing Cities and Suburbs*, T. Fisher Unwin, 1909.

28 Warren, H. and Davidge, W. R. (eds), *Decentralization of Population and Industry: A New Principle in Town Planning*, P. S. King & Son, 1930.

29 Wood, W., *Planning and the Law*, Percival Marshall, 1949.

Chapter II

THE NEW AGENCIES OF PLANNING

THE CENTRAL AUTHORITY

The new conception of town and country planning raised the difficult problem as to how the extended responsibilities were to be fitted into the organization of central government. Was the Ministry of Health – the department responsible for housing and other local government matters – to retain its existing executive powers in relation to town and country planning, and, at the same time, expand its activities into the broad policy fields of regional and national planning? Should there be a separate Ministry of Town and Country Planning, and, if so, should it be responsible both for the framing of policies and for their implementation? Would it be preferable to leave the latter with the Ministry of Health and set up a separate National Planning Authority which could also have certain responsibilities in the field of industrial location and transport? Should Scotland be dealt with in the same way as England and Wales?

Such questions were not quickly answered. Indeed the problems they pose are still with us, and it is doubtful whether any ideal solution exists. Town and country planning in its wider sense embraces a large part of the activities of government. A separate all-embracing Ministry is a contradiction in terms. An all-powerful 'grand co-ordinating' Ministry does not square with the facts of administrative and political life. There must be some division of responsibilities and, at the same time, some means of co-ordination which is acceptable to the individual Ministries. The *modus operandi* devised at any one point of time will reflect not only the particular urgencies of the existing situation, but also the views and personalities of the politicians and administrators whose task it is to interpret them. The importance of these factors is highlighted by the story of the setting up of the Ministry of Town and Country Planning.

The new town and country planning was born in the ancient Office of Works – a department which had become increasingly active with

Government building since the rearmament programme started. In September 1940 this Office became the Ministry of Works and Buildings – responsible for 'the proper co-ordination of building work, the carrying out of Government building programmes, the control of building materials, and research into building and conservation of materials'. At the invitation of Ernest Bevin, then Minister of Labour, Sir John (later Lord) Reith became the first Minister of this Department – an appointment which exercised considerable influence on later developments in the organization of planning. Reith was not only enthusiastic about the new post: he was already 'looking beyond the war to the problems of planning and reconstruction[6] and was hoping that however much responsibility the Ministry of Works and Buildings might initially be given, 'it would acquire still more – by doing things that had not been thought of and for which no one else had staked claims'. Indeed almost immediately he proposed that his Ministry 'should be ready to take up responsibility for . . . planning and reconstruction arising out of the war and post-war period'. This met with objection from the Ministry of Health (the department then responsible for town and country planning). This dispute was only settled after the Lord Privy Seal (Mr Attlee) had acted as arbiter:

'It is clear that the reconstruction of town and country planning after the war raises great problems and gives a great opportunity. The Minister of Works has, therefore, been charged by the Government with the responsibility for consulting the departments and organizations concerned with a view to reporting to the Cabinet the appropriate methods and machinery for dealing with the issues involved.'[6]

Thus the Ministry of Health retained its normal town and country planning functions while Lord Reith was to plan for the future. This he did by means of a Reconstruction Group in his Department, as well as by setting up two committees – the Uthwatt Committee on Compensation and Betterment and the Scott Committee on Land Utilization in Rural Areas. The reports of these committees together with that of the Barlow Commission constituted the famous trilogy which had a great influence on post-war planning.

Relationships between Lord Reith and Mr Arthur Greenwood (who had been appointed as Minister without Portfolio with special responsibility for all post-war reconstruction problems) and with the Ministry of Health were not easy. The boundaries between town and country planning on the one hand and general social and economic planning were not always clear. Lord Reith, however, was authorized to proceed on the assumptions:

'(1) That the principle of planning will be accepted as national policy and that some central planning authority will be required;
(2) that this authority will proceed on a positive policy for such matters as agriculture, industrial development and transport;
(3) that some services will require treatment on a national basis, some regionally and some locally.'[4]

For a while Lord Reith retained his personal responsibility for long-term planning while the Minister of Health retained his statutory planning functions. Following an interim report of the Uthwatt Committee, and 'to ensure that the administration of the Town and Country Planning Act and any legislation implementing the recommendations made in the first report of the Uthwatt Committee shall proceed in conformity with long-term planning policy as it is progressively developed' a Committee of the Privy Council was appointed – Lord Reith (as chairman), the Minister of Health, and the Secretary of State for Scotland.

The next development was the fusion of Lord Reith's Reconstruction Group and the Town and Country Planning Division of the Ministry of Health. This created some misgivings, particularly on the part of the Minister without Portfolio. A proposal to create both a new department for town and country planning and a new executive council for policy and development was rejected by the Cabinet: instead all the town and country planning functions of the Ministry of Health were transferred to a reorganized Ministry of Works and Planning. Lord Reith's apparent victory proved to be a hollow one: within a fortnight of the Cabinet decision he was asked to resign.* With the exit of Lord Reith (and his replacement by Lord Portal who 'disliked planning') the sands shifted. Furthermore, the Ministry of Health was now overburdened. The alternatives were now to create a new department or a non-departmental body. The latter proposal – on which a four-man committee set up under Lord Samuel's chairmanship could not agree – was rejected by the Cabinet on the ground that planning policy was essentially political and could not be removed from parliamentary control. Furthermore, experience which had been gained with the Ministry of Works and Planning, showed that the subject required 'the whole time services of a front-rank Minister'[5] and also that this Minister 'should not only be, but should

* According to Reith's autobiography Churchill had apparently been told 'that the Conservatives demanded my expulsion and that I be replaced by a good Tory. Moving too fast, too much planning all round; even fear of land nationalization perhaps. And this was at the time when Churchill was "yielding to public pressure".' *Into the Wind*, pp. 445–6.

also appear to be, entirely impartial in his judgment as to the right use of any particular piece of land: if he can be regarded as a Minister already predisposed by reason of his other Ministerial duties to lean to a particular type of land use he will for that very reason be less able to exercise his influence'.

In short, the decision was taken to set up a separate Ministry of Town and Country Planning.

The decision was not unanimously applauded, especially since the legislation merely dealt with machinery: 'the way in which it will be used will depend on the powers which the House confers on the Minister hereafter'. Mr Greenwood was particularly concerned about what he considered to be the implicit assumption that town and country planning could neatly be made the responsibility of a single department:

'I cannot overemphasize what I think Government inquiries and enlightened public opinion . . . have undoubtedly proved, namely the complexities of the issues involved and the paramount importance of collective responsibility for policy by the Ministers whose departments will have to take a hand in carrying the plans into effect. You cannot make a super-department which will take the life blood of the Ministry of Agriculture, the Board of Trade and the Ministry of Health and so on.'[5]

But the general discussion was inconclusive – as it had to be, since the legislation did little more than establish the new Department, with a Minister charged with the study of 'securing consistency and continuity in the framing and execution of a national policy with respect to the use and development of land throughout England and Wales'.

The new Ministry had responsibilities only for England and Wales. In Scotland central responsibility remained with the Department of Health for Scotland. Neither of these two Departments was responsible for the location of industry. The 'Barlow policy' for industrial location was accepted, as was the Beveridge principle of full employment, but

'no single Department could undertake the responsibility for formulating and administering the policy for the distribution of industry. . . . This is essentially a policy of the Government as a whole, and its application in practice will involve action by a number of different Departments, each of which will adapt its administration to conform with the general Government policy. The main responsibility will rest with the Board of Trade, the Ministry of Labour and

National Service, the Ministry of Town and Country Planning and the Scottish Office. Standing arrangements will be made for supervising and controlling, under the Cabinet and as part of the central Government machinery, the development and execution of the policy as a whole.... It is necessary, however, that there should be a single channel through which Government policy on the distribution of industry can be expressed.... (This) shall be the Board of Trade.'[12]

In short, the Ministry of Town and Country Planning was to be responsible for town and country planning, the Ministry of Health for housing and the Board of Trade for industrial location, but there would be 'standing arrangements' for co-ordination where necessary.

LOCAL PLANNING AUTHORITIES

The shaping of a local government structure to meet new needs raises problems of an acute nature. There are inherent problems of devising units which are viable in terms of size and financial resources for the administration of different services.[3] But of even greater practical importance is the problem of securing political agreement for change – at the level of both national and local politics. The need for reform at any one point of time may be clear to the reformers, but to demonstrate and prove the beneficial effects (which are often of a long-term nature) is quite a different matter. Usually local government reform is a matter of real interest only to academics, politicians and local government officers. Since these cannot agree (even on the necessity for change) the result is commonly a deadlock. Local government may then be bypassed, and services transferred to government departments or *ad hoc* authorities – as has happened, for example, with the licensing of passenger road services, trunk roads, hospitals, public assistance, valuation for rating, and the major public utilities of gas and electricity. Post-war attempts to reorganize local government have generally been abortive and it is only in the last few years that the problem has been tackled. The tone was set in 1944 when the then Minister of Health stated that it was clear from the views put forward by the various Local Government Associations and 'other authoritative sources' that there was no general desire to disrupt the existing structure of local government: in the view of the Government no case had been made out for any drastic change. However, there was scope for improvements, and a White Paper (*Local Government in England and Wales during the Period of Reconstruction*) published the following year outlined the Government's proposals for a Local Government Boundary Commission. This was set up in the same year, but in fact achieved nothing more than the publication of three annual reports. The Commission was set up to consider the *boundaries* of local authorities – in spite of the general agreement that the question of boundaries could be usefully considered only in relation to *functions*. In their second report, they argued cogently that they could not, within their terms of reference, make proposals which would result in 'effective and convenient units of local government administration'. Such units 'cannot everywhere be procured without a fresh allocation of functions among the various types of local authorities, particularly where the larger towns are concerned'. They therefore had to decide whether to make second-best alterations to the existing structure (i.e. boundary adjustments) within the limits of their powers or to outline the case for radical reorganization in the hope that this would be followed by legislation widening their powers. They chose the latter.

Briefly, their plan envisaged three types of local authorities. The whole of England and Wales *including the areas of existing county boroughs*, would be divided into new counties. These would be formed on the basis of existing counties (combined or divided where necessary) and county boroughs (combined or extended as necessary) The smaller of the new counties would be administered on the one-tier system and the larger on the two-tier system. Second tier authorities would be either 'new county boroughs' ('most-purpose' authorities) or county districts ('minor-purpose' authorities).

So far as town and country planning was concerned responsibility for preparing over-all development plans would rest with the counties. They would thus be responsible for general policy issues such as determining main lines of communication, and the location of new developments, green belts and major open spaces. Within the framework of the county plan, the new most-purpose authorities would be responsible for the preparation of the detailed plans for their areas.

To the advocates of local government reform these proposals were regarded as a step forward, but the absence of a 'regional outlook' was criticized. Robson, for example, complained that 'the Commissioners never for a moment turned their eyes towards the regional movement which has wrought havoc with local government. They did not ask why responsibility for electricity and gas supply, civil airfields, hospitals, trunk roads, passenger road services, and other services, has recently been taken away from local authorities and given to regional or central bodies; or under what conditions it might be practicable for these functions to be restored to the realm of local self-government.'[7] Though the proposals did 'abolish the fatal separation of town and country in watertight compartments which was made in 1888', they gave too little attention to the size of areas and types of authorities needed to carry out services which require large scale planning and administration.

But to the Government of the day the proposals were either too radical or too embarrassing. There was little political support for them and the Government took the easy way out by simply abolishing the Commission.

Since local government was not to be reorganized the question of the local administration of planning resolved itself into a choice between giving responsibility to the existing local government units or setting up *ad hoc* planning bodies on the lines followed in the case of hospitals or the nationalized utilities. The latter would have had the advantage of allowing the boundaries of planning authorities to be drawn on a rational basis, but in fact it was never seriously entertained. The 1947 Town and Country Planning Act gave responsibility to the major authorities – the counties and county boroughs. This reduced the number of local planning authorities from 1,441 to 145 – a reduction of 90 per cent. This obviously greatly enlarged the area over which local planning was to be effected, but two further steps were required.

First, as the Scott Committee pointed out:

'the local planning authority should be the same authority or combination of authorities as executes the principal local government functions involving the use of land. Within this framework the extremely important functions will devolve on the smaller authorities of affording the county planning authorities the benefit of their local knowledge in the formulation of plans, and the county authorities must consult the district councils accordingly; whilst in due course the responsibility for the execution of works within the approved scheme may fall on the district councils.'

Accordingly the 1947 Act required county councils to consult with district authorities in the preparation of their plans and enabled them to delegate powers of controlling development to district councils (or to decentralize these powers to sub-committees charged with responsibility for certain areas).

Secondly, though the Act enlarged the areas over which planning powers were to be exercised by single authorities, the need still existed, in some parts of the country (particularly in the case of conurbations) for larger planning areas. The Act therefore gave the Minister power to set up Joint Planning Boards for combined areas. This could be done either with the agreement of the local authorities concerned, or following a local inquiry, by the Minister. In fact this power has never been used. A similar power to establish joint advisory committees, on the other hand, has been used.

REGIONAL ADMINISTRATION

Within the new structure there was no formal place for regional authorities. The need for wider planning areas was recognized in the provision made for joint planning boards and joint advisory committees, but these constituted a typical English compromise which excited little enthusiasm. Mr Bevan, when Minister of Health, echoed the general feeling: a joint board, he said, 'has no biological content; it has no mother and it has no progeny; it is a piece of paper work'.[7] In the absence of a formal creation of executive, financially responsible, organs of regional government it was left to the Ministry itself to undertake such regional planning as was to be effected – by co-ordinating the efforts of the separate planning authorities and reconciling and amending the plans prepared by them and submitted to the Ministry for approval. This, indeed, was one of the functions implied by the duty with which the Ministry was charged of 'securing consistency and continuity in the framing and execution of a national policy with respect to the use and development of land throughout England and Wales'.

What might at first sight have been regarded as a clear advance towards regionalism was the war-time establishment of civil defence regions and the appointment of Regional Commissioners. These were set up to deal with the conditions which might have arisen had communications been disrupted. This organization – into eleven regions – was retained after the war, but the regions were (and still are) 'no more than civil service creations, established for the dispatch of business; they are not, in any sense, "organic" units'. The Ministry of Town and Country Planning appointed regional planning officers as early as 1943. As the scope and complexity of planning legislation grew the regional machinery was expanded. By 1948 there was an office in each region under the control of a Regional Controller. The initial object of the regional offices was to give advice to local authorities, but the establishment of Regional Controllers marked a new step towards solving the increasing number of conflicting claims over land use from Government Departments. The Regional Controllers presided over Regional Planning Committees composed of representatives from the various other Government Departments in the region. But this was simply an administrative device to cope with inter-departmental frictions.

In view of the absence of regional machinery in the final outcome it is interesting to note Reith's original proposals (submitted to Churchill in 1940) for:

'a central authority to frame and be responsible for the execution of a national plan covering the basic objectives; to lay down the general principles of planning; to supervise planning, design, finance, execution; regional machinery to apply the national plan and to co-ordinate and control the work of local authorities; Exchequer assistance to supplement local funds in approved development.'[6]

Since there was now no middle tier it followed that the central authority would be greatly concerned with the day-to-day work of local authorities (and the time-consuming business of appeals against local authorities), and thus face the danger of paying insufficient attention to 'basic objectives' and 'general principles' – a point to which we return in later chapters.

REFERENCES AND FURTHER READING

1 Chester, D. N. and Willson, F. M. G., *The Organisation of British Central Government, 1914–1964*, Allen & Unwin, 2nd edition, 1968.
2 Cole, G. D. H., *Local and Regional Government*, Cassell, 1947.
3 Lipman, V. D., *Local Government Areas 1834–1945*, Basil Blackwell, 1949.
4 Parliamentary Debates, *H.L. Debates*, Vol. 118, February 26, 1941.
5 Parliamentary Debates on the Minister of Town and Country Planning Bill, *H.C. Debates*, Vol. 386, January 1943.
6 Reith, Lord, *Into the Wind*, Hodder & Stoughton, 1949.
7 Robson, W. A., *The Development of Local Government*, Allen & Unwin, 2nd edition, 1948; 3rd edition, 1954.
8 Scott Report: *Report on the Committee on Land Utilisation in Rural Areas*, Cmd. 6378, HMSO, 1942.
9 Self, P., *Regionalism*, Fabian Publications and Allen & Unwin, 1949.
10 Smith, B. C., *Regionalism in England I: Regional Institutions – A Guide*, Acton Society, 1964.
11 Smith, B. C., *Regionalism in England II: Its Nature and Purpose 1905–1965*, Acton Society, 1965.
12 White Paper, *Employment Policy*, Cmd. 6527, HMSO, 1944.

Chapter III

THE ROLE OF CENTRAL GOVERNMENT

THE MINISTRY OF HOUSING AND LOCAL GOVERNMENT

The Ministry of Housing and Local Government is the central authority for the administration of planning.* The Minister is charged with the duty of 'securing consistency and continuity in the framing of a national policy with respect to the use and development of land throughout England and Wales'. The powers are very wide and, in effect, give the Ministry the final say in all policy matters (subject, of course, to Parliamentary control). The extent of these powers is too wide to permit an adequate summary: they are discussed in detail at appropriate points in other chapters. For many matters the Minister is required or empowered to make regulations; this delegated legislation covers a wide field. For example, one Order (the Use Classes Order) classifies industrial and commercial uses and permits 'changes of use' within each of the categories without the need for planning permission. Similarly the advertisement regulations specify certain types of advertisement for which planning permission is 'deemed' to be given, and the General Development Order provides a detailed list of types of development which do not require planning permission. One function of the Ministry is thus (within the limits laid down by Parliament) to make legislation.

In a wide range of matters, ministerial approval is necessary for proposals made by a local authority. The Development Plan, for example, does not become operative until it has been approved by the Minister. This approval can stipulate modifications in the plan; the Minister has great discretionary powers here since he is acting administratively and quasi-judicially. If a local planning authority fail to produce a plan (or a plan 'satisfactory to the Minister'), he

* The Welsh Office has executive responsibility for town and country planning including new towns, as well as housing, roads, water resources and local government in Wales.

can act in default. Decisions of a local planning authority on applications for planning permission can, on appeal, be modified or revoked by the Minister – even if the development proposed is contrary to the Development Plan. Proposals which the Minister regards as being sufficiently important can be 'called in' for his decision.

In spite of all these powers it is not the function of the Minister to decide detailed planning policies. This is the business of local planning authorities. The Minister's function is to co-ordinate the work of individual local authorities and to ensure that their Development Plans and development control decisions are in harmony with broad planning policies. That this often involves rather closer relationships than might *prima facie* be supposed follows from the nature of the governmental and administrative processes. The line dividing policy from day-to-day administration is a fine one. Policy has to be translated into decisions on specific issues, and a series of decisions can amount to a change in policy. This is particularly important in the British planning system where a large measure of administrative discretion is given to central and local government bodies. This is a distinctive feature of the planning system. The development plan is prepared by and administered by the same local body (unlike the position in the United States where there is a traditional separation of functions). There is virtually no provision for external judicial review of local planning decisions: instead there is the system of appeals to the Minister. A foreign observer sees the position clearly:

'The absence of a written constitution makes the statute controlling in England. External review of the merits of local planning decisions is afforded by the Minister of Housing and Local Government. His ministry is a national agency exercising a supervisory power over local government and having no exact counterpart in the United States. Appeals are taken to the minister from local refusals of planning permission and from permissions with onerous conditions. English courts can review ministerial decisions, but their role in the determination of planning policy is peripheral.

'The area of discretion in English planning administration is enlarged further by the lack of separation of function which is traditional to American government. In America, the zoning ordinance is enacted by the local legislative body but is usually administered by the executive department and by nonelective boards created for this purpose. In England, the local elected council which adopts the development plan also administers it. The failure to separate function in English planning has the healthy effect of forcing attention to the relationship between the individual decision and the general objectives to which, in a small way, it contributes. But this institutional framework blurs the distinction between policy making and policy applying and so enlarges the role of the administrator who has to decide a specific case.'[18]

It is this broad area of discretion which brings the Ministry in close contact with local planning authorities (though, as is explained later, it is not the only factor). The Ministry in effect operates both in a quasi-judicial capacity and as a developer of policy.

The Ministry's quasi-judicial role stems in part from the vagueness of planning policies. Even if these policies are precisely worded, their application can raise problems. Since a local authority has such a wide area of discretion, and since the courts have only very limited powers of action, the Ministry has to act as arbiter over what is fair and reasonable. This is not, however, simply a judicial process. A decision is not taken on the basis of legal rules as in a court of law: it involves the exercise of a wide discretion in the balancing of public and private interest within the framework of planning policies.[4] The procedure basically consists of the lodging of objections either to proposals in a draft development plan or to the decision of a local authority on a planning application. Such objections (or appeals, as the latter are called) are made to the Minister of Housing, who then holds an inquiry in public. These inquiries are carried out by departmental inspectors of the Ministry but the final decision is the formal responsibility of the Minister. There is no appeal against his decision except on a question of law.

The Ministry's role in policy formulation is not easy to summarize. Policies are usually couched in very general terms – preservation of amenity, restraining urban sprawl and so on – which give local authorities considerable leeway. Formal ministerial guidance (circulars, memoranda, bulletins, etc.) often does not provide a clear indication of the action which should be followed in any particular case. Proposals have to be considered 'on their merits' within the broad framework of a set of principles. These principles can – and do – change, at least in emphasis. Usually the change is gradual, perhaps even coming without a conscious step. And the motivating power may well be the local authorities themselves rather than the Ministry. All this makes it very difficult to present a clear-cut picture of central-local government relationships. The truth is that the position is not clear cut. What is clear is that there is little approaching a situation in which the central department determines policy while local governments carry the policy into effect as agents. The larger authorities 'have built up local administrations that can properly be regarded as citadels of local power'. Though central government may lay down national policies, 'it is in the twists and emphases which councils give to central policies, and the degree of co-operation or unwillingness which they show, that their own power lies. They do not have the paper guarantees of local sovereignty which states in a federal system possess, but they have some of the reality of power which comes from being on the spot, knowing the special qualities and demands of the local people, and being costly and difficult to replace if the central government finds them unsatisfactory.'[20] The general conception of local government in this country was succinctly set out in the *First Report of the Local Government Manpower Committee:*

'. . . local authorities are responsible bodies competent to discharge their own functions and . . . though they may be the statutory bodies through which Government policy is given effect and operate to a large extent with Government money, they exercise their responsibilities in their own right, not ordinarily as agents of Government Departments. It follows that the objective should be to leave as much as possible of the detailed management of a scheme or service to the local authority and to concentrate the Department's control at the key points where it can most effectively discharge its responsibilities for Government policy and financial administration.'[15]

It is common to talk of central-local government relationships as constituting a 'partnership', and though any such single term must oversimplify the situation, the description is apposite. Certainly there is no pressure (at least so far as town and country planning is concerned) for a take-over of functions by the Ministry. Their attitude was expressed in 1960 by the then Permanent Secretary, Dame Evelyn Sharp, in her evidence to the Royal Commission on Local Government in Greater London: 'I certainly could not accept, and I should be rather horrified if local authorities expressed a considered and deliberate view . . . that the main outlines of their plan ought to be a matter for central government'.[36] Indeed, it can be argued that the Ministry plays too passive a role!

The positive powers and functions of the Ministry should not, however, be minimized. Reference has already been made to the way in which it can override the decisions of a local authority on particular cases. It is worth examining this in more detail.

Planning Appeals

An unsuccessful planning applicant can appeal to the Minister, and a large number do in fact do so. Appeals* decided during 1968 numbered 7,081, of which 25 per cent were allowed (many subject to conditions) and 75 per cent dismissed. Here the Minister has very wide powers. He may reverse the local authority's decision or subject it to conditions. He may quash or modify conditions which they have imposed. He may make those conditions more onerous, or he may even go to the extent of refusing planning permission altogether if he decides that the local authority should not have granted it.†

Though each planning appeal is considered and determined on its merits, the cumulative effect is an emergence of the Ministry's views on a wide range of planning matters. These have been made more explicit in 'statements of policy' published in the *Bulletin of Selected Planning Appeals* and in the *Development Control Policy Notes*. The effect of these on the policy of individual authorities may be difficult to assess, but clearly they are likely to have a very real influence. A local planning authority is unlikely to refuse planning consents for a particular type of development if it is convinced that the Ministry would uphold an appeal.

It is not, of course, every planning application that raises an issue of policy. Yet, until recently, all had to be dealt with by the Ministry's inspectorate. Nearly a half of appeals are settled by correspondence after an informal visit to the site and without a local inquiry. (This is termed *the written representations procedure*.) The Franks Committee on Administrative Tribunals and Inquiries argued that it was not satisfactory 'that a Government Department should be occupied with appeal work of this volume, particularly as many of the appeals relate to minor and purely local matters, in which little or no departmental policy entered'. An analysis of the subject-matter of appeals undertaken by the Ministry (and reported in the

* This discussion relates particularly to appeals under Section 23 of the Town and Country Planning Act, 1962. It does not deal specifically with advertisement appeals, appeals against enforcement notices, appeals to determine whether in doubtful cases planning permission is required, or appeals against certificates of alternative development for the purposes of assessing compensation under Section 18 of the Land Compensation Act, 1961 – though the principles discussed are generally the same. Section 23 of the 1962 Act covers appeals:

(1) against a decision of a local planning authority to *refuse* planning permission for the development of land;
(2) against their decision to grant it *subject to conditions*: in this case the appeal is against one or more of the conditions;
(3) against their *failure* to issue a decision within the period prescribed – two months for ordinary applications and three months for applications affecting trunk roads.

See Ministry of Housing and Local Government, *Planning Appeals: A Guide to Procedure 1969*, HMSO, 4th ed., 1969, p. 7.

† See Appendix for some illustrative appeal decisions.

TABLE III.1

*Planning appeals in England and Wales, 1962–8**

	In hand at beginning of year	*Received*	*Withdrawn*	*Decided*						*Outstanding at end of year*
				Allowed		*Dismissed*		*Total*	*Percentage of total decided by written representation*	
				Number	*Percentage*	*Number*	*Percentage*			
1962	7,382	12,352	4,170	2,359	*27·2*	6,302	*72·8*	8,661	*34·0*	6,903
1964	6,797	14,345	4,429	2,001	*22·9*	6,725	*77·1*	8,726	*39·0*	7,987
1966	9,004	11,725	4,485	1,982	*21·9*	7,053	*78·1*	9,035	*46·0*	7,209
1968	6,545	10,250	2,976	1,778	*25·1*	5,303	*74·9*	7,081	*53·6*	6,738

* Ministry of Housing and Local Government: *Handbook of Statistics* (annual). The figures relate only to appeals under Section 23 of the Town and Country Planning Act, 1962, i.e. against decisions, or failure to give decisions within the statutory period, of local planning authorities on application made to them for planning permission for development. See footnote on p. 53.

1967 White Paper *Town and Country Planning*) confirmed this. About 60 per cent concerned small-scale development; many of these raised issues of purely local significance. They included such matters as minor residential development, small groups of shops, small caravan sites, betting shops, garages and minor changes of use. Rather more than a quarter related to single houses.

Another relevant point is that of all appeals made during the five years 1962 to 1967, 97·5 per cent were decided as the inspector recommended.

In view of the delay which is inevitable in this appeals system (on average it has taken nine months to issue decisions) and the huge administrative burden it has placed on the Ministry, considerable thought has been given to possible alternatives. The solution adopted by the 1968 Planning Act is for the determination of certain classes of appeals by inspectors. The classes are determined by regulation and can thus be amended in the light of experience. This is a highly novel innovation and one on which caution is necessary. The first set of regulations prescribe only five very limited classes:

1. Residential development on not more than two acres.
2. Erection or alteration of not more than ten dwelling-houses.
3. Building, etc., operations ancillary to residential use or development of land.
4. Change in use of building(s) to not more than ten dwelling-houses.
5. Change in use of not more than ten dwelling-houses to other residential use.

Even these restrictive classes are further limited in the detailed regulations. Furthermore, the Minister can 'call in' appeals within these classes if he sees good grounds for so doing, for example in controversial cases.

The objectives of this new system are to speed up the appeal procedure and to relieve the central government of detailed work which takes up far too much of their effort, thereby prejudicing the work which the central government should be doing – for example on major issues of policy. In short, the intention is that the Ministry will be better able to fulfil its essential role.

'Call in' of Planning Applications

The power to 'call in' a planning application for ministerial decision is quite separate from that of determining an appeal against an adverse decision of a local planning authority. This power is not circumscribed: the Minister may call in any application, and his decision is final. Though there is no general statement of policy as to which applications will normally be called in, there are several categories which are particularly liable. In the first place, all applications for development involving a substantial departure from the provisions of a development plan which the local planning authority intend to grant must be sent to the Minister together with a statement of the reasons for which they wish to grant the permission. This procedure enables the Minister to decide whether the development is sufficiently important to warrant it being called in for his own determination. Secondly, mineral workings often raise problems of more than local importance and the national need for particular minerals has to be balanced against planning issues. Such matters cannot be adequately considered by local planning authorities, and, in any case, involve technical considerations requiring expert opinion of a character more easily available to the Ministry. For these reasons large numbers of applications for permission to work minerals have been called in. Furthermore, there is a general direction calling in all applications for the winning and working of ironstone in certain counties where there are large-scale ironstone workings. Thirdly, the power of call-in is generally used when the matter at stake is (as in the case of minerals) of more than local importance or interest. Examples of applications called in are the proposal by Hull County Borough to build on over 400 acres of land in an area of East Riding adjacent to the city, the proposed new buildings on the Monico site at Piccadilly Circus, and the application of Richard Thomas and Baldwins to extract ironstone from an area of 2,900 acres in north Oxfordshire.

When an application is called in, the Minister must, if either the applicant or the local planning authority so desire, hold a hearing or public inquiry. The public inquiry is more usual, particularly in important cases.

The Minister now has power, under the Town and Country Planning Act, 1968, to refer development proposals of a far-reaching or novel character to an *ad hoc* Planning Inquiry Commission.

Further reference must also be made to the circulars, bulletins and handbooks published by the Ministry, and the studies on which some of them are based. Quite apart from straightforward statements of broad policies, these contain a great deal of technical guidance. It needs to be stressed that planning policies often raise technical issues which are beyond the competence of local authority staffs, or at least need a wider background of experience than is always to be found in a planning authority.

Then again there are the controls operated by the Ministry over capital expenditure. These controls have tended to increase as economic and regional planning tools have gradually developed.

For instance, 'in order that redevelopment plans could be based on more realistic assumptions of what can be afforded, local authorities in England and Wales were asked in September 1966 to submit their proposals for redevelopment schemes for the next five years, so that a programme of approved schemes could be drawn up'.[27]

It must be repeated, however, that local planning authorities are not agents of the Ministry. Though the Ministry can – and does – exercise many direct controls, it prefers (in accordance with British traditions) to wield its power in a gentlemanly fashion by way of exhortation, advice and informal contacts. This is particularly important at officer level. The chief planning officers of local authorities are not strangers to the Ministry officials: on the contrary, relationships between them are close. And they are members of a small (but active) profession in which policy issues are constantly being discussed.*

The Organization of the Ministry of Housing and Local Government†

The Ministry of Housing and Local Government is responsible, as the name suggests, not only for town and country planning but also for housing and a range of local government services. These include water and sewerage, refuse collection and disposal, burial grounds and crematoria, clean air and river pollution, together with the general structure (including reorganization) and finance of local government.

As far as planning is concerned there are two broad groupings – administrative and professional. The administrative group deal with development plans, development control, new and expanding towns, national parks and so on. The organization is partly functional and partly geographical: there is, for example, one Division which deals with all general planning matters in London and the Home Counties, while a second Division deals with the remainder of the country; but some specialist matters (e.g. historic buildings, tree preservation and acquisition of land under the Planning Acts) are divided between them without regard to area. The professional group includes the specialist officers responsible for giving advice to the administrators on planning techniques, principles and

* For a recent statement of central-local relationships see Chapter 3 of P. G. Richards, *The New Local Government System*, Allen & Unwin, 1968.

† For a more detailed account and a valuable discussion of the role of the Ministry in relation to local planning authorities see J. A. G. Griffith, *Central Departments and Local Authorities*, Allen & Unwin, 1966, Chapter 5. An up-to-date summary of the Ministry's organization and a detailed account of its work is to be found in E. Sharp, *The Ministry of Housing and Local Government*, Allen & Unwin, 1969.

standards. They are also responsible for a critical evaluation of development plans and for such research as is carried out at the central government level. Within this technical group are the housing and planning inspectorate responsible for the holding of public inquiries, hearings and inspections, and the estate staff, responsible for advice on estate development and management.

The Ministry's regional organization was largely disbanded in 1956, but was resuscitated in the mid-'sixties when the new economic planning regions were set up. In each of the economic planning regions an advisory Economic Planning Council is served by a Board consisting of senior regional officers of the main Government Departments – including the Ministry of Housing and Local Government.* The planning functions of the Ministry's regional offices are to assist the local planning authorities, to act as the regional 'eyes and ears' of the Ministry, and to contribute to the work of the regional economic planning boards and councils. They play an important role in the preparation and review of the regional studies which are assuming an increasingly significant role in both economic and physical planning.†

This sketch of the position of the Ministry of Housing will be considerably elaborated in later chapters. A fuller account at this stage would involve repetition in the more detailed discussion which these chapters contain. The position of two other Government Departments is, however, different. The Ministry of Transport and the Board of Trade have different relationships with local authorities, and their role in policy making is much more positive. It is, therefore, appropriate to discuss their position and powers more comprehensively.

THE MINISTRY OF TRANSPORT

Transport is, of course, inseparable from town planning. The volume, nature and even mode of transport is governed by land use. Indeed, the relationship between town planning and transport is so close that it has been argued that they should be the responsibility of a single Ministry.‡ The division of responsibility carries the danger of inadequate co-ordination. On the one hand, inadequate consideration may be given to transport needs in the planning process, while, on the other hand, road planning may be so much

* See Chapter XII.

† The Ministry's *Annual Report* for 1965 and 1966 contains a convenient summary of the studies undertaken in the West Midlands, the North-West, the Northern, the Yorkshire and Humberside, and the East Midlands Regions.

‡ For a note on recent developments, see Appendix to this chapter.

concerned with providing for traffic flows that wider planning issues become submerged.

There has been increasing recognition in recent years of the need to 'integrate' planning and transport policies. In 1962 the Ministries of Housing and Transport set up a Joint Urban Planning Group (later joined by the Scottish Development Department), comprising both administrative and technical staff. This is both a study group and an advisory body (to the three Departments). It has been responsible for a number of Planning Bulletins, including *Town Centres: Approach to Renewal* (1962), *Town Centres: Cost and Control of Redevelopment* (1963), *Town Centres: Current Practice* (1963), and *Parking in Town Centres* (1965). Following the Buchanan Report on *Traffic in Towns* (1963) this initial emphasis on town centres was broadened to a consideration of wider issues of urban form and structure. The need for much greater (and more sophisticated) data on traffic generation and flows led to the mounting of major combined land use and transport surveys in all the conurbations and in many large towns. For a time, however, it seemed that the two Ministries were adopting a more independent approach. (*Traffic and Transport Plans*,[34] for instance, which appeared in 1968, was a publication of the Ministry of Transport.) But developments were afoot for a much more systematic and basic linking of land use planning and transportation. Legislatively, these culminated in the Town and Country Planning Act of 1968 with its emphasis on *structure plans*.

A major feature of the new planning system is to be a greater integration of transport planning and land use planning. Regulations and circulars are to be issued on this. In the debates on the Bill it was stated that the new system 'will involve from the very earliest – from the survey stage – close co-operation between the planning authority and the Ministry of Transport and its local offices – divisional road engineers, and so on. Equally, when the time comes for consideration of structure plans at our level, we will consult the Ministry of Transport and ensure that the plans that are approved contain proposals which, from a transport point of view, are realistic and fit in with the broader national picture.'

The movement of both Ministries into their new building in Horseferry Road will no doubt provide the framework for the necessary central co-ordination. It remains to be seen whether this will be as effective as the Scottish solution: there the Scottish Development Department is responsible for all local government, roads and industry functions of the former Scottish Home Department as well as the town and country planning, housing and environmental functions of the former Scottish Department of Health.

For the present,* the Ministry of Transport is consulted by the Ministry of Housing on the highway proposals in development plans, and agreement is achieved before the plans are approved. Furthermore, the Planning Acts require local planning authorities to consult the Ministry of Transport before they grant permission for development which will affect trunk roads. After consulting the Ministry, the local planning authorities must comply with any direction given concerning the restriction of the permission. Table III.2 shows the number of such applications on which the Ministry were consulted in 1966–8.

TABLE III.2

Planning applications on which the Ministry of Transport was consulted, 1967–9[33]

	1967–8	*1968–9*
Applications outstanding on April 1st	1,083	640
Applications during the year	9,712	10,521
	10,795	11,161
Dealt with as follows:		
Directions not considered necessary	4,581	4,847
Direction issued:		
(i) that consent be restricted	3,129	3,144
(ii) that consent be refused	2,445	2,387
Applications outstanding on March 31st	640	783
	10,795	11,161

Under administrative arrangements made with the Ministry of Housing, appeals made under the Planning Acts can be referred to the Ministry of Transport where one of the issues in the appeal is the effect of the development on the use and safety of an actual or proposed highway. During 1967–8 the number of such appeals was 330.

Trunk Roads

The Ministry of Transport is not however a passive body. It is responsible for designating the lines of trunk roads. It has a major influence in determining road priorities by means of grants to local authorities for road construction and improvement. Indeed, in the

* No longer the present: see the end of this chapter for a note on changes made in October 1969.

relationship between local authorities and the Ministry 'the trend has been one of increasing centralized control of broad planning and strategy, with execution and management falling to the county boroughs and county councils'.[8]

In their evidence to the Royal Commission on Local Government in Greater London, the Ministry of Transport stated that 'the choice and order of priority of individual schemes on trunk roads is completely under the control of the Minister, and on classified roads priority is virtually determined by his control of grants – although in general he can only choose from among schemes which are out to him'. Both trunk roads and classified roads have been the subjects of investigation by the Estimates Committee to which the reader in search of a wealth of detail is referred.[9, 11] The subject of transport planning is discussed in a later chapter. Here attention is concentrated on providing a summary of the organization of the Ministry in so far as its work relates to town and country planning, and the Ministry's role in the planning process.

It is important at the outset to make clear the distinction between trunk and other roads. Trunk roads form a national system of routes for through traffic. The 'highway authority' for these roads is the Ministry of Transport. It is the Minister's responsibility under the Trunk Roads Act of 1946 to keep under review the national system of routes for through traffic in Great Britain. (Responsibility for road administration in Scotland and Wales now rests with the respective Secretaries of State.) He can construct new trunk roads and designate existing roads as trunk roads. Motorways are 'special' trunk roads. Most new constructional work and improvement schemes are designed and supervised by local authorities acting as agents for the Ministry. All expenditure on trunk roads is met by the Ministry.

The programming of trunk road schemes is the responsibility of the central department:

'The road programme should be thought of as a continuous process extending over a number of years. Trunk road schemes take a long time to prepare up to contract letting stage, perhaps three or four years in the case of larger schemes, and the detailed planning of schemes is normally commenced some four years in advance of the time it is expected that constructional work on these will start. A provisional selection of schemes for several years ahead is also made, so that a certain amount of preliminary work, such as making orders setting out the line of route, can be undertaken. Looking even further ahead there is a special planning section in the Department with the task of working out in the light of the latest information about traffic trends, what the country's long-term road requirements are likely to be.'[11]

In short, so far as trunk roads are concerned, the Ministry of Transport is the policy-making body. It determines the programme, approves estimates and allocates money to individual authorities. The local authorities are merely the agents for carrying out the Ministry's policy.

TABLE III.3

Mileage of public highways in England and Wales, April 1, 1969[33]

	Trunk roads				
	Motorway	*All-purpose*	*Principal roads*	*Other roads*	*Total*
England					
County Boroughs	14	133	1,857	17,769	19,773
Greater London	16	134	876	6,800	7,826
Counties	501	5,155	11,461	105,928	123,045
Total England	531	5,422	14,194	130,497	150,644
Wales					
County Boroughs	7	21	90	870	988
Counties	16	996	1,388	15,700	18,000
Total Wales	23	1,017	1,478	16,570	19,088
Total England and Wales	554	6,439	15,672	147,067	169,732

For other roads a different system operates. The responsibility for these lies with local highway authorities. The Ministry's position is largely dependent upon its power to make grants. Up to 1967, specific grants for both improvement and maintenance were payable to local highway authorities for 'classified' roads. These grants were paid at rates of 75 per cent, 60 per cent and 50 per cent on Class I, II and III roads respectively.

Since April 1967, a new, simplified system has operated. This was conceived within the general framework of a comprehensive review of central-local government financial relationships.[26] The purpose of the revised grant structure (introduced by the Local Government Act, 1966) is threefold[32]:

(i) to concentrate specific Exchequer aid on roads which make an important contribution to the national highway system;

(ii) to strike a better balance of responsibility between central and local government, and to keep detailed control to the essential minimum;

(iii) to simplify the system of grants and classification to streamline highway administration.

Under the new system, highway works are divided into two categories: improvements and maintenance. Capital grants, at a rate of 75 per cent, are payable for improvements (not maintenance) on 'principal roads' only. (Principal roads are roughly equivalent to the previous Class I system.) All other grant aid (for improvements and maintenance) is given through the Rate Support Grant which is a non-specific revenue grant for (nearly) all local government services.

THE BOARD OF TRADE

The Board of Trade is the central department responsible for controlling the location of industry. This is entirely a central government responsibility. Though certain local authorities have appointed industrial development officers and many act in concert through industrial development associations, they have no statutory responsibility for industrial location policy. This may appear to be an overstatement, since an important part of a local authority's development plan will be concerned with industrial sites, and authorities in areas of unemployment will seek to attract new industry, while those in congested areas (particularly London) operate a policy of encouraging industrial dispersal. Nevertheless, the powers here are limited and in practice are much more concerned with siting than with general issues of location. The distinction is important. Though local authorities can erect factories in an attempt to encourage industrial growth and can buy up existing factories in order to reduce the level of employment, their real power lies in approving or rejecting a planning application for industrial development on particular sites. The question as to whether this industrial development should take place at all in the area is a matter for the Board of Trade. In short, the Board is responsible for the *location* of industry, whereas local authorities are responsible for the *siting* of industrial developments. It follows that the Board of Trade has an extremely important role to play: it is an executive as well as a policy-making body.

The Board operates in two ways. First, it administers the Industrial Development Certificate scheme under which any industrial building or extension above a certain size requires the Board's certification that it is consistent with the proper distribution of industry. Since 1965, the Board has also administered an Office

Development Permits scheme in certain 'congested' areas. Secondly, it has powers to attract industries to areas of high unemployment.

The general policy of the Board is to encourage industrial expansion in areas of high unemployment and to restrict it in congested areas. This has been the interpretation of 'the proper distribution of industry' – a phrase which is nowhere defined in the legislation, though the Local Employment Act of 1960 does require the Board (when considering whether an industrial development certificate should be granted) to have 'particular regard to the need for providing appropriate employment in development districts'.

Development Areas

Policy relating to areas of high unemployment has changed considerably over the post-war years in response to changing conditions. The Special Areas of the pre-war legislation were converted into Development Areas by the Distribution of Industry Act of 1945. They were enlarged and added to, but the basic concept of large areas of persistent large-scale unemployment remained. By the end of the 'fifties the official view was that 'the steps which had been taken to rehabilitate these areas had achieved a large measure of success and many districts within the scheduled development areas – which contained nearly 20 per cent of the insured population – were no longer in any need of special assistance'.[10] On the other hand the rate of economic and technical change had increased. Pockets of unemployment were occurring in small isolated places. A new and more flexible approach was needed. The first recognition of this was the 1958 Distribution of Industry (Industrial Finance) Act, which extended some of the Board's powers to non-development areas in which the Board considered that high unemployment was likely to persist. The 1960 Act went much further: the former statutory schedule of development areas gave way to a new concept of administratively determined districts. These were defined as localities in which, in the opinion of the Board of Trade, a high rate of unemployment exists, or is to be expected, and in either case is likely to persist, whether seasonally (e.g. in seaside resorts) or generally.

In the mid-'sixties, however, the concepts of 'growth areas' and more selective regional development policies gradually took shape. Increasingly it was felt that measures to relieve unemployment ought to be set within a framework of policy geared to facilitate growth in areas with the greatest economic potential. The change in focus can be clearly seen by comparing the definition of 'development districts' in the Local Employment Act, 1960, with that of 'development areas' in the Industrial Development Act, 1966:

Local Employment Act, 1960

In this Act *development district* means any locality in Great Britain in which in the opinion of the Board . . . a high rate of unemployment exists, or is to be expected within such a period that it is expedient to exercise the said powers, and (in either case) is likely to persist, whether seasonally or generally.

Industrial Development Act, 1966

The areas to be specified by the Board [as *development areas*] shall be those parts of Great Britain where, in the opinion of the Board, special measures are necessary to encourage the growth and proper distribution of industry; and in exercising their powers . . . the Board shall have regard to all the circumstances actual and expected, including the state of employment and unemployment, population changes and the objectives of regional policies.

In 1969 the development areas were the whole of Scotland (excluding the Edinburgh, Leith and Portobello Employment Exchange areas), the Northern Region (plus Furness and Grange-over-Sands), Wales (excluding parts of the south-east and north), and the westernmost parts of the South-Western Region (Cornwall and north Devon). The development areas cover a very extensive part of the land area of the country and contain a fifth of the employed population. In 1965–6 their average unemployment rate was 2·7 per cent, but this increased to 3·0 per cent in 1966–7 and to 3·9 per cent in 1967–8. As a proportion of the Great Britain total unemployed,

TABLE III.4

Unemployment in Great Britain, 1966–8

	Average of wholly unemployed for 12 months ending March					
	1966		*1967*		*1968*	
	Number (thousands)	*Per cent*	*Number (thousands)*	*Per cent*	*Number (thousands)*	*Per cent*
Development area:						
Northern	33·2	2·4	38·8	2·8	55·3	4·0
Merseyside*	19·7	2·4	20·5	2·5	26·3	3·2
South-Western	4·9	3·7	5·5	4·0	6·3	4·6
Welsh	20·0	3·1	23·5	3·6	29·0	4·4
Scottish	57·2	2·9	61·9	3·2	77·9	4·0
All development areas*	134·9	2·7	150·2	3·0	194·9	3·9
Non-development areas	174·3	0·9	232·0	1·3	341·0	1·8
Great Britain	309·2	1·3	382·2	1·6	535·9	2·3

* Excluding Skelmersdale and Winsford.

the development areas constituted 43·6 per cent, 39·3 per cent and 36·4 per cent in these three years.

The positive powers of the Board of Trade (as distinct from regulatory powers through the granting of industrial development certificates and office development permits) can, in general, only be used in development areas. Under these powers, the Board can buy

TABLE III.5

Board of Trade factory statistics

(A) Approvals for factory building by the Board in Development Areas 1.4.60 to 31.3.68

Development area	*Projects (No.)*	*Area in square feet (thousands)*	*Estimated cost in £ (thousands)*
Northern	245	5,559	21,212
Merseyside	20	1,404	5,761
South Western	15	165	620
Total England*	285	7,412	28,502
Welsh*	125	3,559	15,826
Scottish	224	7,610	28,131
Total*	634	18,581	72,459

(B) The Board's industrial property

	In Development Areas			*Outside Development Areas*		
	Area owned in square feet (thousands)	*Under construction in square feet (thousands)*	*Total employment*			
England	20,921	809	95,305	1,584	Nil	5,837
Wales	13,842	983	59,391	360	Nil	2,836
Scotland	23,538	440	92,839	—	—	—
Total	58,301	2,232	247,535	5,866	2,807	8,673

* Includes former development districts not included in the development areas.

or build factories for sale or renting; make grants to firms providing their own premises; and advance loans and give grants for 'general purposes'. There are further powers for other Government Departments to give grants for clearing derelict land and for improving basic services.

Under the 1960 Act, Industrial Estates Management Corporations were established in England, Scotland and Wales to manage the industrial estates and factories built under earlier legislation. These Corporations also act as agents of the Board in undertaking the building and management of new premises. Table III.5 shows the amount of building approved during the period 1960–8 and the total industrial property owned by the Board at March 31, 1968. About a quarter of a million workers in the development areas are employed by firms who are tenants of the Board.

Of particular importance is the power of the Board to build 'advance factories' in order to attract new firms. During 1967–8, forty-five such factories were completed and twenty-eight were let or sold.

Factory rents are negotiated on the basis of current market value – as assessed by the District Valuer – which may, in a development area, be well below cost. Firms wishing to build a new factory (or buy a new one from the Board) can apply for a building grant. The benefit to the industrialist is roughly equivalent to that given to a tenant in a Board factory. In the year 1967–8, 1,548 offers of grant were made, totalling £18,510,000. During the eight years up to March 31, 1968, 4,609 grants totalled £75 million.

The Board have a general power to make loans and grants to firms providing or proposing to provide employment in development areas. The objective is to assist firms who incur unusual initial expenses in moving to a development area. Expenses which would have been incurred irrespective of the location chosen are thus excluded. The assistance covers such things as transport, duplication of machinery, special costs of training labour and costs of abnormal site preparation.

Various other incentives are provided for industrialists to move to development areas. The details vary from time to time. For instance, the 1963 Local Employment Act enabled the Board to offer grants of 10 per cent of the cost of acquiring and installing plant and machinery in industrial undertakings. The 1963 Budget introduced a new system of 'free depreciation' which allowed manufacturers who invest in development areas to write off, for tax purposes, expenditure on most new plant and machinery at any rate they chose. Following the White Paper on *Investment Incentives*, the Industrial Development Act, 1966, introduced a new system of special incentives including investment grants for plant and machinery at 40 per cent (as compared with the national rate of 20 per cent) to manufacturing and extractive industries in development areas. In November 1967, certain areas where exceptionally high unemployment might arise through colliery closures were designated 'special development areas'. Additional incentives were provided for firms moving to such areas, e.g. rent-free periods of up to five years for firms renting Board of Trade factories and providing suitable employment.

These incentives add up to a significant total. Between April 1960 and March 1968 the financial cost amounted to £269 million and provided an estimated 428,000 jobs.

Increasing attention has been given in recent years to what has become known as 'infrastructure' – basic public services such as roads, water supplies and sewerage schemes. These are, of course, normal responsibilities of local authorities and statutory undertakers. However, the Local Employment Acts provide for special grants in development areas where existing services are inadequate 'and it is expedient for the purpose of providing employment appropriate to the needs of the district that they should be improved.'

The Annual Reports of the Board of Trade are none too clear on how much financial aid is actually given under these powers, but it seems that in 1967–8 it was of the order of £75,000 for six water supply schemes, £220,000 for twenty-one sewerage schemes, and an unstated amount for road schemes.

Grants are also available for the purchase and rehabilitation of land which is derelict, neglected or unsightly. These grants are available to all local authorities at a rate of up to 50 per cent (under the Local Government Act, 1966). In development areas, however, if the Board of Trade agrees that schemes will contribute directly or indirectly to the development of industry in the area the grants are payable at the higher rate of 85 per cent. Again, adequate figures are difficult to come by, but in 1967–8, final approval was given to forty-four schemes in England covering 997 acres. These were estimated to attract grants amounting to £906,000. A further eleven schemes covering 359 acres and estimated to cost £297,000 received preliminary approval.

Finally, yet another Government Department has powers under the Local Employment Acts: this is the Department of Employment and Productivity, which was known until 1968 as the Ministry of Labour. These powers enable the Department to give grants and allowances to key workers (and their dependants) who move to a development area. In the eight years ended March 31, 1968, 885 lodging allowances and 2,017 grants for removal expenses were paid.

The Department also administers a resettlement transfer scheme under which unemployed or redundant workers who move their homes to take up employment can receive financial assistance towards the cost of fares, lodgings, removal and legal expenses.

Industrial Development Certificates

Industrial development is, of course, subject to planning control by local authorities. But no application for planning permission for the erection of an industrial building (normally exceeding 5,000 square feet – but less in some areas, particularly in Southern England and the West Midlands) can be made unless it is accompanied by an industrial development certificate. This is a negative control and, furthermore, is limited in extent. There is no control over existing buildings. A firm which is refused permission for development in, say, the London area, may be able to purchase a vacant factory and thus create the very increase in employment which it was the Board's objective to prevent. This stems from the fact that the control is applied to building and not directly to employment. Under current powers the only alternative is the purchase by the local authority of the property – an extremely costly undertaking.

An IDC is generally made valid for the area of a local authority. The Board does not inquire whether the proposed site – if one has been chosen – is suitable. This is an issue of land use which falls within the scope of the local planning authority's functions. It thus follows that the granting of a certificate by the Board does not guarantee that the authorized development will – or can – take place.

Recent legislation has been directed towards a tightening up of the controls. Thus the Control of Office and Industrial Development Act, 1965, extends the meaning of 'related development' to effect greater control over the creation of a substantial area of floor space by the accumulation of individual pieces of development, each of which is below the exemption limit. Similarly, the Industrial Development Act, 1966, extends the meaning of 'industrial building', thereby bringing under IDC control all buildings used or designed for use for scientific research. ('Scientific research' is defined as 'any activity in the fields of natural or applied science for the extension of knowledge'.) This Act also provides powers which ensure that planning permission is needed before space approved for 'ancillary purposes' such as storage can be converted to production use.

The most important recent change, however, has been the introduction of controls over office development.

Office Development Permits

Pressures for the control of office development were resisted throughout the late 'fifties and early 'sixties on the ground that it would be impracticable. The 1963 White Paper, *London – Employment: Housing: Land*, argued the case well:

'The machinery for controlling the issue of industrial development certificates depends on knowledge of the firm which occupies the factory and on an assessment of the need for that firm to carry on its manufacture in a particular area. Many new factories are purpose-built and have heavy machinery installed; occupiers do not change often. New office blocks, on the other hand, are more often than not built for letting; this is, indeed, often the only way in which modern accommodation can be provided in units of a suitable size for small and medium-sized firms. Consequently, when the developer seeks planning permission he may not know how many tenants he will have or who his tenants will be; and these tenants may change at frequent intervals. A Government Department trying to administer a control of this sort would, therefore, be without the basic information needed for the purpose. Even when a tenant was known it would be extremely difficult to judge the case put forward in support of an office in the central area by a commercial or professional firm. The Government do not believe that it would be practical to administer a system of control of office occupation either effectively or equitably.'[23]

Action along three lines was proposed. First, planning controls over new office building were tightened. The issue here was a complicated legal one. In brief, the existing legislation allowed a 10 per cent increase in cubic capacity to owners rebuilding their premises. Since new buildings have lower ceilings and less circulation space, a 10 per cent increase in cubic capacity could involve as much as a 40 per cent increase in floor space. Attempts by local planning authorities to restrict this involved the risk of paying heavy compensation. The Town and Country Planning Act, 1963, removed any compensation liabilities which may arise when permission is refused for an increase in *floor space* of more than 10 per cent.

Secondly, an attempt was made to disperse more Government offices. It had been Government policy for many years to disperse Headquarters Departments and self-contained branches which could function away from London without loss of administrative efficiency. In 1962, of the total headquarters staff of 125,000, some 25,000 already worked outside London, and there were plans for moving a further 7,000. It was felt, however, that it was time for a thorough re-examination of the situation. A review was undertaken by Sir Gilbert Flemming. His (unpublished) report recommended the transfer of some 18,000 jobs from central London.

Thirdly, a new agency, the Location of Offices Bureau, was set up to encourage the decentralization of office employment from central London. (Ministerial responsibility for the Bureau rested with Housing and Local Government until April 1969, when it was transferred to the Board of Trade.) The Bureau's main function is to provide an information service. Its operations are summarized in its annual reports.[16]

The return of the Labour Government in 1964 was followed by an introduction of direct controls over office building through 'Office Development Certificates'. The legislation (Control of Office and Industrial Development Act, 1965) applied the control only in the Metropolitan Region, but provided for its extension by Order to any other part of Great Britain. In August 1965 it was extended to the Birmingham conurbation, and in July 1966 to major parts of Southern England and the East and West Midlands.

The controls are very similar in form to the industrial development certificate control. In the areas to which the Act applies an office development permit (like the industrial development certificate) must be obtained before planning permission can be given. In deciding whether to grant such a permit, the Board of Trade 'shall have particular regard to the need for promoting the better distribution of employment in Great Britain'. The Board has complete discretion and there is no right of appeal or compensation if a permit is refused.

In considering an application for an ODP, the Board are guided by three principles: first, the activity for which new accommodation is sought must be one which cannot be carried on outside the area of the control; secondly, there must be no suitable alternative accommodation available; and thirdly, the development must be essential in the public interest.

The controls have been operated with particular stringency in the Greater London area. When office control was first introduced it was estimated that 37 million square feet of office space were being created or at least had received planning permission. The control reduced this amount substantially: by the spring of 1968 about 11½ million square feet of new and potential office space were in the pipeline.

The controls have not escaped criticism. The London Chamber of Commerce, for example, have argued that rents are rising to very high levels, that small firms are forced by these high rents to occupy outmoded and uneconomic premises, and that there is a real danger that international companies may by-pass London when they choose locations for offices to control their European operations.

THE DEPARTMENT OF ECONOMIC AFFAIRS*

Since it was established in 1964, the Department of Economic Affairs has been responsible for regional economic planning. Its role and functions are more appropriately discussed within the

* See appendix to this chapter for recent changes in the machinery of central government.

context of regional planning which is the subject of Chapter XII. Here a brief account is given of its organization.

The DEA is smaller than most Government Departments and has a higher proportion of administrators and economists, together with a team of industrial advisers seconded for short periods from private industry. It is organized in three main groups: industrial policies, economic forecasting and regional policies.

The industrial group, led by an Industrial Policy Co-ordinator, consists of a number of industrial advisers and a staff of career civil servants. It is concerned with the co-ordination of policies which affect the management of industry in both the public and private sectors such as monopolies, mergers and rationalization. (DEA is the sponsor Department for the Industrial Reorganization Corporation.)

The economic group is staffed largely by professional economists and statisticians. It is concerned with the allocation of national resources and the role played by particular industries in economic growth. The division contributes to the discussion within the Government of general problems of economic policy, especially those of a structural character. Among its tasks is the designing and up-dating of a mathematical model of the development of the UK economy.

The regional group is concerned with regional problems, research and planning. It provides the Chairman and Secretaries of the Economic Planning Boards in the English regions. This group is also the base for the interdepartmental Central Unit for Environmental Planning.

The Central Unit for Environmental Planning

Established in 1966, the CUEP is a research team staffed from DEA, the Board of Trade, the Ministry of Housing and Local Government, the Ministry of Transport and the Department of Employment and Productivity. Its first major work has been a detailed study of the Humberside area.

The objectives of the Unit's work are to:

(i) consider the kind of questions which need to be answered in providing feasibility studies for Government;
(ii) work out the best means of conducting such studies, so as to make the best use of work already done, and of staff resources;
(iii) within the general framework, collect and analyse the facts and forecasts relevant to the areas under study, and to make recommendations.

For the Humberside study the CUEP were assisted by a physical planning unit located in the area. This was composed of staff seconded from the four local planning authorities in the study area, together with two nominees of the Ministry of Transport. This physical planning unit worked under the direction of a Principal Planning Officer of the Ministry of Housing and Local Government who was also a member of the CUEP thus facilitating liaison between the two units.

Appendix

THE 1969 MACHINERY OF GOVERNMENT CHANGES

The structure of local government is painfully slow to change, but the machinery of central government can alter at a rate which defeats the chronicler who attempts to provide an up-to-date picture. Indeed, one Government Department – the Ministry of Land and Natural Resources* – was so short-lived (April 1965 to February 1967) that it failed to gain a mention in any edition of this book. The Department of Economic Affairs (October 1964 to October 1969) was established in time to receive an appendix note in the second edition and was abolished just too late to be deleted from the current edition. It is not without good reason that the best reference book on planning law – Heap's *Encyclopedia of Planning* – is published in loose-leaf form!

The October 1969 changes are, at the time of writing (October 1969), far too recent to permit a useful assessment, particularly since there is still a baffling movement of chairs and personnel both in the Government and in Whitehall – with promises of more to come.

All that can be attempted here is a summary of the major changes in so far as they are relevant to this book. The record is largely taken from the Downing Street statement of October 5 (and the Prime Minister's statement in the House of Commons on October 13).

The most important change is the creation of an 'overlord' for local government and regional planning. This is the appointment of a Secretary of State for Local Government and Regional Planning, with major responsibilities for local government reorganization and 'environment pollution in all its forms'. (The first incumbent is Mr Anthony Crosland.) He has rather unclear (probably inevitably unclear) federal powers in relation to the Ministries of Housing and Transport and more direct responsibility for the Regional Planning Councils and Boards which have been transferred to him from the now defunct Department of Economic Affairs.

The Board of Trade's responsibilities in the field of regional

* During its short existence, it took over MHLG functions relating to water resources and the countryside, including responsibility for the Water Resources Board and the National Parks Commission. Its claim to historical record lies in its responsibility for the Land Commission and Leasehold Enfranchisement Bills.

economic development, however, go to another super-Ministry: the Ministry of Technology. This Ministry has reponsibility for industrial development certificates, advance factories, industrial estates in development areas, building grants and loans. The rationale here is that the Ministry which is responsible for dealing with the greater part of private and public industry is also responsible for executive decisions concerning the location of industry.

Relevant extracts from the Statement are given below:

Technology, Industry and Trade

'The Ministry of Technology becomes the Government Department with the main responsibility for industry both in the public and private sectors.

The merger with the Ministry of Power will bring together in one Department responsibility for all primary fuels and plant industries for electricity generation, together with other power and energy supply and plant industries.

The expanded Department will also be concerned with the structure of industry and with industrial productivity. It will therefore assume responsibility for the Industrial Reorganization Corporation.

The industries concerned with mineral development in both the public and private sectors (except those which are closely linked with the construction industry) will also be brought together under the Ministry of Technology. The Ministry will thus have the main responsibility for all general questions relating to mineral development.

The Ministry of Technology will assume the Department of Economic Affairs' responsibilities in the field of regional economic development and also the related distribution of industry functions of the Board of Trade. The regional organizations of the Ministry of Technology and of the Board of Trade will be adjusted so as to reflect the new division of responsibilities between the two Departments.

The Board of Trade will concentrate on overseas trade and export promotion, including the many activities which contribute invisible earnings to the balance of payments. Thus, in addition to its responsibilities for external commerical policy (including tariff policy) and export policy and services, the Board of Trade will retain responsibility for civil aviation, shipping, tourism, hotels and insurance.

Local Government and Regional Planning, after the Maud Report

The new Secretary of State for Local Government and Regional Planning will co-ordinate the work of the Ministries of Housing and Local Government and Transport. He will be particularly concerned with following up the recommendations in the Maud Report. He will take personal charge of the negotiations for carrying through the reform of Local Government in England. Responsibility for the Regional Planning Councils and Boards will pass, with their staffs in the regions, from the Department of Economic Affairs to the new Secretary of State.

The Secretary of State will also have special responsibility in relation to all aspects of environmental pollution. He will co-ordinate the activities of the executive Departments in this field. The Prime Minister has asked him as a matter of urgency to submit recommendations for improving the machinery for dealing with pollution problems. The Secretary of State's responsibilities in this field cover England, but he will have the task of securing co-ordination with the Secretaries of State for Scotland and for Wales, whose responsibilities and statutory functions remain unchanged in this and in all other matters.'

REFERENCES AND FURTHER READING

1 *Board of Trade, Control of Office and Industrial Development Act, 1965: Annual Reports by the Board of Trade*, House of Commons Papers, HMSO, annual.
2 Board of Trade, *Local Employment Acts: Annual Reports by the Board of Trade*, House of Commons Papers, HMSO, annual.
3 Brown, H. J. J. 'Digest of Planning Decisions', Part V of Heap, D., *Encyclopedia of the Law of Town and Country Planning*, Sweet & Maxwell, 1959. (In loose-leaf form with regular supplements.)
4 *Committee on Administrative Tribunals and Enquiries: Report* (Franks Report), Cmnd. 218, HMSO, 1957.
5 Cowan, P. *et al.*, *The Office – A Facet of Urban Growth*, Heinemann, 1969.
6 Daniels, P. W., 'Office Decentralization from London – Policy and Practice', *Regional Studies*, Vol. 3, No. 2, September 1969, pp. 171–8.
7 Department of Economic Affairs and Board of Trade, *Investment Incentives*, Cmnd. 2874, HMSO, 1966.
8 Dunnett, Sir James, 'The Relationship between Central and Local Government in the Planning and Execution of Road Schemes', *Public Administration*, Vol. 40, Autumn 1962.
9 Estimates Committee, Session 1961–2, *Classified Roads*, H.C. Paper 227, HMSO, 1962.
10 Estimates Committee, Session 1962–3, *Administration of the Local Employment Act, 1960*, H.C. Paper 229, HMSO, 1963.
11 Estimates Committee, Session 1968–9, *Motorways and Trunk Roads*, H.C. Paper 102, HMSO, 1969.
12 Griffith, J. A. G., *Central Departments and Local Authorities*, Allen & Unwin, 1966, Chapter 5.
13 Hammond, E., *London to Durham: A Study of the Transfer of the Post Office Savings Certificate Division*, University of Durham, Rowntree Research Unit, 1968.
14 Hammond, E., 'Dispersal of Government Offices: A Survey', *Urban Studies*, Vol. 4, No. 3, November 1967, pp. 258–75.
15 Local Government Manpower Committee, *1st Report*, 1950, *Second Report*, 1951, HMSO.

16 Location of Offices Bureau publications (obtainable from the Bureau, 27 Chancery Lane, London WC2):
Annual Reports.
Commuters to the London Office: A Survey, 1966.
White Collar Commuters: A Second Survey, 1967.
Offices in a Regional Centre: A Study of Office Location in Leeds, 1968.
Relocation of Office Staff: A Study of the Reactions of Office Staff Decentralised to Ashford, 1969.
Offices: A Bibliography, 1969.
17 McCrone, G., *Regional Policy in Britain*, Allen & Unwin, 1969.
18 Mandelker, D. R., *Green Belts and Urban Growth*, University of Wisconsin Press, 1962.
19 Marriott, O., *The Property Boom*, Hamish Hamilton, 1967.
20 Miller, B., 'Citadels of Local Power', *The Twentieth Century*, Vol. 162, October 1957.
21 MHLG, *Bulletin of Selected Appeal Decisions*, HMSO, 1947–63.
22 MHLG, Planning Bulletins, HMSO, 1962 and continuing.
23 MHLG, *London – Employment: Housing: Land*, Cmnd. 1952, HMSO, 1963.
24 MHLG, Circular No. 47/63, *Town and Country Planning Act, 1963*, HMSO, 1963.
25 MHLG, Circular No. 64/65, *Control of Office and Industrial Development Act, 1965*, HMSO, 1965.
26 MHLG, *Local Government Finance, England and Wales*, Cmnd. 2923, HMSO, 1966.
27 MHLG, *Report for 1965 and 1966*, Cmnd. 3282, HMSO, 1967.
28 MHLG, *Town and Country Planning*, Cmnd. 3333, HMSO, 1967.
29 MHLG, *Development Control Policy Notes*, HMSO, 1969 and continuing.
30 MHLG, *Planning Appeals: A Guide to Procedure 1969*, HMSO, 1969.
31 MHLG, *Report for 1967 and 1968*, Cmnd, 4009, HMSO, 1969.
32 Ministry of Transport, *Roads in England 1965–66*, H.C. Paper 232, HMSO, 1966.
33 Ministry of Transport, *Roads in England 1968–69*, H.C. Paper 1, HMSO, 1969.
34 Ministry of Transport, Roads Circular No. 1/68, *Traffic and Transport Plans*, HMSO, 1968.
35 Richards, P. G., *The New Local Government System*, Allen & Unwin, 1968.
36 *Royal Commission on Local Government in Greater London: Minutes of Evidence* and *Report*, Cmnd. 1164, HMSO, 1960.

37 Select Committee on Estimates, Session 1958–59, *Trunk Roads*, H.C. Paper 223, HMSO, 1959.
38 Self, P., *Town Planning in Greater London*, London School of Economics, Greater London Papers No. 7, 1962.
39 Sharp, E., *The Ministry of Housing and Local Government*, Allen & Unwin, 1969.

Chapter IV

THE LEGISLATIVE FRAMEWORK

The Town and Country Planning Act, 1968, represents a landmark in the development of planning policy and administration. It is a major attempt to bring the planning system up to date, to shed the cumbersome and inflexible procedures of the established system, to redefine the respective roles of central and local government (with far less central concern with detailed planning matters) and to provide the framework for a far greater degree of citizen-participation in the planning process.

The changes in law are to be implemented by Ministerial Order. The intention (to quote from the Debates on the Bill) is to bring the provisions of the Act into operation selectively 'as and when the administrative machine at both governmental and local authority level is able to cope with them'. The majority of the provisions of the Act became operative during 1969; the major exception being those relating to the new development plan system. Apart from this exception, the following account has been up-dated to include the new provisions.

The new system of 'structure', 'action area' and 'local' plans is more difficult to deal with, for two reasons. First, it is intended that this system will be introduced 'into those parts of the country where it can usefully be operated in advance of its general introduction when local government is reorganized'.[20] *Secondly, even in areas where the new plans are being formulated, the existing system will continue in operation until the structure plans have been formally approved by the Minister. In short, the current development plans will continue in operation for some considerable time. It follows that it is necessary to discuss both systems fully.*

It should be noted that there will be a spate of regulations and circulars from the Ministry during the transition to the new system. These are collated in the supplements to the 'Encyclopedia of the Law of Town and Country Planning'. Summaries are provided in the monthly 'Journal of Planning and Property Law'. (Both are published by Sweet & Maxwell.)

This chapter only briefly touches on the role of citizen-participation in the new system; the main discussion is to be found in the final chapter, where a more appropriate framework can be provided.

DEVELOPMENT PLANS

Under the pre-war system of planning, an operative planning scheme was in effect a zoning plan. A developer could visit a local town hall and ask to see the planning scheme: he would be shown a written document and a series of coloured maps, each colour representing some particular use. From the published scheme the developer would find that particular pieces of land were zoned for industry, for open space, for residential development at not more than eight houses to the acre, and so on. The great advantage of this system to the developer was that there were no doubts as to what development would be permitted: it was all written down and had the force of law. But therein lay one of its gravest shortcomings: certainty for the developer meant inflexibility for the local authority. One way of circumventing this was for planning authorities to take advantage of the time-consuming and cumbersome procedure for preparing and obtaining approval to their schemes by remaining at the draft stage for as long as possible. Yet this had the opposite danger: the flexibility thereby attained could easily become mere expediency. The new system attempted to achieve a balance between these two extremes by the introduction of the flexible development plan. A development plan is essentially a statement of development proposals. It is intended to show, for example,

'which towns and villages are suitable for expansion and which can best be kept to their present size; the direction in which a city will expand; the area to be preserved as an agricultural Green Belt and the area to be allocated to industry and to housing'.[30]

The legislation, however, defined a development plan as 'a plan indicating the manner in which a local planning authority propose that land in their area should be used, whether by the carrying out thereon of development or otherwise, and the stages by which any such development should be carried out'. Furthermore, it was required that the development plan should 'define the sites of proposed roads, public and other buildings and works, airfields, parks, pleasure grounds, nature reserves and other open spaces, or allocate areas of land for use for agricultural, residential, industrial or other purposes'.

Unlike the pre-war 'operative scheme', the development plan does not of itself imply that permission will be granted for particular developments even if it appears that they are clearly in harmony with the plan. Development control is achieved by a system of planning permissions. The development plan merely sets out the intentions of the local planning authority. Though a developer is able to find out from the plan where particular uses would be likely to be permitted, his specific proposals still need to be considered by the local planning authority. When considering applications the authority are expressly directed to 'have regard to the provisions of the development plan', but the plan is not binding in any way, and, indeed, authorities are instructed to have regard not only to the development plan but also to 'any other material considerations'. Furthermore, in granting permission to develop the authority can impose 'such conditions as they think fit'.

But though local planning authorities have considerable latitude in deciding whether to approve applications, they have to be clear on the planning objectives for their areas: otherwise they have no adequate basis on which they can judge the merits and shortcomings of particular applications. This is the purpose of the development plan – on which great stress is laid in the legislation. A meaningful plan can be prepared only on the basis of an intensive study of existing conditions, trends and needs.

Some idea of the comprehensive approach required in the survey is given by the following list of matters on which the Ministry required the collection of information.[31]

1. Existing land use; age and condition of buildings; quantities of building uses; residential density; land unsuitable for building purposes.
2. Ancient monuments and buildings of architectural or historic interest.
3. Rural community structure.
4. Population – natural change and migration.
5. Industry and employment.
6. Minerals.
7. Agriculture and forestry.
8. Communications – roads, railways, docks, harbours and canals; airports and airfields.
9. Proposed developments by Government Departments.
10. Public utilities – water supply and sewerage; electricity; gas; land drainage.
11. Social services.
12. National parks, conservation and amenity areas.
13. Holiday development.

This is merely a list of the main headings. The full list is a formidable one. An indication of the amount of detailed work involved can be given by considering one heading – the age and condition of buildings:

'The physical condition of buildings will be an important factor in determining the need for redevelopment. Maps should, therefore, be prepared for each area in respect of which a town plan is being prepared, distinguishing buildings as follows:

(*a*) Buildings which have suffered extensive war damage.
(*b*) Buildings already condemned or which would be scheduled for demolition under the Housing Acts if demolition were immediately practicable.
(*c*) Buildings of architectural or historic interest.
(*d*) Other buildings, classified by age as follows:
 (i) Erected before 1875.
 (ii) Erected between 1875 and 1914.
 (iii) Erected since 1914.

This classification should give a first index to the areas to be considered for redevelopment. From the information so obtained, considered with other factors such as density, mixture of uses, layout, structural condition, and subjection to periodic flooding, other maps should be prepared to show:

(i) areas requiring early development;
(ii) areas becoming obsolete but which still contain some years of useful life;
(iii) areas not likely to require redevelopment for many years.'

On the basis of this information and after all the necessary consultations with Government Departments, statutory undertakers and (in the case of counties) district councils, the local planning authority prepares a development plan. Strictly speaking this is a totally separate series of documents. The 'Report of Survey' provides the background to and the basis of the plan, but it has no statutory effect. The legal documents consist of a 'Written Statement' and a series of maps. The Written Statement is a short, formal (some would say excessively short and formal) document containing little more than a summary of the main proposals of the plan. It does not contain any argument for or against the proposals, or, indeed, the factual material on which these are based. Thus, the Written Statement to the Cambridgeshire Development Plan[1] lists seven 'basic proposals'.

'The principal proposals upon which the Development Plan was based were:

(*a*) That Cambridge should remain predominantly a University Town.
(*b*) To reduce the rate at which the City is growing and to stabilize the population within the Town Map Area at not more than about 100,000 persons.
(*c*) At the same time to accelerate the development of villages surrounding Cambridge to accommodate an additional population up to approximately 7,500 persons.
(*d*) The provision of a comprehensive road system capable of satisfying traffic requirements in the City.
(*e*) In the rural areas of the County, to safeguard the interests of agriculture and to provide improved conditions for the agricultural population.
(*f*) To limit industrial expansion in and near Cambridge, and to discourage the establishment of large industries of the mass-production type, within the County.
(*g*) To encourage the development of those larger villages which are on good lines of communication and which form suitable centres for the surrounding rural areas.

The bulk of the document is taken up with proposals for school building, roads, public utilities and so on.'

DESIGNATED LAND

An important part of the Written Statement is a list of sites 'designated for compulsory acquisition'. This can be a source of some confusion since on the one hand it is not a complete list of sites that are to be compulsorily acquired during the period of the plan, and on the other hand, designation does not imply that the land will in fact be compulsorily acquired. What is achieved by designation is simply a considerable extension of the powers of compulsory purchase, not only for local authorities but also for Government Departments and statutory undertakers. All these public authorities have specific powers of compulsory purchase for defined purposes, but if land is designated 'for the purpose of any of their functions', they become freed from the restrictions imposed by their existing powers. Normally, of course, the existing powers would be adequate, but designation provides a means whereby land can be acquired which otherwise could not have been acquired. This is particularly important in connection with the proposals of the Development Plan, since the local planning authority can designate any land which they decide needs to be developed comprehensively, and any land which needs to be compulsorily acquired 'in order to secure its use in the manner proposed by the plan'. In short, provided that the use is defined in the plan, land may be designated and thus compulsorily acquired.

These are extremely wide powers and have been subject to considerable criticism. In the Committee Stage Debates on the Bill, the Minister argued that 'it is in the interests of owners that they should know what land is likely to be required by the planning authority, by statutory undertakers or by Government Departments within a reasonable period', but in fact since these public authorities still retain their existing powers (and can thus compulsorily acquire land under these powers at any time whether or not the land in question is designated) and, since designated land might not in the event be acquired, this is little consolation either to the owners of designated land or to the owners of non-designated land. Nevertheless, development plans cannot be put into effect without some use of compulsory powers and the proposals of the plan itself contain the threat of compulsory acquisition (particularly in relation to public works). The designation of an area does confirm that it is likely to be compulsorily acquired within a certain period and to that extent gives the owners of land some knowledge of what is to happen.

Designation creates another difficulty: it puts a 'dead hand' on land, which may become unsaleable to anyone other than the authority for whom it is designated. As the Ministry have pointed out, 'this is one of the most serious difficulties associated within planning. Advance notice of intention may, temporarily, blight land needed in future for particular development: yet not to give the notice may result in a waste of money.'[10]

There is, however, a number of safeguards. For instance the Minister must, in approving a designation, be satisfied that the proposal is reasonable and that it will take place within ten years. The designation can be challenged if the land is not acquired within twelve years (eight years in the case of agricultural land), and designation lapses if the owner carries out the development for which the land is designated.

A few local authorities have made extensive use of designation. The draft London Development Plan (1951), for example, contained proposals for 343 designation areas totalling 660 acres. (This was reduced to 219 areas covering 347 acres in the plan as approved by the Minister.) The policy at this time was to designate *all* land which was likely to be required in the first five years of the plan or shortly afterwards. This extensive use of designation was partly responsible for the great number of objections to the plan. (Nearly 7,000 objections were heard at the public inquiry which lasted for 153 days.)

In the draft First Review of the London Plan (1960) the policy has been to designate a much smaller amount and designation has been used only if no other means of compulsory acquisition are possible, or if there are reasons why designation is particularly advantageous. (The actual acreage is not given in the published report, but 138 of the original 219 areas designated in the approved plan have been deleted.)

Generally, planning authorities have used designation sparingly. Its most common use has been for land definitely needed in the near future for developments for which other powers are not available, e.g. small parcels of land needed as sites for post offices and telephone exchanges. The Cambridgeshire Written Statement contains 32 areas of designated land, of which the following are examples:

4·78 acres of land allocated to HM Postmaster General for Post Office Engineering Scheme;
6·20 acres of land allocated to County Council for school playing fields; 0·3 acres of land allocated to the Cambridge City Council for road widening to provide improved access to car park;
25·07 acres of land allocated to the County Council for a village college.

Designated Land and the 1968 Act

The 1968 Act repeals the requirement that land to be compulsorily acquired under the powers of the Town and Country Planning Acts shall previously be designated in an approved development plan. As the White Paper concluded, 'experience has shown that it adds procedural complications without compensating benefits for anybody'.[20] But though designation is no longer required, this is not the case with the powers of compulsory acquisition for planning purposes. The designation provisions have therefore been replaced by new provisions empowering local authorities to compulsorily acquire land needed in connection with development or for other planning purposes. These new powers are more extensive than those which they replace and they include the extension to all public authorities of the 'vesting procedure' available to the Land Commission.*

Local authorities now have power to compulsorily acquire any land in their area if the Minister is satisfied:

(*a*) that the land is required in order to secure or assist the treatment as a whole, by development, redevelopment or improvement or

* See Chapter VI, p. 160.

partly by one and partly by another method, of the land or of any area in which the land is situated; *or*

(*b*) that it is expedient in the public interest that the land should be held together with land so required; *or*

(*c*) that the land is required for development or redevelopment, or both, as a whole for the purpose of providing for the relocation of population or industry or the replacement of open space in the course of the redevelopment or improvement, or both, of another area as a whole; *or*

(*d*) that it is expedient to acquire the land immediately for a purpose which it is necessary to achieve in the interests of the proper planning of an area in which the land is situated.

COUNTY, TOWN AND PROGRAMME MAPS

Accompanying the Written Statement is a series of maps. For a county these include County Maps and a related Programme Map (at a scale of 1 inch to the mile) covering the whole of the administrative county. For areas requiring more detailed planning there will be Town and Programme Maps at the larger scale of 6 inches to the mile. The Cambridgeshire plan has a Town Map for the City of Cambridge – the most important urban area in the County.

In the case of a county borough there is, of course, no county map: the principal maps are the Town Map and its related Programme Map.

The County and Town Maps indicate the developments which are expected in the twenty-year period of the plan (and possibly some important developments which are expected somewhat later) and the pattern of land use proposed at the end of the period. (In areas for which no notation is given – which may be extensive in counties – it is intended that the main existing uses should remain undisturbed.) A Programme Map shows the stages by which the proposed development is to be achieved. This usually distinguishes at least between the first five years and the remainder of the plan period. In this way private and public development is programmed in a co-ordinated way. Thus the development of housing estates is viewed in relation to the school-building programme and proposals for new roads. At the same time the various needs of an area can be seen as a whole and a set of priorities determined. During the period when the initial surveys were being undertaken, building resources were severely limited and a system of licensing was in operation. It was therefore necessary to relate the programme to the anticipated availability of resources. Furthermore, an estimate was required of the total cost of that part of the plan which was likely to be undertaken by the local authority. These financial estimates were necessarily very crude, but they did encourage a realistic approach to planning proposals.

As an example to programming, the following extract is reproduced from the Written Statement of the Development Plan for East Ham[3]:

'The Programme Map accompanying the Town Map gives a broad indication of the principal development, expected to be undertaken and substantially completed during the first five years and during the remainder of the period of the plan. The map also indicates proposals of major importance in the Development Plan, the construction of which may not be undertaken within the period of the plan.

'In the preparation of the programme a broad assessment has been made of the amount of development which can be carried out having regard to the labour resources available in the Borough and the progress of development during recent years. It is emphasized, however, that this assessment can only be of the broadest possible character because of the mobility of labour in the London area.

'In formulating the Programme Map an assessment has been made of the relative urgency of the principal development proposals and thus of the approximate order in which they should be undertaken. Regard has been paid as far as possible to the condition of property and to the rehousing liability of the Council and the fulfilment of the programme is subject to the provisions of paragraph 22. (This states that for progress and continuity of the Council's housing programme it is essential that further land be allocated outside the Borough for housing development.)

'It has been estimated that the gross capital outlay of realizing that part of the plan likely to be undertaken by the Council is about £23 million.'

A formidable amount of work is involved in the preparation of development plans. The 1947 Act required local planning authorities to submit plans to the Minister for approval within three years (by July 1, 1951), 'or within such extended period as the Minister may in any particular case allow', but not surprisingly most authorities could not meet the deadline. (Only twenty-two did, in fact, do so.)

The Ministry's task is to assess the general provisions of the plan, to weigh all objections to it, to hold a public local inquiry, to consider the report of the Inspector on the inquiry, and finally to approve the plan with or without modification. Every plan has been modified in some degree before approval, sometimes very substantially.

Local authorities themselves often propose modifications in order to meet objections. About half the plans had been approved by 1951 and the bulk had been approved by 1959; but three were not approved until the early 'sixties: Denbighshire, part of Glamorgan and Manchester.

Development plans, unlike the old 'operative schemes', are not intended to be final statements – even of broad intentions. Local planning authorities are obliged to review them at least every five years, and additionally can propose amendments at any time.

The impossibility of coping with the preparation and approval of plans on the original time-scale has greatly delayed the review procedure and many local authorities were still engaged on their first review in the mid-'sixties.

This was one of the major reasons for introducing the new (1968) system. However, since the new system is to be introduced gradually, provision has had to be made for the 'transition'. Existing development plans remain operative until superseded, but no further reviews or amendments are to be submitted to the Ministry (except without prior approval).

The reviews followed the same process as the initial plan: survey, draft written statement and maps, submission to the Ministry, local public inquiry, and approval with or without modification. Alterations or additions to development plans could be made at any time. Often these 'amendments' amounted to more detailed plans for particular areas. In counties, the Town Maps for the districts were commonly submitted in this way. Another type of detailed planning often submitted as a formal amendment was a Comprehensive Development Area plan.

COMPREHENSIVE DEVELOPMENT AREAS

In its consideration of the problems of post-war reconstruction the Uthwatt Committee examined the existing powers (under the Town and Country Planning Act, 1932, and the Housing Act, 1936) of local authorities to undertake redevelopment. These they found quite inadequate. In their view, 'the simplest and only effective method of achieving the desired results is to confer on the planning authority compulsory powers of purchase, much wider and more simple in operation than under existing legislation, over any land which may be required for planning or other public purposes'. In particular they recommended that there should be powers for the compulsory acquisition of the whole of war-damaged and of obsolete areas – later popularly termed 'blitz' and 'blight' areas. Only by such a means would it be possible to cut through the tangle of separate ownerships and make the whole of an area immediately available for comprehensive redevelopment. Some idea of the problems involved is provided by the well-known example of the 267-acre Duddeston and Nechells area in Birmingham.*

'Nearly 11 miles of existing streets, mostly narrow and badly planned. 6,800 individual dwellings, the density varying locally up to eighty to the acre.

'5,400 of these dwellings classified as slums to be condemned.

'15 major industrial premises or factories, several of them comparatively recent in date.

'105 minor factories, storage buildings, workshops, industrial yards, laundries, etc.

'778 shops, many of them hucksters' premises.

'7 schools.

'18 churches and chapels.

'51 licensed premises.

'Many miles of public service mains, water, gas and electricity, including over a mile of 42-inch trunk water main, nearly all land under carriageways and consequently in the wrong places for good planning. Add to these a railway viaduct, a canal, a railway goods yard and a gas works and you have a beautiful problem in redevelopment.'

The procedure for dealing with areas such as this was lengthy and tortuous, and involved dealing with the separate problems under separate powers and persuading different Government Departments (Health, Education, Transport) to give approvals without regard to their separate Departmental priorities. Yet comprehensive redevelopment was obviously necessary if modern layouts and adequate provision for transport and amenities was to be made. (A trial layout for the area showed that a saving of twenty acres of land could be made on the street pattern alone.)

Many of the Uthwatt recommendations were incorporated in the Town and Country Planning Acts of 1944 and 1947. Local authorities were given powers to define 'comprehensive development areas' where it is desirable to develop or redevelop an area as a whole.† Such an area could include areas of war damage, areas of obsolete development or bad layout, land required for accommodating population displaced in connection with the redevelopment of the area or *any* land to be developed as a whole for *any* purpose defined in the development plan.

* The quotation comes originally from a 1937 report of the City Engineer (Sir Herbert Manzoni). It is also to be found on page 6 of the Uthwatt *Report*.[34]

† For further discussion see Chapter XI.

The principle underlying the comprehensive development area procedure was that 'because of the multiplicity of ownerships usually involved, the key to proper redevelopment of towns is public acquisition, to be followed either by the disposal of the land to private developers, under conditions ensuring that they will themselves carry out development in accordance with the plan for the area, or by direct development by the local authority'.[29]

The comprehensive development area procedure is replaced in the 1968 Act by the 'action area' procedure discussed below.

THE CONTROL OF DEVELOPMENT

With certain exceptions, all development requires the prior approval of the local planning authority. The authority have considerable discretion in this matter. Though they must 'have regard to the provisions of the development plan' they may take 'any other material considerations' into account. Indeed they can approve a proposal which 'does not accord with the provisions of the plan'. If the proposal does not involve a substantial departure from the plan and does not 'injuriously affect the amenity of the adjoining land' their discretion is unlimited. In other cases they require prior approval of the Ministry.

The planning decisions of the authority can be one of three kinds: unconditional permission, permission 'subject to such conditions as they think fit', or refusal. The practical scope of these powers is discussed in a later section. Here it is necessary merely to stress that there is a right of appeal to the Ministry against conditional permissions and refusals. If the action of the authority is thought to be *ultra vires* there is also a right of appeal to the courts. Furthermore, planning applications which raise issues which are of major importance, or are of a particular technical nature, can be 'called in' for ministerial decision.

Development control necessarily involves some procedure for enforcement. This is provided by 'enforcement notices' under which an owner who carries out development without permission or in breach of conditions can be compelled to 'undo' the development – even if this involves the demolition of a new building. A 'stop notice' can also be used in conjunction with an enforcement notice to put a rapid stop to the carrying out or continuation of development which is in breach of planning control.

These are very strong powers and clearly it is important to establish the meaning of 'development', particularly since the term has a legal meaning far wider than in ordinary language.

TABLE IV.1

Decisions on planning applications, 1967 (a)

	No.	%
Planning applications decided in 1967	422,553	100·0
Permissions granted	358,338	84·8
Refusals	64,215	15·2

(*a*) Ministry of Housing and Local Government, *Statistics of Decisions on Planning Applications 1967*, HMSO, 1968. (Additionally there were 40,509 advertisement applications. See Table VII.1, p. 173 below.) Conditional permissions or permissions for a limited period are counted as 'permissions granted' except for caravan sites, where a distinction is made between consents given with and without a time limit.

THE DEFINITION OF 'DEVELOPMENT'

In brief, development is 'the carrying out of building, engineering, mining or other operations in, on, over or under the land, or the making of any material change in the use of any buildings or other land'.* There are some legal niceties attendant upon this definition with which it is fortunately not necessary to deal in the present outline. Some account of the breadth of the definition is, nevertheless, needed. 'Building operations', for instance, include rebuilding operations, structural alterations of or additions to buildings and – somewhat curiously – 'other operations normally undertaken by a person carrying on business as a builder'; but maintenance and improvement works which affect only the interior of the building or which do not materially affect the external appearance of the building are specifically excluded. The demolition of a building does not *of itself* constitute development, though, of course, it may form part of a building operation, or lead to the making of a material change in the use of the land upon which it stood.

The second half of the definition introduces quite a different concept: development here means not a physical operation, but a change in the *use* of a piece of land or a structure. The change has to be 'material', i.e. substantial – a concept which it is clearly difficult to define; and which, indeed, is not defined in the Act. A change in *kind* (for example from a house to a shop) is material, but a change in *degree* is material only if the change is very substantial. For instance, the fact that lodgers are taken privately in a family dwelling-house does not of itself constitute a material change so long as the main use of the house remains that of a private residence. On the other hand, the change from a private residence

* Town and Country Planning Act, 1962, Section 12. (This Act is a consolidating measure which repealed and re-enacted most of the provisions of the 1947 Act, together with much of the later legislation.)

with lodgers to a declared guest-house, boarding house or private hotel would be material. Difficulties arise with changes of use involving part of a building with secondary uses and with the distinction between a material change of use and a mere interruption. Two changes of use are specifically declared in the legislation to be material. First, if a building previously used as a single dwelling-house is used as two or more dwelling-houses (thereby making decisions under the Rent Restriction Acts on what constitutes a 'separate dwelling' relevant to planning decisions).[33] Secondly, the deposit of refuse or waste material on land 'notwithstanding that the land is comprised in a site already used for that purpose, if either the superficial area of the deposit is thereby extended, or the height of the deposit is thereby extended and exceeds the level of the land adjoining the site'; in other words the deposit of refuse or waste material always constitutes development unless the deposit is made in a hole – and the shape of the hole is important because though a hole can be filled to the level of the adjoining land the superficial area must not be increased.

This is by no means the end of the matter, but enough has been recorded to show the breadth of the definition of development and the technical complexities to which it can give rise. Reference must, nevertheless, be made to one further issue. Experience has shown that complicated definitions are necessary if adequate development control is to be achieved, but the same tortuous technique can be used to exclude matters over which control is not necessary. Apart from certain matters which are specifically declared not to constitute development (e.g. internal alterations to buildings, works of road maintenance or improvement carried out by a local highway authority within the boundaries of a road), and others which though possibly constituting development are declared not to require planning permission, there is provision in the Act for the Minister to make a 'Development Order' specifying classes of 'permitted' development, and a 'Use Classes' Order specifying groups of uses within which interchange is permissible.

To deal first with the latter. The Use Classes Order prescribes classes of use within which change can take place without constituting development. Thus Class X is 'use as a wholesale warehouse or repository for any purpose', and Class XII is 'use as a residential or boarding school or residential college'. For some classes particular uses which would otherwise fall into a category are specifically excluded: for example, Class I is 'use as a shop for any purpose except as (i) a fried fish shop, (ii) a tripe shop, (iii) a shop for the sale of pet animals or birds, (iv) a cat's-meat shop, (v) a shop for the sale of motor vehicles'. As a result, to change a sweet shop into a bookshop does not constitute development, but to change a shoe shop into a 'noxious trade' such as a tripe shop does. These categories, it should be stressed, refer only to changes of use – not to any building work. Furthermore, the Order gives no freedom to change from one class to another; whether such a change constitutes development depends on whether the change is 'material'. It should also be noted that in granting permission for a particular use, a local planning authority may impose conditions restricting that use and thus preventing the changes in use allowed by the Order. For instance a local planning authority may decide that an office of a special character might be allowed in a residential area but at the same time may not wish the premises to be available for any type of office use. Conditions could be imposed on the planning permission which would overrule the general permission given for such a change in use by the Use Classes Order (Class II is 'use as an office for any purpose').

The General Development Order gives the developer a little more freedom by listing classes of 'permitted development'. If a proposed development falls within these classes then no application for planning permission is necessary – the General Development Order itself constitutes the permission.* The Order includes certain developments by public authorities and nationalized industries, the erection of agricultural buildings (other than dwelling-houses), and permits the change of use from a fried fish shop, a tripe shop, etc. (as listed in Class I of the Use Classes Order), to any type of shop – but not, of course, the other way round.

Permissions given under this Order are not unqualified. Apart from two 'standard conditions' relating to development which involves making or altering the means of access to a trunk or classified road or which 'creates an obstruction to the view of persons using any road by vehicular traffic at or near any bend, corner, junction or intersection so as to be likely to cause danger to such persons', particular conditions are laid down for each of the different classes of development listed. Thus, under Class I the enlargement, improvement or other alteration of a dwelling-house is permitted

* The distinction between the Use Classes Order and the General Development Order is that the former lists changes of use which do not constitute development, while the latter lists activities which, though constituting development, do not require *ad hoc* permission. The distinction was of importance during the time when development charges were imposed, since if there was no 'development' then no development charge was payable, whereas development was, by definition, eligible for a charge. (In fact, however, exemption from development charge was specifically made for many of these permitted developments.) These complexities are now mainly of historical interest and are not discussed further in this book.

(including the building of a garage) subject to limitations of size and elevation.*

This by no means complete account of 'development' is sufficient for present purposes. The cynic may perhaps be forgiven for commenting that the 'freedom' given by the Use Classes Order and the General Development Order is so hedged by restrictions, and frequently so difficult to comprehend (though he may note with relief that painting is not subject to control – unless it is 'for purposes of advertisement, announcement or direction') that it would be safer to assume that any operation constitutes 'development' and requires planning permission. The framers of the legislation have here been helpful. Application can be made to the local planning authority (either as part of an application for planning permission or as a separate application) for a 'determination' as to whether a proposed operation constitutes 'development' and, if so, as to

* To give an illustration of the detailed way in which the law of planning is drawn up, the following is the full text of Class I of 'permitted development':

Class I: Development within the curtilage of a dwelling-house

Description of development	*Conditions*
1. The enlargement, improvement or other alteration of a dwelling-house so long as the cubic content of the original dwelling-house (as ascertained by external measurement) is not exceeded by more than 1,750 cubic feet or one-tenth whichever is the greater, subject to a maximum of 4,000 cubic feet; provided that the erection of a garage, stable, loosebox, or coach-house within the curtilage of the dwelling-house shall be treated as the enlargement of the dwelling-house for the purposes of this permission.	1. The height of such building shall not exceed the height of the original dwelling-house. 2. No part of such building shall project beyond the forwardmost part of the front of the original dwelling-house. 3. Standard conditions 1 and 2.
2. The erection, construction or placing, and the maintenance, improvement or other alteration, within the curtilage of a dwelling-house, of any building or enclosure (other than a dwelling, garage, stable, loosebox or coach-house) required for a purpose incidental to the enjoyment of the dwelling-house as such, including the keeping of poultry, bees, pet animals, birds or other livestock for the domestic needs or personal enjoyment of the occupants of the dwelling-house.	1. The height shall not exceed, in the case of a building with a ridged roof, 12 feet, or in any other case, 10 feet. 2. Standard conditions 1 and 2.

Standard Conditions 1 and 2 are:

1. This permission shall not authorize any development which involves the formation, laying out or material widening of a means of access to a trunk or classified road.
2. No development shall be carried out which creates an obstruction to the view of persons using any highway used by vehicular traffic at or near any bend, corner, junction or intersection so as to be likely to cause danger to such persons.

whether planning permission is required. Should the local planning authority determine that the proposals do constitute or involve development, they have to inform the applicant of the grounds on which they have reached this decision and also of his rights of appeal. Most planning decisions are administrative acts against which appeal lies only to the Minister, but in the case of a determination of whether planning permission is required, the question is a mixed one of fact and law: thus not only is there the normal right of appeal against the local authority's decision to the Minister, there is also a right of appeal against the Minister's decision to the High Court.

CONDITIONAL PERMISSIONS

A local planning authority can grant a planning permission subject to conditions. This can be a very useful way of permitting development which would otherwise be undesirable. Thus residential development in an area liable to subsidence can be permitted subject to the condition that the foundations are suitably reinforced, or a garage may be approved in a residential area on condition that 'no panel beating or paint spraying is carried out, and the hours of business are kept within reasonable limits'. The local planning authority's power to impose conditions is a very wide one. The legislation allows them to grant permission subject to 'such conditions as they think fit' – but this does not mean 'as they please'. The conditions must be appropriate from a planning point of view: 'the planning authority are not at liberty to use their powers for an ulterior object, however desirable that object may seem to them to be in the public interest. If they mistake or misuse their powers, however *bona fide*, the court can interfere by declaration and injunction.'* Three types of condition are specifically referred to in the 1962 Act:

(1) Conditions can be imposed for regulating the development or use of *any* land under the control of the applicant, whether or not it is land to which the application relates, so long as there is a definite relationship between the object of the condition and the development permitted.
(2) A 'time condition' can be imposed on a permission. This is referred to in the legislation as 'permission granted for a limited period only'. Such a condition is particularly appropriate where the proposed development is undesirable on a long-term view, but there is no reason why a temporary permission should not

* *Pyx Granite Co. Ltd.* v. *Ministry of Housing and Local Government*, 1 Q.B. 554, p. 572. This famous case is widely reported in legal texts.

be granted. This would occur where a local authority had definite plans for redevelopment in the near future.

(3) A condition can be imposed requiring operations to commence within a specified time. (Under the pre-1968 legislation that planning permissions normally ran with the land and had no time limit.) This particular condition can be imposed where the planning proposals for the area will require substantial revision, but the degree of risk that the proposed development will conflict with these proposals is not sufficient to justify outright refusal.[28]

Until the passing of the 1968 Act, there was no general time-limit within which development had to take place: unless a specific condition was imposed, planning permission development could take place at any time. The 1968 Act, however, made all planning permissions subject to a condition that development is begun within five years. If the work is not begun within this time limit, the permission lapses. The Minister or the local planning authority can vary the period, and there is no bar to the renewal of permission after the period (whether it be five years or more or less) has elapsed.

The purpose of this new provision is to prevent the accumulation of unused permissions and to discourage the speculative land hoarder. (For this reason they apply to pre-1968 Act permissions as well as later ones.) Accumulated unused permissions could constitute a difficult problem for some local authorities: they created uncertainty and could make an authority reluctant to grant further permissions which might result in, for example, too great a strain on public services. The new provision is directed towards the bringing forward of development for which permission has been granted and thus to enable new allocations of land for development to be made against a reasonably certain background of pending development.

The provision relates, however, only to the beginning of development and this apparently includes 'digging a trench or putting a peg in the ground'. But (if the permission is not a pre-1968 Act one) the trench-digger may be brought up against a further new provision: he may be served with a *completion notice*. Such a notice states that the planning permission lapses after the expiration of a specified period (of not less than one year). Any work carried out after then becomes liable to enforcement proceedings.

ENFORCEMENT OF PLANNING CONTROL

If the machinery of planning control is to be effective some means of enforcement is essential. Under the pre-war system of interim development control there were no such means. A developer could go ahead without applying for planning permission, or could even ignore a refusal of permission. He took the risk of being compelled to 'undo' his development (e.g. demolish a newly built house) when – and if – the planning scheme was approved, but this was a risk which was often worth taking. And if the development was inexpensive and lucrative (e.g. a petrol station or a greyhound racing track) the risk was virtually no deterrent at all. This flaw in the prewar system has been remedied. There is now machinery for dealing with development carried out without planning permission or in contravention of conditions laid down in a grant of permission.

Development undertaken without permission is not an offence in itself; but ignoring an 'enforcement' notice is – there is a maximum fine following conviction of £100 and a penalty of £20 for each day during which the requirements of the notice remain unfulfilled.

These are very drastic powers; but there is a number of safeguards. In the first place a local authority can serve an enforcement notice only 'if they consider it expedient to do so having regard to the provisions of the development plan and to any other material considerations' – in short, they must be satisfied that enforcement is necessary in the interests of good planning. Secondly, in the case of building or other operations (but not of material changes of use) the notice must be served within four years of the development being carried out. (Prior to the 1968 Act this 'four year rule' applied to all development including change of use.) Thirdly – and this meets the case of development carried out in good faith, or ignorance – application can be made for retrospective permission. It is hardly likely that a local authority would grant permission for a development against which they had served an enforcement notice, but they could, of course, attach conditions; and for the owner there is the usual right of appeal. Fourthly, there is a right of appeal against an enforcement notice to the Minister and to the courts. Appeals can be made on several grounds, e.g. that permission ought to be granted, that permission has been granted, and that no permission is required.

The 1968 Act introduced a further enforcement device: the *stop notice*. This is an attempt to prevent delays in the other enforcement procedures (and advantage being taken of these delays) resulting in the local authority being faced with a *fait accompli*. Previously, when an appeal was lodged against an enforcement notice there was nothing to stop development continuing while the appeal was being 'determined'. The appeal could take several months, particularly in cases where a local inquiry was held. No liability was involved since, until the enforcement order was made (if it was), no offence was being committed. The stop notice prohibits the continuation of development which is alleged (in the enforcement notice) to be in breach of planning control. Development carried out in contravention of a stop notice constitutes an offence. Local authorities must, however, use this new power with circumspection, since if the enforcement notice is quashed on appeal they are liable to pay compensation for loss due to the stop notice.

REVOCATION, MODIFICATION AND DISCONTINUANCE

The powers of development control possessed by local authorities go considerably further than the granting or withholding of planning permission. They can interfere with existing uses and revoke a permission already given even if the development has actually been carried out.

A revocation or modification order is made when the development has not been undertaken (or before a change of use has taken place). The local authority must 'have regard to the development plan and to any other material considerations', and an order has to be confirmed by the Minister. Compensation is payable on two grounds: first for any expenditure or liabilities incurred after the permission has been granted (e.g. expenditure on the preparation of plans); and, secondly (following the 1954 Act), for the loss in the development value of the land. The logic in the latter is based on the curious situation caused by the abolition of development charges. The granting of planning permission increases the value of the land in question, but since no development charge is now levied, the development value is thus given to the owner along with the planning permission. The revocation of that permission deprives the owner of a value which had been specifically given to him – hence compensation is payable. (Before the 1954 Act logic demanded otherwise. The fact that revocation thereby deprived the owner of potential development value did not in itself warrant compensation, since if permission had been given the development value would be transferred to the State through the development charge.)

A revocation or modification order is not very often made. One case which attracted some attention was that of the Eton Fish and Chip Restaurant. This concerned an application for planning permission to use premises in the Eton High Street as a fish and chip restaurant. The Eton Urban District Council granted permission (under delegated powers), but after a petition, mainly from local shopkeepers, decided to seek a revocation order on the ground that 'the existence of a fish and chip restaurant in the High Street would be detrimental to the amenities, would cause nuisance, offence and annoyance to occupiers of properties in the vicinity and to users of the public highway, and would adversely affect the general appearance of the High Street'. The order was confirmed by the Minister. In this particular case it would seem that planning permission had been given after inadequate consideration of publicity. The revocation was therefore a rectification of a 'mistake'.

Quite distinct from these powers is the much wider power to make a Discontinuance Order. This power is expressed in extremely wide language: an order can be made 'if it appears to a local planning authority that it is expedient in the interests of the proper planning of their area (including the interests of amenity)'. Again ministerial confirmation is required and compensation is payable – for depreciation, disturbance and expenses incurred in carrying out works in compliance with the order. Under this power action can be taken against any development (or use) whether it was specifically permitted under the post-war planning Acts or established prior to the Acts. It would appear that an order will be confirmed by the Minister only if the case is a strong one. In recently rejecting a discontinuance order on a scrap metal business in an 'attractive residential area', for instance, the Minister has said: 'the fact that such a business is out of place in an attractive residential area must be weighed in the light of an important distinction between the withdrawal of existing use rights, as sought in the discontinuance order, and the refusal of new rights'. In this particular case the Minister did 'not feel justified in overriding the proper interests of the objector as long as his business is maintained on an inoffensive scale'. Other cases have established the principle that a stronger case is needed to justify action to bring about the discontinuance of a use than would be needed to warrant a refusal of permission in the first instance.

It needs to be stressed that English planning legislation does not assume – as does American planning – that existing non-conforming uses must disappear if planning policy is to be made effective. This may often be the avowed policy, but the Planning Acts explicitly permit the continuance of existing uses.

This problem of non-conforming uses is an extremely difficult one. As the Uthwatt Committee pointed out:

'The question whether the right to maintain, replace, extend and use an existing building is to subsist in perpetuity, notwithstanding that the building does not conform to the provisions of the scheme is fundamental in relation to the replanning of built-up areas. On the one hand, it would not be equitable, without compensation, at any time and for any reason to remove, or to prohibit the maintenance, replacement, extension or use of an existing building. On the other hand, an unqualified right, unless compensation is paid, to replace non-conforming buildings and to maintain existing uses permanently is inconsistent with the present conception of planning.

'The problem is one of finding a proper balance between the two considerations.'[34]

The Committee proposed that a 'life' should be placed on non-conforming uses and that at the expiration of that life the use should be brought to an end without compensation. This recommendation was not accepted and thus local planning authorities can extinguish a non-conforming use only by paying compensation. That this can be an expensive business is shown by the experience of the London County Council (now the Greater London Council) in purchasing non-conforming industrial premises. The Council estimated in 1956 that there were 1,950 acres occupied by non-conforming industry in the Administrative County, of which 500 were in office or commercial zones and were unlikely to be disturbed. The cost of acquiring the whole of the remaining 1,450 acres was thought to be of the order of £150 million. Some £500,000 a year (increased in 1963 to £750,000 a year) is spent on acquiring such premises by agreement, and by April 1959 nearly fifty had been bought at a cost of £2¼ million. Clearly by such means only the fringe of the problem is touched. Yet purchase by agreement (though involving time consuming and involved negotiations) is preferable to the use of discontinuance orders. Indeed a discontinuance order is rarely used since it gives rise to liability for the payment of compensation without the advantage of securing any interest in the property. The Council has evolved a policy of carefully selecting sites for purchase; according to the First Review of the London Plan factors which are taken into consideration include:

(i) whether the site can be redeveloped for housing, schools, open space, etc.;
(ii) whether purchase would reduce employment in the inner parts of the County;
(iii) the possibility of buying when vacant, thus avoiding payment for disturbance;
(iv) the degree of nuisance caused;
(v) the possibility of assisting a firm wishing to move to a new or expanded town.

A similar situation existed in Middlesex, where there were about 3,000 non-conforming firms, having a total site area of 788 acres. Between January 1957 and March 1962 over £400,000 was spent on the displacement of thirty firms.

CONTROL OF DEVELOPMENT UNDERTAKEN BY GOVERNMENT DEPARTMENTS, LOCAL AUTHORITIES AND STATUTORY UNDERTAKERS

Development by Government Departments does not require planning permission, but there are special arrangements for 'consultations'. The formal procedure is for the Government Department to submit to the local authority a 'Notice of Proposed Development'. 'Representations' can be made to the Department, and 'if the local planning authority has some substantial objection to the proposal which the developing department is unable to meet, the department will inform the Ministry of Housing and Local Government, and the two departments will discuss with the authority whether anything can be done to meet the authority's point of view'.[32]

Certain classes of development are excluded from the requirement for consultation, namely:

(*a*) secret development;
(*b*) minor operations and unimportant changes of use in which the local planning authority is unlikely to be interested because what is proposed will not materially affect the character of the neighbourhood;
(*c*) proposals for further buildings similar in type and demands on public services to those already existing on a site in their possession unless the buildings abut on a public highway or might be considered to affect amenity (either directly or in relation to eventual removal).

It is the Government Department which has the final say in any matters affecting their land. The legislation merely allows agreements to be made to ensure that, so far as is possible, their developments will be in harmony with the provisions of a development plan or the requirements of good planning.

Development undertaken by local authorities and statutory undertakers is subject to special planning procedures. ('Statutory undertakers' are defined as 'persons authorized by any enactment to carry on any railway, light railway, road transport, water transport, canal, inland navigation, dock, harbour, pier or lighthouse undertaking, or any undertaking for the supply of electricity, gas, hydraulic power or water'.) Where a development requires the authorization of a Government Department (as do developments involving compulsory purchase orders, work requiring loan sanction, and developments such as local authority housing on which government grants are paid) the authorization is usually accompanied by 'deemed planning permission'. Much of the normal development of local authorities and statutory undertakers (e.g. road works, laying of underground mains and cables) is 'permitted development' under the General Development Order. Local planning authorities are also 'deemed' to have permission for any development in their area which accords with the provisions of the development plan. The Minister has power, however, to require them to apply for his permission in any particular case. Other local authorities (including those exercising delegated powers) are normally required to obtain planning permission from the local planning authority. If a local planning authority wishes to develop in the area of another planning authority they must apply to that authority for planning permission in the same way as would a private developer. Thus a county borough which wishes to develop an overspill housing estate in the adjacent county has to obtain planning permission from that county. In all these cases there is the right of appeal to the Minister.

Statutory undertakers wishing to carry out development which is neither 'permitted development' nor authorized by a Government Department have to apply for planning permission to the local planning authority in the normal way, but in the case of 'operational land' appeals are considered jointly by the Minister of Housing and the 'appropriate Minister,' e.g. in the case of electricity and gas undertakings, the Minister of Fuel and Power; and in the case of transport undertakings, the Minister of Transport. ('Operational land' is land which, in respect of its nature and situation, is not 'comparable with land in general'. This is a rather imprecise definition, but land used for railway sidings or a gas works is operational land whereas land used for showrooms or offices is not.) Until recently statutory undertakers could be 'controlled' only on the payment of compensation by the local planning authority.

The privileged position of statutory undertakers has not escaped criticism, and two highly controversial developments proposed in 1967 created a public outcry. The first was the proposal by the Southern Gas Board to erect a 128 feet high gasholder in the historic centre of Abingdon. The second was the proposal by the Gas Council for a terminal at Bacton in East Anglia to process North Sea Gas.

In the former case, the Minister withdrew the Gas Board's right of 'permitted development' and planning permission for the gasholder was refused. Compensation of £250,000 was involved and this was met on a 50–50 basis between the local authorities concerned and the Gas Board.

In the Bacton case, permission for development was given after two exhaustive public inquiries, but subject to rigorous conditions.

These brought matters to a head. The original justification for the special position of statutory undertakers was that they are under an obligation to provide services to the public and cannot, like a private firm in planning difficulties, go elsewhere. If a planning authority wished to restrict their activities, it was held that it was only right for the extra costs to be reimbursed.

In the debates on the 1968 Town and Country Planning Bill, the Minister said that the climate of opinion had now changed. It was still necessary for planning to pay sensible attention to the need to provide essential public services economically. But modern industrial undertakings had to be prepared to conduct their businesses in a way which minimized ugliness and to accept any reasonable cost involved in making their buildings, plant and operations acceptable to public opinion.

A working party of officials of statutory undertakers and Government Departments was set up to consider the planning implications of developments by statutory undertakers and to review the relevant planning legislation. The first fruits of their work were new provisions now incorporated in the 1968 Act. The Act provides that no land which is not already operational can become such unless certain planning requirements are met. The most important of these is that there shall be a specific planning permission for development for operational purposes. The Act also breaches the long-standing compensation principle. Compensation for refusal of planning permission is abolished in certain types of case.

At the time of writing the working party was reviewing other aspects of the planning control of statutory undertakers.

In the previous edition of this book this section ended with the comment that though statutory undertakers and Government Departments must consult with local planning authorities, they are either exempted from planning provisions or are effectively beyond their reach. This statement is no longer true, and it is likely that it will become even less so in the future.

CARAVANS

Caravan sites are subject to special provisions contained in Part I of the Caravan Sites and Control of Development Act, 1960, and the Caravan Sites Act, 1968.

Sir Arton Wilson's report, *Caravans as Homes*, highlighted the problems of residential caravanning. In 1959, about 60,000 caravans in England and Wales were being used as homes by some 150,000 people – mainly young married couples, often with small children. About 80 cer cent of caravan dwellers hoped to move into normal dwellings. To quote the report, they live in caravans 'because they could not get other dwellings in the right places or on the right terms; or because caravans meet their needs for cheapness, convenience or mobility'. Some simply like caravan life.

The report estimated that about 38,000 of the 60,000 caravans were on sites for which permission, usually conditional and temporary, had been given; about 12,000 had 'existing use' rights; and about 10,000 were on sites which appeared to contravene planning control. With some notable exceptions, local authorities tended to regard caravans as a substandard form of accommodation and (less debateably) difficult to control. (It was the publicity given to a case in Egham which led to the setting up of the Arton Wilson Committee.) The caravan interests, on the other hand, argued the case for recognition of caravanning as an acceptable way of life and pressed for more positive approaches by the local authorities.

The 1960 Act gave local authorities new powers to control caravan sites, including a requirement that all caravan sites had to be licensed before they could start operating (thus closing loopholes in the planning and public health legislation). These controls over caravan sites operate in addition to the normal planning system: thus both planning permission and a licence has to be obtained. Most of the Act dealt with control, but local authorities were given wider powers to provide caravan sites.

The Ministry's *Policy Note* on caravans states that: 'Planning policy recognizes the demand for sites. The main objectives of policy are, first, to enable the demand to be met in the right places, while preventing sites from springing up in the wrong places; and, second, to allow caravan sites, where permitted, to be established on a permanent or long-term basis, in order to facilitate the provision of proper services and equipment and to allow the occupants reasonable security of tenure.'

In fact, of the 6,374 residential caravan planning applications decided in 1967, a quarter were refused and two-thirds were granted for a limited period only. Only 641 were granted without a time limit. Local authorities face strong pressure from their ratepayers 'to preserve local amenities and property values' – to which caravans are seen as a threat. The Ministry may be clear as to what 'planning policy recognizes' but the reality differs considerably from the official statement.

One group of caravanners is particularly unpopular: gypsies, or to give them their less romantic statutory description 'persons of nomadic life, whatever their race or origin' (but excluding 'members of an organized group of travelling showmen, or persons engaged in travelling circuses, travelling together as such'). The appalling conditions in which the majority of the 15,000 gypsies live were portrayed in the 1967 report of the Ministry's Sociological Research Section, *Gypsies and Other Travellers*. As the Ministers stated in their foreword to this report, the basic problem is that no one wants gypsies around: 'all too often the settled community is concerned chiefly to persuade, or even force, the gypsy families to move on'. Under Part II of the Caravan Sites Act, 1968, local authorities will have a duty to provide adequate sites for gypsies 'residing in or resorting to' their areas – but no date has yet been set for this part of the Act to become operative.* When it does, the main responsibility for providing these sites will lie with local authorities. In the meantime local authorities are exhorted to do as much as they can, and applications for loan sanction for sites will receive 'sympathetic consideration'.

Holiday caravans are subject to the same planning and licensing controls as residential caravans. To ensure that a site is used for holidays only (and not for 'residential purposes'), planning permission can include a condition limiting the use of a site to the holiday season. Conditions may also be imposed to require the caravans to be removed at the end of each season or to require a number of pitches on a site to be reserved for touring caravans.

The Ministry's *Policy Note* states that it is the aim 'to steer holiday caravan development to a limited number of areas, usually those in which caravans are already established, rather than allow them to be scattered more widely'.

In 1967, of the 1,627 planning applications for holiday caravan sites, 45 per cent were refused, 36 per cent granted for a limited period, and 19 per cent granted without a time limit.

PURCHASE NOTICES

Planning considerably affects the value of land. The granting of planning permission carries with it the liability (on sale or development) to pay a betterment levy, but a major part of the development value accrues to the owner. A planning refusal does not of itself confer any right to compensation. On the other hand, revocation of planning permission or interference with existing uses do rank for compensation, since they involve a taking-away of an existing right. There are other circumstances in which planning controls so affect the value of the land to the owner that some means of reducing the hardship is clearly desirable. For example, the allocation of land in a development plan for a school will probably reduce the value of houses on this land or even make them completely unsaleable. In such cases the affected owner can serve a notice on the local authority

* 1st April 1970 has now been fixed as the operative date.

requiring them to purchase the property at an 'unblighted' price. Broadly, a purchase notice can be served, if, as a result of a planning action, land becomes 'incapable of reasonably beneficial use'. In all cases Ministerial confirmation is required. The cases in which a purchase notice can be served include*:

(i) refusal or conditional grant of planning permission;
(ii) revocation or modification of planning permission;
(iii) discontinuance of use;
(iv) 'planning blight'.

Normally if an owner is refused permission to develop his land (or, if onerous conditions are laid down) there is nothing he can do about it – except, of course, to appeal to the Minister. But if the refusal or the conditions prevent him from obtaining 'reasonably beneficial use' of the land, he can serve a purchase notice. 'The question to be considered in every case is whether the land in its existing state and with its existing permissions (including operations and uses for which planning permission is not required) is capable of reasonably beneficial use. In considering what capacity for use the land has, relevant factors are the physical state of the land, its size, shape and surroundings, and the general pattern of use in the area. A use of relatively low value may be reasonably beneficial if such a use is common for similar land in the neighbourhood.'[12]

A purchase notice is not intended to apply to a case in which an owner is simply prevented from realizing the full potential value of his land. This would imply the acceptance in principle of paying compensation for virtually all refusals and conditional permissions. It is only if the existing and permitted uses of the land are so seriously affected as to render the land incapable of reasonably beneficial use that the owner can take advantage of the purchase notice procedure.

Blight Notices

The redress by way of a purchase notice provided for owners affected by planning blight was introduced in 1959 (and extended in 1968, since when it has been termed a *blight notice*). The object is to deal with the problem presented to certain classes of owners by the fact that a development is planned to take place on their land at some future (probably uncertain) date. A development plan may, for instance, show the line of a proposed road, though not necessarily the year in which it is to be constructed. In the meantime an owner

* The 1968 Act makes corresponding provisions in relation to listed building consent. See p. 177.

who wishes to move and sell his property has to wrestle with the problem of 'blight'. These purchase notice provisions are restricted to owner-occupiers of houses and small businesses who can show that they have made reasonable attempts to sell their property but have found it impossible to do so except at a substantially depreciated price because of certain defined planning actions. These include land designated for compulsory purchase or allocated or defined by a development plan for any functions of a Government Department, local authority, statutory undertaker or the National Coal Board; and land on which the Minister of Transport has given written notice of his intention to provide a trunk road or a 'special road' (i.e. a motorway).

The gradual introduction of the new type of development plan under the 1968 Act has involved new provisions in relation to planning blight. Briefly, the effect of these is that in those areas where a structure plan comes into force, blight caused either by the structure plan or the previous development plan is covered by the planning blight provisions until a local plan allocating land succeeds the old development plan. That local plan then becomes the relevant plan for the blight provisions. Since local plans will provide a much more precise indication of the possibility of public acquisition of land, the structure plan will no longer be relevant.

Structure plans, however, will lack this precise indication. Whether they will give rise to more or to less planning blight than the old development plan system remains to be seen. The Planning Advisory Group thought it unlikely that there would be any more and, 'in so far as they show less detail (e.g. town map primary school and minor open space allocations) it may be less'. On the other hand, in the debates on the Bill, it was officially stated that:

'When we are dealing with the structure plan for which there is no local plan in force, we have a new problem which is that, owing to the diagrammatic nature of the plans, no one will be able to say with certainty that this does or does not affect the claimant's property, but that nevertheless, because of that very uncertainty, a wider number of properties may be affected.'

But how far is it possible to go with compensation for planning blight? Or, to put the matter in its broader context, how far ahead is it possible to plan in a democratic society? Some discussion of the problem is to be found in the last chapter; here it is sufficient to note that the 1968 Act effects a compromise. Compensation is payable for blight, except in cases where a planning proposal is not precisely defined and the local authority have a genuine doubt as to whether they will eventually need the land, yet are sure that they will not require it for at least fifteen years. In such cases a blight notice is met by a *counter-notice*, known in jargon as the 'fifteen-year counter-notice'.

It is at points such as this that even complex legislation reaches its limit and resort has to be had to ministerial exhortation and discretionary powers. Hardship cases should, according to official statements and ministerial circulars, be treated as sympathetically as possible. Unless there is little likelihood of a proposal being implanted in the foreseeable future (in which case this should be clearly and firmly stated 'so that prospective purchasers are not unnecessarily deterred'), hardship cases should be dealt with by 'discretionary purchase'. Loan sanction and any relevant Exchequer grant is normally given in such cases.

THE NEW DEVELOPMENT PLANS

The Report of the Planning Advisory Group

The system of development plans and development control set up under the Town and Country Planning Act of 1947 operated for almost two decades without significant change. During this time the system has proved its value but it would be surprising if what was appropriate for the mid-'forties was equally relevant to the 'seventies. Furthermore, not only has the tempo of social and economic change increased but also the system has tended to develop its own rigidities. This is particularly the case with development plans. Unlike the 1932 Act 'schemes', they were intended to show only broad land-use allocations. But the definition of 'development plan' in the 1947 Act is a plan 'indicating the manner in which the local planning authority propose that land in their area should be used'. This, together with the way in which plans are mapped, has led inexorably towards greater detail and precision. 'The plans have thus acquired the appearance of certainty and stability which is misleading since the primary use zonings may themselves permit a wide variety of use within a particular allocation, and it is impossible to forecast every land requirement over many years ahead.'

Above all, 'it has proved extremely difficult to keep these plans not only up to date but forward looking and responsive to the demands of change. The result has been that they have tended to become out of date – in terms of technique in that they deal inadequately with transport and the interrelationship of traffic and land use; in factual terms in that they fail to take account quickly enough of changes in population forecasts, traffic growth and other economic and social trends; and in terms of policy in that they do not reflect more recent developments in the field of regional and urban planning. Over the years the plans have become more and more out of touch with emergent planning problems and policies, and have in many cases become no more than local land use maps.'[18]

In short, the system has become out of tune with contemporary needs and forward thinking, and it is becoming bogged down in details and cumbersome procedures. The quality of planning is suffering and delays are beginning to bring the system into disrepute. As a result public acceptability – which is the basic foundation of the system – is beginning to crumble.

Certain changes could be – and were – made within the framework of the existing legislation,[16, 17] but these did not go far enough.

It was within the context of thinking that the Planning Advisory Group was set up in May 1964 to review the broad structure of the planning system and, in particular, development plans. Their report, *The Future of Development Plans*, published in 1965, proposed a basic change which would distinguish between the policy or strategic issues and the detailed tactical issues. Only the former would be submitted for ministerial approval: the latter would be for local decisions within the framework of the approved policy.

For urban areas with populations over 50,000 a new type of *urban plan* was proposed which concentrated on the broad pattern of future development and redevelopment and dealt with the land-use/transport relationships in an integrated way, but which excluded the detailed land-use allocations of the present town maps. Similarly for the counties a new form of *county plan* was proposed which dealt with the distribution of population and employment, the major communications network, the main policies for recreation and conservation, green belts, and the general development policy for towns and villages.

These were to provide a coherent framework of planning policy and would be submitted to the Minister for his approval. Each would identify *action areas* which would require comprehensive planning and on which action would be concentrated over the next ten years or so.

Local planning authorities would have power to prepare *local plans*, which would not be submitted for ministerial approval, but would conform with the policies laid down in the urban plan or county plan. These would serve as a guide to development control and a basis for the more positive aspects of environmental planning. The most significant of local plans would be those for the action areas. The Minister's approval of the action areas would be limited to the policy proposed, and the local planning authorities would prepare *action area plans*, which would provide the detailed basis for implementation.

These types of plans could not be produced by planning authorities acting in isolation: they needed to form part of a regional strategy and also of what was termed a sub-regional pattern. Here – assuming a continuation of the present structure of local government – the regional context would be provided by the Economic Planning Councils and Boards:

'These are likely to be primarily concerned with creating the conditions for economic growth in some regions and controlling the pace of growth in others, within the framework of national economic planning. As a part of this process they will have to be concerned with physical planning issues which are of regional significance, with the overall distribution of population and employment, green belt policy and any other limitation on growth in the conurbations. They must also encompass other physical factors of regional significance such as communications, water resources and major industrial projects; the economic implications of major development projects (motorways, docks, airports); and the impact of economic decisions on physical planning. It will consequently be necessary to associate local planning authorities with the regional planning process and to ensure that their development plans give effect to the intentions of the regional plan.'[18]

The 1968 Planning Act

Following a White Paper, *Town and Country Planning*, published in June 1967, legislative effect to the Planning Advisory Group's proposal was given by the Town and Country Planning Act. The Act provides for structure plans and local plans; among the latter an important category is the action area plan.

A *structure plan*, which has to be submitted to the Minister for his approval, is primarily a written statement of policy, accompanied by diagrammatic illustrations for counties and major towns. Its range is considerably wider than the present development plans. It deals with broad land-use policies (but not with detailed land allocations) and with policies for the management of traffic and the improvement of 'the physical environment'. The legislation provides that the written statement *must:*

(*a*) formulate the local planning authority's policy and general proposals in respect of the development and other use of land in that area (including measures for the improvement of the physical environment and the management of traffic);

(*b*) state the relationship of those proposals to general proposals for the development and the other use of land in neighbouring areas which may be expected to affect that area; and
(*c*) contain such other matters as may be prescribed or as the Minister may in any particular case direct.

The term 'plan' is perhaps misleading since it might be expected to involve a map. But there is to be no map. Unlike the previous development plans (which required county and town maps, with related programme maps), the structure plan has to be accompanied only by 'diagrams, illustrations, and descriptive matter'.

The plan has to 'have regard to current policies with respect to the economic planning and development of the region as a whole' and 'to the resources likely to be available' for its implementation. High ideals must therefore be tempered by the facts of life.

Of particular note is the character of the survey which is to precede the plan. Differences in the content and scope of the surveys required under the earlier and the new legislation highlight the major change in planning philosophy. The earlier legislation is largely concerned with land use: 'a *development plan* means a plan indicating the manner in which a local planning authority propose that land in their area should be used'. The 'survey' required as a preliminary to this dealt predominantly with physical matters. In the 1968 Act, emphasis is laid on major economic and social forces and on broad policies or 'strategies' for large areas. The 'survey' becomes a major part of the planning process. Unlike the earlier legislation, the 1968 Act spells out the coverage of the survey. In the forefront are 'the principal physical and economic characteristics' of the area and, to the extent that they are relevant, of neighbouring areas as well. In formulating the structure plan, particular attention has to be paid 'to current policies with respect to the economic planning and development of the region as a whole' and to likely availability of resources. It is within this strategic framework that 'local plans' are to be drawn up.

The structure plan is essentially a statement of general policy designed to channel major forces in socially and economically desirable directions.

Another major change follows from this. Under the '1947 philosophy', a development plan had to be reviewed 'at least once every five years' and, for this purpose, fresh surveys had to be carried out. This proved totally impracticable for reasons already outlined. Under the new system the 'survey' is a continuing operation. Though some authorities already adopt this approach, the 1947 concept implied an assembly and interpretation of 'survey material' which was reviewed quinquennially and which led to an amendment of the development plan. The 1968 concept sheds a mass of detail and focuses attention on major trends: the continual review is designed to ensure that the strategy remains appropriate and adequate. The review relates essentially to the survey; when the review indicates that the structure plan is in need of alteration, the local planning authority will take the initiative of drawing up a new plan. Alternatively, the Minister can direct an authority to submit proposals for an alteration to its structure plan if he regards it to be necessary in view of, for instance, major proposals in another area which will have an impact in the authority's area.

There is another significant difference in the wording of the requirement for a survey in the new Act. Whereas the earlier legislation required a local authority 'to carry out' a survey, the 1968 Act refers to the duty to *institute* a survey. This change was deliberately designed to facilitate the employment of consultants. As the Minister stated in the Debates, 'the kind of surveys which we envisage would have to be made for some plans will require considerable expertise in fields where manpower is scarce. Some authorities will have been fortunate and have been able to recruit staff with those skills, but others will not. If there are outside consultants available who are able and willing to do the job, that will be satisfactory.'

Structure plans will 'indicate' *action areas* where major change, by development, redevelopment or improvement may be expected. This, ideally, will involve more than simply picking out areas where the local authority think that action is needed. The intention is that the survey will identify and outline problems which require action; the written statement of the structure plan will discuss these problems, determine priorities and indicate areas where action is required not only on a comprehensive basis, but also at an early date. It will also discuss the nature of the required action, its extent and its feasibility in financial terms.

Action areas, it should be noted, are to be *indicated* not *defined.* This deliberate wording was chosen for two reasons. First, if the boundaries of an action area were to be defined precisely and be subject (as part of the structure plan) to ministerial approval, this would involve the very thing which the new system is designed to avoid: detailed consideration by the Ministry and the embodiment of inflexible proposals in a statutory document. Secondly, it was thought likely that it would intensify the problems of planning blight. If boundaries were drawn on a map they would most probably have to be redrawn when more detailed plans were prepared. Thus some people who thought they would be affected would find that they had been misled, and others who thought they would not be affected would find that they were in fact within an action area. Objections would be made to a structure plan on the basis of individual interests rather than on the basis of the general nature of the proposals.

In short, the definition of an action area would be foreign to the essential concept underlying the structure plan – that it deals with general issues in broad terms; it is a policy document not a physical design plan. Fundamentally it is a matter of words and diagrams, not of maps.

Having given 'adequate publicity' to a structure plan (a matter which is discussed at length in Chapter XIII) it is submitted to the Minister (who may approve it in whole or in part and with or without modifications and reservations; or reject it). Objections can be made, as with the old development plans, and a local inquiry may be held. All these issues are subject to ministerial regulations which, at the time of writing, have not yet been published.

Local Plans

Essentially, a local plan is a detailed elaboration of proposals sketched out as matters of broad policy in a structure plan. It will consist of a written statement, a map on an ordnance survey base, together with 'diagrams, illustrations and descriptive matter'. Regulations are to be made regarding the form and content of local plans. The Act provides for a great deal of flexibility – a matter which, in the Debates, the Minister pleaded was essential to the underlying conception. It is envisaged that local plans will vary greatly. Where the proposed development is to be undertaken by a local authority, the local plan will be detailed. Thus those affected will know clearly what is proposed. But where the intention is that the development is to be undertaken privately, the local plan will simply provide broad guide-lines. To quote a ministerial statement:

'I think we are agreed that one of the defects of the present system is its negative nature and that planning authorities are not able to play the useful and constructive role in positive planning which we would like to see them play. We believe that some of the local plans of the kind that I have been indicating – that would give general broad indications for the developer – would take the form, as it were, of a brief for the developer and his architect. It might, for example, state the general objectives of the plan and the broad outlines of the way in which the planning authority envisaged that they would be achieved. The proper grouping of usages within the area, the density and height of buildings on the site, provision for proper circulation of vehicles and foot passengers – matters of this kind will be indicated in the plan. It does not follow by any means that in such a case the planning authority would need to, or would want to, lay down at the plan-making stage the details of the buildings that it wants to see on the site to achieve the objectives of good design and satisfactory treatment of the environment. I think it will generally be considered advantageous to leave scope within the main framework for the imagination and initiative of private developers.'

The legislation *empowers* a local authority to make local plans, but they have no duty to do so except in the case of action areas in a structure plan. This raises the question, what is a 'non-action' area plan? In the absence of regulations and advice on this from the Ministry (which are, however, in the pipeline), enlightenment has to be sought in the Debates on the Bill. It was there explained that an action area local plan would 'typically' be for an area requiring comprehensive treatment – and at an early date. Other local plans will have the primary function of providing a guide for development control.

The most radical feature of a local plan is that at no time does it require to be approved by the Minister.* The policy which it embodies has to be set out in an approved structure plan but its elaboration and adoption are entirely a matter for the local authority (though future regulations and directions may qualify this). This revolutionary innovation goes to the very kernel of the philosophy underlying the 1968 Act – that the Ministry should be concerned only with important issues, and that local responsibility in local matters should become a reality.

There are four safeguards. First, this part of the Act applies only to selected authorities ('We propose to give these powers only to those local authorities which we believe will operate them responsibly'). Secondly, the local plans must be drawn up within the framework of the approved structure plan and must conform with the policy which is there set out. Thirdly, the local authority are required to give 'adequate publicity' to their proposals *before* they are included in a local plan and to give 'adequate opportunity' for the making of representations on their proposals. In these and similar ways 'citizen-participation' is actually written into the legislation. Fourthly (with one important difference), the normal statutory procedure will apply for the deposit of plans, the making

* The Minister has the power to direct that a local plan 'shall not have effect' unless he approves it. This is a reserve power intended to be used only in the exceptional case.

of objections, and the holding of a hearing or inquiry by an independent inspector. This will include the publication of the inspector's report.

The important difference from the traditional procedure is that the inspector will report to the local authority, not to the Minister. This follows, of course, from the principle that the local plan is a local authority, not a central authority, matter.

Important details remain to be settled by regulation (e.g. the professional qualifications of inspectors and procedures at local plan inquiries) but it is clear that citizen participation is more than a desirable adjunct to the new system – it is an essential feature. If citizen participation fails, so will the system.

Citizen participation is discussed, within a wider context, in the final chapter of this book.

Implementing the 1968 Planning Act

The new development plan system cannot be instituted quickly. Quite apart from the difficulties of changing over to a new style of plan, many local authorities are quite incompetent to handle the new system, either because of staffing or because of the irrelevance of their boundaries to the problems which beset them. To use the more diplomatic words of the White Paper, 'some local planning authorities lack the resources to make an immediate start on the new system, and some well-organized authorities administer areas which make it difficult for them to draw up a satisfactory structure plan of the new type'. But to await the reorganization of local government would have involved a very considerable delay (how long only time will show) and would have held back those authorities who are keen and able to make a start – including London. Furthermore, gradual introduction of the new system would have the positive advantage of enabling experience to be gained before it became operative over the country as a whole. Thus the decision was taken to go ahead in advance of the establishment of an appropriate local government system. As a result the central government has the delicate task of deciding which local authorities shall be selected to prepare the first wave of structure plans. Since few (even of the 'best' authorities) operate over a meaningful area this presents a difficult problem. The solution has been to select groups of authorities who could work together voluntarily and whose areas taken together provide a reasonable planning area – but, of course, without prejudice to any decisions on future local government reorganization! Hence what might be called 'conurbation structure plans' are under way in the West Midlands (Birmingham, Dudley, Solihull, Walsall, Warley, West Bromwich and Wolverhampton);

Teesside (Teesside CB, Durham County and North Riding); Tyneside (Gateshead, Newcastle, Sunderland, South Shields, Tynemouth, Durham County and Northumberland); South-East Lancashire and North-East Cheshire – the SELNEC area – (Manchester, Salford, Cheshire and Lancashire); Merseyside (Bootle, Birkenhead, Liverpool, Wallasey, Cheshire and Lancashire); South Hampshire (Portsmouth, Southampton and Hampshire). With a number of other authorities in Leicestershire (Leicester and Leicestershire), Norfolk (Norwich and Norfolk) and South Wales (Cardiff, Newport, Swansea, Glamorgan and Monmouthshire), a total of thirty-five authorities had been invited (by the end of April 1969) to prepare the new plans.

So far as London is concerned, the 1968 Act provides that 'the Greater London development plan shall be treated for the purposes of this Act as a structure plan'. This is precisely what the 'strategic development plan' for London is, though in this area local government reorganization preceded the new planning Act.*

* See Chapter V.

REFERENCES AND FURTHER READING

1 Cambridge County Council, *County Development Plan: Written Statement* (as Approved by the Minister of Housing and Local Government, September 9, 1954).

2 Consumer Council, *Living in a Caravan*, HMSO, 1967.

3 East Ham County Borough Council, *Development Plan 1952: Written Statement*.

4 Gray, P. G. and Parr, E. A., *A Survey of Residential Caravan Life*, Government Social Survey, 1959.

5 Heap, D., *Encyclopedia of the Law of Town and Country Planning*, Sweet & Maxwell, 1959, and periodic supplements.

6 Heap, D., *The New Town Planning Procedures*, Sweet & Maxwell, 1968.

7 Heap, D., *An Outline of Planning Law*, Sweet & Maxwell, 5th edition, 1969.

8 Karslake, H. H., *An Annotated Text of the Town and Country Planning Act, 1968*, Rating and Valuation Association, 1968.

9 Megarry, R. E., *Lectures on the Town and Country Planning Act, 1947*, Stevens, 1949.

10 MHLG, *Report for the Period 1950/51 to 1954*, Cmd. 9559, HMSO, 1955.

11 MHLG, *Caravans as Homes* (Arton Wilson Report), Cmnd. 872, HMSO, 1959.

12 MHLG, Circular No. 49/59, *Purchase Notices*, HMSO, 1959.

13 MHLG, Circular No. 42/60, *Caravan Sites and Control of Development Act, 1960*, HMSO, 1960.

14 MHLG, *Caravan Paris*, HMSO, 1962.

15 MHLG, Circular No. 6/62, *Gypsies*, HMSO, 1962.

16 MHLG, Circular No. 58/65, *Development Plans*, HMSO, 1965.

17 MHLG, Circular No. 70/65, *The Town and Country Planning (Development Plans) Direction, 1965*, HMSO, 1965.

18 MHLG, *The Future of Development Plans: A Report by the Planning Advisory Group*, HMSO, 1965.

19 MHLG, *Gypsies and Other Travellers*, HMSO, 1967.

20 MHLG, *Town and Country Planning*, Cmnd. 3333, HMSO, 1967.

21 MHLG, Circular No. 5/68, *The Use of Conditions in Planning Permissions*, HMSO, 1968.

22 MHLG, Circular No. 49/68, *Caravan Sites Act, 1968*, HMSO, 1968.
23 MHLG, Circular No. 15/69, *Town and Country Planning Act Part IV—Acquisition and Disposal of Land*, HMSO, 1969.
24 MHLG, Circular No. 26/69, *Purchase Notices*, HMSO, 1969.
25 MHLG, *Development Control Policy Notes*, 1969:
1. General Principles.
2. Development in Residential Areas.
3. Industrial and Commercial Development.
4. Development in Rural Areas.
5. Development in Town Centres.
6. Road Safety and Traffic Requirements.
7. Preservation of Historic Buildings and Areas.
8. Caravan Sites.
9. Petrol Filling Stations and Motels.
26 MHLG, *Handbook of Statistics* (Annual), HMSO.
27 MHLG, *Statistics of Decisions on Planning Applications* (Annual), HMSO.
28 Ministry of Local Government and Planning, Circular No. 58/51, *The Drafting of Planning Permissions*, HMSO, 1951.
29 Ministry of Local Government and Planning, *Town and Country Planning 1943–1951: Progress Report by the Minister of Local Government and Planning on the Work of the Ministry of Town and Country Planning*, Cmd. 8204, HMSO, 1951.
30 Ministry of Town and Country Planning, *Town and Country Planning Bill 1947: Explanatory Memorandum*, Cmd. 7006, HMSO, 1947.
31 Ministry of Town and Country Planning, Circular No. 40, *Survey of Development Plans*, HMSO, 1948.
32 Ministry of Town and Country Planning, Circular No. 100, *Development by Government Departments*, HMSO, 1950.
33 Parkes, W., 'Planning Control of Converted Dwellings', *Journal of Planning and Property Law*, 1968, pp. 6–11 and 160–1.
34 *Report of the Expert Committee on Compensation and Betterment* (Uthwatt Report), Cmd. 6386, HMSO, 1942.

Chapter V

THE LOCAL PLANNING MACHINE

THE ADMINISTRATIVE FRAMEWORK

For purposes of local government England and Wales is divided first into county boroughs and administrative counties. Administrative counties are further divided into three types of county districts – municipal (or 'non-county') boroughs, urban districts and rural districts. Rural districts are themselves divided into parishes, but as these have no planning function (except in relation to footpaths, which are discussed in Chapter IX), they can be ignored here.

County boroughs are 'all-purpose' authorities: they are responsible for all local government functions within their areas. A county borough is thus the education, health, housing, highway and planning authority inside its boundaries. In administrative counties functions are shared between the county and the districts. (The differences between the various types of district are unimportant for the present discussion.) All the major functions except housing are the responsibility of the county. Districts are responsible for housing, open spaces, sanitation, cemeteries and burial grounds, refuse collection and disposal, and so on. However, in certain services, of which town and country planning is one, there is a delegation of certain functions from counties to the larger districts.

To summarize the position so far as town and country planning is concerned: the planning authorities are county boroughs and administrative counties, but with some delegation within the latter to the larger districts. In London, planning powers are shared between the Greater London Council and the thirty-two Greater London Boroughs and the ancient City.

In England there are (in 1968) forty-five administrative counties and seventy-nine boroughs outside Greater London, ranging in population from 30,000 (Rutland CC) and 33,000 (Canterbury CB) to 2,428,000 (Lancashire CC) and 1,075,000 (Birmingham CB). In Greater London, the Greater London Council has a population of 7,764,000 with thirty-two Greater London Boroughs (all with populations between 145,000 and 329,000) and the City of London (4,210). In Wales, there are thirteen county councils, ranging in population from 18,000 (Radnor CC) to 743,000 (Glamorgan CC); and four county boroughs: Merthyr Tydfil (56,000), Newport (112,000), Swansea (171,000) and Cardiff (287,000). Table V.1 lists the number of local authorities by size of population. This illustrates not only the wide variation in size but also the large number of small authorities. Forty – nearly a quarter – have populations of 100,000 or less. At the other extreme, there are seventeen authorities within the 500,000 to 1 million range, and six with populations exceeding a million.

Local government has a long history, which can be traced back to Saxon times, but the present structure dates back to the end of the nineteenth century. Though there have been considerable changes in functions since then, and though the number of county boroughs has increased, the basic structure remains largely unchanged except in London.

The large variation in the size of local planning authorities has obvious implications both for the problems confronting them and the organization which they are able to adopt. The large authority is able to establish a separate planning department with a chief planning officer wholly concerned with planning. In the small authority there is neither the scope nor the resources for this; planning has to be combined with other functions, usually roads and engineering or architecture.

So far as the problems facing different sized authorities are concerned, the relationship is not so clear; indeed some small authorities, particularly in the older industrial areas, have acutely difficult planning problems. These have often to be tackled on an inadequate rate and grant income by a small staff. In the larger authorities there are at least the advantages which flow from large-scale organization – the opportunity to employ specialists in, for example, industrial and estate development, and landscaping, as well as research officers.

Rather clearer is the concentration of problems in different types of area: the huge problems of slum clearance, redevelopment and overspill in the conurbations, large-scale suburban development in the rural and semi-rural areas surrounding the big towns, preservation problems in historic towns, mineral workings in the countryside, the pressures for development in beauty spots and, in particular, on the coast. In growing areas there is the problem of dealing with a spate of development applications and ensuring that plans are adequate to meet the needs. In static and declining areas the problem

TABLE V.1

Local planning authorities in England and Wales, 1968

	ENGLAND				WALES			ENGLAND AND WALES	
	Counties	*County Boroughs**	*Greater London Boroughs*	*Total*	*Counties*	*County Boroughs*	*Total*	*Total*	
Population	No.	No.	No.	No.	No.	No.	No.	No.	%
Less than 50,000	1	1	1	3	3	–	3	6	3
50,000–100,000	1	29	–	30	3	1	4	34	20
100,000–250,000	7	35	20	62	5	2	7	69	40
250,000–500,000	19	9	12	40	1	1	2	42	24
500,000–1,000,000	12	4	–	16	1	–	1	17	10
Over 1,000,000	5	1	–	6	–	–	–	6	3
	45	79	33	157	13	4	17	174	100

* Including the City of London

is not so much a matter of controlling development as of encouraging it. Some areas have plenty of room for new development (though they may have problems of inadequate water supply or sewage disposal), while others suffer from an acute shortage of space.

The list could be lengthened almost indefinitely, but the point is obvious. Though most authorities are faced with some difficult problems of redevelopment or development control, preservation, roads, transport and parking, housing and so on, these are unevenly distributed throughout the country. And often the sheer size of these problems bears little relationship to the staffing and financial resources of the planning authority which bears the responsibility for dealing with them. Generalization is therefore difficult.

PLANNING DEPARTMENTS

There is, however, one generalization which can be made: most counties have separate planning departments, whereas most county boroughs administer planning within an architect's or engineer's department. The reason for this is in part historical. County boroughs have been responsible for town and country planning throughout its evolution: it developed gradually within the existing departmental structure. In the counties, on the other hand, planning did not become a general responsibility until the passing of the 1947 Act, when powers were transferred to them from the county districts. In recent years, however, several of the larger towns (Leicester, Liverpool, Newcastle upon Tyne and Sunderland for example) have established separate planning departments with a chief officer in charge, and professional pressures encouraging this are mounting. In some of the large authorities there may be *de facto* a separate department even though there is no separate designation. But the important point still stands: an adequately staffed planning machine cannot be achieved in a small authority.

It needs to be repeated, however, that the essential issue is one of size, not of status. The reports of the Local Government Commissions abound with references to the inadequacies of small planning authorities, whether they be counties or county boroughs. The County of Carmarthenshire (population 165,000), for example, though having a chief planning officer, has only three qualified officers: the County Planning officer, his Deputy and one planning assistant. In fact, in most of the Welsh counties the size of the area is too small for the establishment of an adequate planning department:

'Few of the authorities employ a team of experts in the various branches of planning. For some of the smaller counties the planning department formed part of the County Architect's department, and even if the staff was adequate for normal day-to-day planning control it is difficult to see how serious consideration could be given to the wider aspects of planning.'[12]

The smaller county borough is in the same position. In Merthyr Tydfil (population 57,000), for example:

'. . . the Planning Department was associated with the Engineer's Department. Such a combination, whilst not ideal, can, it is true, be paralleled in many county boroughs and even a few counties, but in Merthyr the chief officer of the combined departments was also the Waterworks Engineer. What was even less satisfactory was that there was little differentiation of function at lower levels; those officers responsible for work in connection with planning also had extensive non-planning duties. The effective control of day-to-day planning was in the hands of a Chief Town Planning Assistant (salary £1,360–£1,535) and three unqualified assistants; two of the three assistants had extensive duties outside the field of planning and, in fact, no single officer was entirely free of extraneous duties. Thus much of the time of the staff of the Planning Department was actually occupied with other duties, for example, street-lighting schemes. No member of the department appeared to have qualifications specially in town planning, though the senior members had qualifications in municipal or civil engineering.'[12]

It is, of course, always tempting to dwell on the deficiencies of an administrative organization: these are easier to discuss, and in any case are usually comparatively well documented. The shortcomings of the present administrative structure of planning, however, justify this emphasis. The problem is particularly acute in the conurbations which, it should be remembered, at present accommodate over a third of the population. The following extract from the report of the Local Government Commission on Tyneside summarizes the structural deficiencies in one conurbation.

'We found that the Tyneside authorities were handicapped in two ways by the existing local government structure. In the first place, a number of authorities had not the strength in population or financial resources to enable them to deal effectively with some of their problems, particularly the big tasks of renewing and improving the whole urban environment, including housing. . . . There was a second handicap, as it seemed to us, under which the Tyneside authorities were labouring, irrespective of their individual strength;

this was the interlocking nature of certain problems over the whole of the urban Tyneside, for instance, problems of town planning, including planning for industry; housing and overspill; communications; sewage disposal. The common factor among all these is the extent to which action taken – or action needed but not taken – in one area can have effects beyond the boundaries of that area and extending to other parts of the conurbation.'[7]

As this quotation clearly indicates, the size of a local planning authority can be important in terms of *area* as well as in terms of *population.* It is only in recent years that this distinction has been given the attention it deserves. The point is nicely made by Derek Senior in his *Memorandum of Dissent* to the *Report of the Royal Commission on Local Government in England*:

'The environmental-service authority must be in charge of a plannable unit, and the scale of such a unit is by definition fixed, within limits, in terms of the *area* served by its main centre. Its size in terms of population is whatever may be the number of people who live in the area from which that centre is more conveniently accessible than any other centre offering a comparable range of opportunities – provided only that this number is enough to sustain an authority with the minimum necessary staff. On the other hand, the scale of a unit responsible for the personal services is related to the *population* that throws up enough cases to keep the necessary professional and administrative staffs economically occupied. Its size in terms of area is whatever may be the acreage over which that population spreads itself – provided only that it forms a reasonably coherent arena of social activity and is not so extensive that its remotest inhabitants cannot easily reach its centre.'[24].

We shall return to this issue in the discussion, later in this chapter, on local government reorganization and again in the chapter on regional planning.

ADMINISTRATIVE ORGANIZATION

It follows from the previous discussion that the organization of planning differs markedly between different areas. At one extreme are small authorities which cannot be said to have any planning organization at all; at the other extreme are the highly organized planning departments of some of the larger authorities. In this section some examples of the latter are given, based on information kindly provided by the Chief Planning Officers.

Liverpool

A separate City Planning Department was formed in Liverpool in 1963. The Department has a total establishment of 157 posts and is organized in four divisions, dealing with development control, policy and research, urban design and development, and administration.

The *Development Control Division* has fourteen planning officers and is responsible for the detailed examination of all proposals and applications for planning permission. These amount to approximately 2,000 a year and are increasing as a result of the large-scale redevelopment in the central area and increasing slum clearance in the outer areas.

The Division is also responsible for work in connection with the relocation of industry, shops, etc., affected by the Council's redevelopment and traffic schemes and for the implementation of the Council's planning policies and redevelopment schemes.

The *Policy and Research Division* is divided into two groups, one dealing with all aspects of research and the other with planning policy. The Research Group's work includes (*a*) socio-economic aspects as they affect planning policies, (*b*) planning standards, (*c*) traffic planning, including planning for vehicular and pedestrian movement and the co-ordination of various means of transport. The Group also services the other Divisions of the Department by providing information necessary for their work. There are seventeen officers in the Group. The Policy Section (eleven officers) is responsible for (*a*) the preparation of planning policies and the continuous review of the City's policy plan, (*b*) the preparation and review of district plans in the areas other than slum clearance areas, (*c*) the planning contribution to the City's capital work programme.

The *Urban Design and Redevelopment Division* is divided into two groups. In the Central Area Group the work involved covers the regular review of the present City Centre Plan policies and proposals and detailed design work connected with all urban design aspects of the renewal of central Liverpool. In the Outer Areas Group the work is involved with the renewal of the City's Inner Residential Area – existing population 200,000, planning for the clearance of 33,000 slums within the next seven years and the consequent comprehensive redevelopment with related social and community facilities. Planning Briefs and District Plans for the areas of major change (Inner Areas of the City) are prepared in this Division. There are sixteen officers in the Central Area Group and ten in the Outer Areas.

The *Administrative and Services Division* provides administrative, clerical and ancillary services throughout the Department. The Division has administrative and clerical units working in each of the Technical Divisions and they are responsible for the processing of development applications, correspondence, reports to Committees, staff records and the preparation of Annual Estimates.

The Department runs a Graduate Training Scheme whereby Graduates are sponsored on Planning and Traffic Engineering Courses at recognized schools and are paid a salary whilst studying. On completion of the course the Graduate is under agreement to remain with the Department for not less than two years.

Newcastle upon Tyne

The City Planning Department of Newcastle upon Tyne is organized in four main divisions. The *Policy and Redevelopment Division*, directed by the Principal Planner, has three sections. The Urban Structure Officer is responsible for all Structure Plan work and Development Plan up-dating and interpretation; planning research, sub-regional and regional planning, the development of computer techniques, and public participation at policy level. The Local Plans Officer is responsible for central area design work, the preparation of District Plans and some Action Areas, the preparation of models and other visual and design aids, and public participation at Local Plan level. The Implementation Officer is responsible for the implementation of all central area redevelopment proposals, the preparation of development briefs for public and private developers in major redevelopment areas, and negotiations with developers in respect of major redevelopment schemes.

The *Development Division* is headed by the Development Officer who exercises control through two Section Heads. The Assistant Development Officer supervises the work of the Design Officer, the Landscape Architect and the Revitalization Officer. He is responsible for the major programme of urban improvement by means of Action Area plans, planning briefs, etc. He is also concerned with up-dating and monitoring the housing programme and securing planning objectives in the housing fields. In addition, he has specific responsibilities in relation to conservation areas.

The Deputy Development Control Officer is responsible for development control and enforcement.

The *Traffic Division*, under the control of the Traffic Engineer, and aided by two Senior Assistants, controls car parking provision and

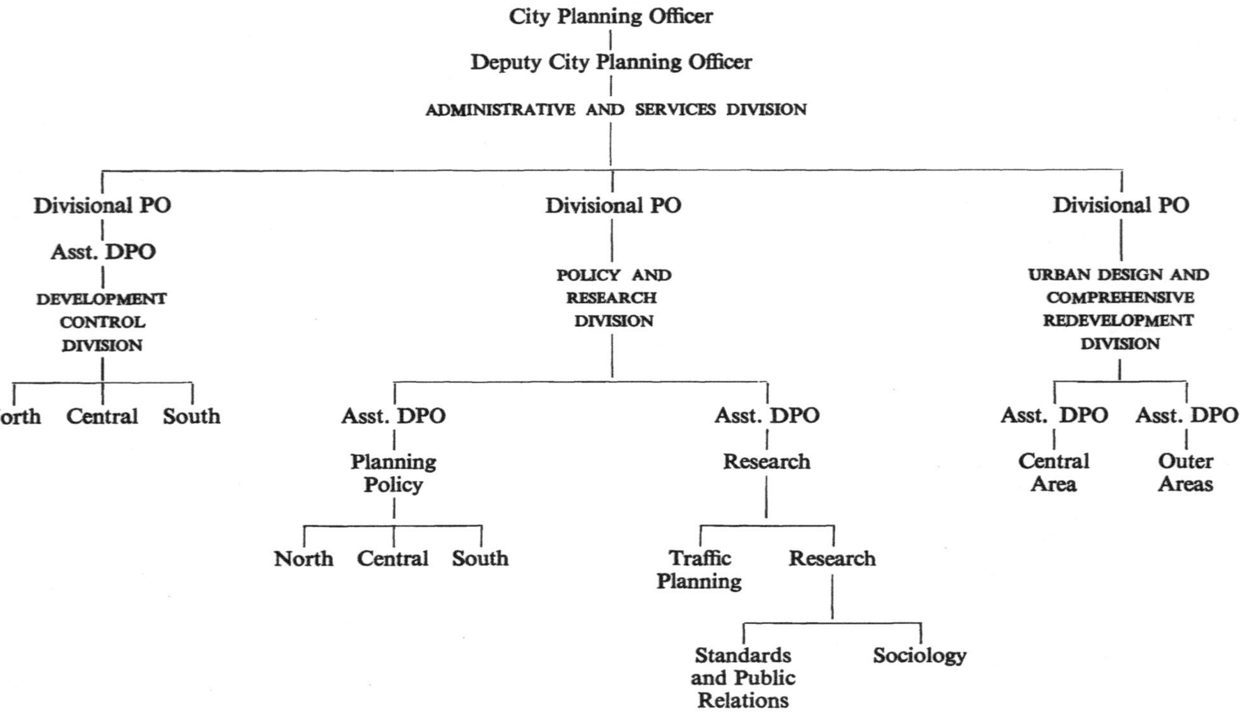
City of Liverpool Planning Department
City Planning Officer
Deputy City Planning Officer
ADMINISTRATIVE AND SERVICES DIVISION
Divisional PO
Asst. DPO
DEVELOPMENT CONTROL DIVISION
North
Central
South
Divisional PO
POLICY AND RESEARCH DIVISION
Asst. DPO
Planning Policy
North
Central
South
Asst. DPO
Research
Traffic Planning
Research
Standards and Public Relations
Sociology
Divisional PO
URBAN DESIGN AND COMPREHENSIVE REDEVELOPMENT DIVISION
Asst. DPO
Central Area
Asst. DPO
Outer Areas

is concerned with the collection and analysis of traffic data for short and long term management and planning.

Finally, the *Administrative Division*, under the Chief Administrative Officer, provides central filing, typing, clerical and administrative services to the Department.

Lancashire County Planning Department

The organization of county planning departments is more complex because of the two-tier structure of local government in administrative counties. Delegation to 'second-tier' authorities is discussed later in the chapter. Here the organization in Lancashire is outlined.

The department is divided into a Headquarters Office in Preston, six Divisional Offices and two sub-offices, situated in Ormskirk, Manchester, Wigan, Bury, Rishton, St Annes, Lancaster and Ulverston. The Headquarters Office is divided into four sections, Architectural, Development, Research and Administrative, each under the leadership of a Section Head. The duties carried out by the various offices are as follows:

Architectural Section (Staff establishment – 42). Detailed layout of residential areas including site surveys in the case of overspill schemes; constructional drawings of roads, sewers and buildings; schemes for the redevelopment of town centres and for conservation areas; protection and preservation of buildings listed as being of architectural or historical importance; elevational control; engineering work on land reclamation schemes; the development of a number of the County's industrial estates. In addition architectural and engineering advice is available to Divisional Offices and Local Authorities.

Development Section (Staff establishment – 36). Preparation, implementation and periodical review of the Development Plan and Town Maps; definition and investigation of development areas; overspill and industrial location; investigation of mining problems in relation to development proposals; exploitation of minerals and mineral workings; protection and preservation of amenities and beauty spots; rural development; landscaping proposals for development and acquisition for tree planting and afforestation of derelict land.

Research Section (Staff establishment – 22). Collection, collation, analysis and interpretation of information relative to the basic problems of planning; organization of surveys; assistance in the industrial aspects of development control; participation in the

City of Newcastle upon Tyne Planning Department

- City Planning Officer
  - Principal Planner
    - POLICY AND REDEVELOPMENT DIVISION
      - Urban Structure Officer
      - Local Plans Officer
      - Implementation Officer
  - Development Officer
    - DEVELOPMENT DIVISION
      - Assistant Development Officer
        - Design Officer
        - Landscape Architect
        - Revitalization Officer
      - Deputy Development Control Officer
  - Traffic Engineer
    - TRAFFIC DIVISION
      - Senior Assistant
      - Senior Assistant
  - Chief Administrative Officer
    - ADMINISTRATIVE DIVISION

Lancashire County Planning Department

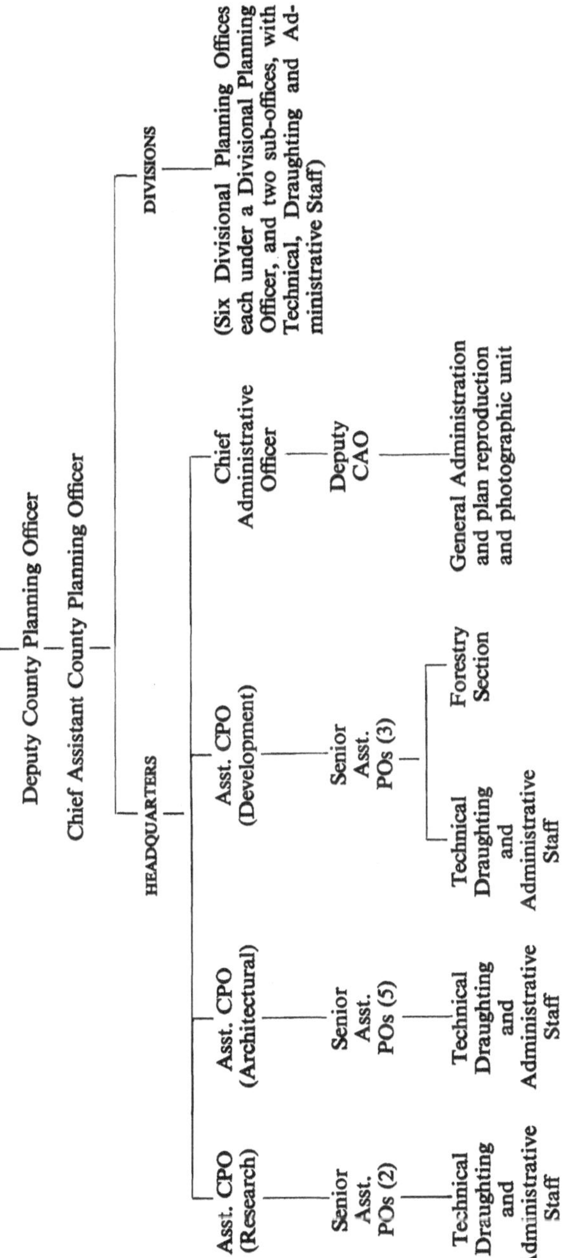

preparation and review of the Development Plan and Town Maps; advice on matters relating to the movement of population, distribution and location of industry and the economic aspects of mineral workings; preparation of programmes for housing developments and the movement of overspill; liaison with Regional Bodies (North-West Economic Planning Council, North-West Sports Council, Standing Conference of Local Authorities in the North-West); advice on the provision and demand for recreation facilities in the County as a whole; and the administration of an Industrial Bureau for the guidance of industrial developers.

Administrative Section (Staff establishment – 36). Preparation of material for the Planning and Development Committee and its various Sub-Committees, budgetary control and administrative and clerical functions associated with Town and Country Planning Acts and other legislations.

Divisional Offices. Control of development, preparation of evidence for Appeals and Public Inquiries, preparation of certain Town Maps in consultation with Headquarters Office. The average establishment is for a technical staff of twelve and an administrative staff of six.

DELEGATION IN COUNTIES

The transfer of planning powers from districts to counties, which was effected by the 1947 Act, was generally agreed to be necessary – except by the districts. Larger authorities were needed to undertake the new and wider planning functions, to plan comprehensively over bigger areas and to hold the balance between any conflicting interests of urban and rural districts, to negotiate with other authorities on questions of regional importance such as the establishment of national parks and the planned provision for overspill from the congested conurbations. At the same time the limited supply of qualified planning officers needed to be rationally distributed and concentrated in a smaller number of departments where their skills could be most effectively utilized. However, the opposition of the district councils to their loss of powers (in education and health as well as in town planning) led to the compromise of delegation. Delegation may be defined as an administrative device whereby some particular function of government is performed partly by one tier of authority and partly by another; it enables the 'upper-tier' authority to be responsible for general policy and finance, and the 'lower-tier' authority for the execution of policy within a given area. The lower-tier authority may be a separate local authority or it may be an organ of the upper-tier authority with or without members drawn from other authorities though the latter might be more accurately termed decentralization (implying the discharge of responsibility by the upper-tier authority on an area basis).

Delegation should not, however, be regarded merely as a political expedient. It has very real advantages. In the first place there is the question of the sheer administrative load on upper-tier authorities. Now that so many functions have been transferred from districts to counties, the latter have become heavily burdened, whereas the districts have insufficient major functions to attract officers and councillors of the desired calibre. So long as the districts can support an adequate number of officials (which implies a certain minimum size) and can therefore cope successfully with delegated powers, delegation at one and the same time relieves the county of some of its administrative load and increases the general effectiveness of the district authority – thereby improving what the Royal Commission on Local Government in Greater London have termed 'the health of representative government'. The second advantage is intimately tied up with this. As the same Royal Commission stressed, there is no antithesis between healthy local government and efficient administration.* The districts have the great asset of fuller acquaintance with local conditions and needs. They are more accessible to the local electorate. They are better placed for facilitating citizen participation in the planning process – a matter which, as is argued in the final chapter, is of considerable importance.

Delegation is thus in principle a positive device for capitalizing the respective advantages of country and district administration. It can work effectively, however, only if two requirements are met. First, the districts must constitute administrative units of adequate population and resources. For nearly a half this is not so. Some 700 districts in England and Wales have populations of less than 15,000; nearly 500 have less than 10,000; and over 200 have less than 5,000. But even if the districts are of the necessary minimum size there remains the question of the relationship between them and the county. A formal 'instrument of delegation' has to be translated

* It can be argued that the Royal Commission accepted this too whole-heartedly and, indeed, laid too much emphasis on their conception of 'healthy local government'. Their philosophy is summed up in the following extract: 'local government is with us an instance of democracy at work, and no amount of potential administrative efficiency could make up for the loss of active participation in the work by capable, public-spirited people elected by, responsible to, and in touch with those who elect them' (*Report*, op. cit., p. 59). For further discussion in relation to housing and planning see J. B. Cullingworth, *Housing in Greater London*, London School of Economics, Greater London Papers No. 4, 1961.

into practice. Where relationships are good few problems may arise, but where relationships are strained and characterized by mistrust and suspicion, delegation may only exacerbate the problems it is designed to alleviate.

It follows that it is not easy to legislate for an effective system of delegation. Nevertheless, increased delegation (in other services as well as town and country planning) was one of the objectives of the Local Government Act of 1958. This Act was an attempt to modernize local government: it considerably altered the system of central government grants, it provided for the machinery for reorganizing local government structure, and it extended the powers and responsibilities of the larger district councils mainly by providing for greater delegation of certain functions from counties.*

Before 1958, the general situation was that delegated powers in relation to planning applications were exercised (in widely varying degrees) by county districts. The normal procedure was (and still is) for an application to be made to the district council, whether or not that district had any delegated powers. Where they had none the application was referred to the county (possibly with any 'observations' the district might wish to make). Some districts had limited powers for approving applications which were in conformity with the approved plan or which did not raise major policy issues. In such cases they would first receive advice from an area or divisional planning officer of the county. The crucial decision to be made here was, of course, on whether an application *was* in conformity with the development plan or whether it did raise *major* policy issues. Usually (but not in all areas) this decision was taken by the county. In some counties there was a system of area planning committees which might consist of equal numbers of representatives from the county and the districts concerned. Some counties had both a scheme of delegation and a series of area committees. In short, there was a wide range of variations. These were, in practice, more marked than the formal published schemes suggested. It was because of this variation and because conditions differed so greatly between counties that the original intention of providing for automatic delegation of planning functions to the larger districts was abandoned.

The post-1958 delegation arrangements allowed districts with popu-

* For a full discussion see G. Seward and G. H. Forster, *The Local Government Act 1958*, Charles Knight & Co., 1959. The legislation was preceded by three White Papers: *Areas and Status of Local Authorities in England and Wales*, Cmd. 9831, 1956; *Functions of County Councils and County District Councils in England and Wales*, Cmnd. 161, 1957; *and Local Government Finance* (*England and Wales*), Cmnd. 209, 1957.

lations of 60,000 or more to claim a wide measure of delegated powers in relation to development control. In 'special circumstances' the Minister could require similar delegation to other districts. This was the only substantive change brought about by the scheme. For the rest there was ministerial exhortation:

'The Minister considers that it would now be right for county councils to review their arrangements for the exercise of planning powers, taking into account the views of their district councils, and, where appropriate, to revise those arrangements in order to give to district councils who so wish, and to whom adequate technical advice is available, an additional measure of delegation and freedom of action bearing in mind the size and characteristics of the county and the county districts, and the need for efficiency and economy in administration.'[16]

So far as town maps were concerned greater freedom of action might be given to districts 'in appropriate circumstances'. Where districts had the necessary staff they should, in the Minister's view, be given 'the fullest opportunity of co-operating with the planning authority'. Where this could not be done (for example where a town map affected more than one district) 'the fullest co-operation between the county and district councils should be maintained from the earliest stage of the preparation of any town map'.

This trend towards greater delegation was a feature of the early 'sixties. Enthusiasm (except on the part of the district council) has definitely waned since then. In their evidence to the Royal Commission on Local Government, the Ministry of Housing and Local Government was highly critical.[21] In their experience delegation did not lead to an improved speed or quality of development control. The advantages which flow from delegating some of the work load to district councils is offset by the shortage of qualified planning staff in most district offices, by the limited range of problems which arise within any one area, the difficulties caused by the natural inclination of district councils to take a 'narrow view', and the extra administrative complications that limited delegation usually entails. The Ministry thought that decentralization of planning control to area committees of the planning authority produced better results than delegation to another elected body. This view is supported by the report of the *Management Study on Development Control*. The management consultants who undertook this study concluded that, within the context of the current two-tier system in administrative counties, area committees provided the best method of reconciling the rights of individuals with speed of decision, low cost and the interests of the wider community.[18]

The Royal Commission's *Report* came out strongly against delegation but maintained that it was an essential corollary of their recommendations for a smaller number of local planning authorities that there should be adequate decentralization and consultation.

Delegation has been a means of attempting to adjust planning machinery to an out-dated local government system. In recent years increasing attention has been focused on the alternative: changing the local government system to meet planning needs. This is a subject to which we now turn.

LOCAL GOVERNMENT REORGANIZATION

Several references have already been made to the inadequacies of the present local government structure and the review which is now under way. A full discussion is inappropriate in the present context and, in any case, is likely to be overtaken by events.* There has been a remarkable change in attitudes over the last decade or so. The 1956 White Paper on *Areas and Status of Local Authorities in England and Wales*, and the review which followed it, had as a basic premise that

'a fundamental alteration of the existing structure could be justified only if it had shown itself to be incapable of meeting present day needs. That is not the situation. The present system has, over many years, stood up to the severest tests.'

Throughout the 'fifties, local government reorganization was conceived in terms of adjusting boundaries. The first major change came with the *Report of the Royal Commission on Local Government in Greater London* (the Herbert Report) and the 1964 London Government Act which followed it at a speed which, in the light of previous experience, was staggering. Henceforth local government reorganization was taken seriously. Change was in the air and debate centred on how radical the change should be. Piecemeal reorganization was brought to a halt and a Royal Commission on Local Government in England (the Redcliffe-Maud Commission) was set up and charged with the task of looking at the local government system (outside London) as a whole.

This was a major change in tactics. No longer could the hopelessly

* Reference may be made to Chapter VIII of P. G. Richards, *The New Local Government System*, Allen & Unwin, 1968, which outlines changes over the period 1945 to 1948; and to 'Local Government Boundaries Since 1888' in Volume III of the Report of the Royal Commission on Local Government in England, *Research Appendices*, HMSO, 1969, Cmnd. 4040–II.

out-dated small authority successfully oppose reorganization. Rutland was no longer alone: the writing was on the wall for all. The evidence submitted to the Redcliffe-Maud Commission reflected a widespread agreement that the local government system needed radical overhaul. And when the Commission reported in June 1969, recommending the abolition of all the 79 county boroughs, 45 counties, 227 non-county boroughs, 449 urban districts and 410 rural districts, and their replacement by an entirely new system, the argument centred on alternative systems rather than on defence of the existing structure.

The Report was 'accepted in principle' by the Government on the day it was published. What this means (according to the Prime Minister's statement in the House of Commons) is that there is to be a fundamental reorganization of local government, a marked reduction in the number of authorities with executive responsibility, and the ending of the 'anachronistic division between town and country'. How far the detailed recommendations of the Commission will be implemented remains to be seen, but at the time of writing the Government have expressed their view that 'decisions should be reached as soon as practicable and the period of uncertainty kept to a minimum'.

It is appropriate here to outline only the major recommendations of the Commission and those arguments which are relevant to town and country planning.

The Commission identified four 'basic faults' in the present pattern of working of local government:

1. Local government areas do not fit the pattern of life and work in modern England. The gap will widen as social, economic and technological changes quicken.
2. The fragmentation of England into 79 county boroughs and 45 counties, exercising independent authority and dividing town from country, has made the proper planning of development and transportation impossible. The result has often been an atmosphere of hostility between the county boroughs and the counties, and this has made it harder to decide difficult questions on their merits.
3. The division of responsibility within each county between the county council and a number of county district councils, together with the position of county boroughs as islands in the counties, means that services which should be in the hands of one authority are split up among several. This greatly complicates the work of meeting comprehensively the different needs of families and individuals.

4. Many local authorities are too small, in size and revenue, and in consequence too short of highly qualified manpower and technical equipment, to be able to do their work as well as it could and should be done.

Their proposed solution is the abolition of all existing authorities and the establishment of sixty-one new areas covering both town and country. In fifty-eight of these a unitary authority would be responsible for all services. In these 'metropolitan areas' (based on Birmingham, Manchester and Merseyside) responsibility for services would be divided between a metropolitan authority whose key functions would be planning, transportation and major development, and a number of metropolitan district authorities whose key functions would be education, the personal social services, health and housing.

These sixty-one new local authorities would form the operational level of local government but two other levels were thought to be needed. Under-pinning and complementing the basic units the Commission saw the need for smaller representative bodies 'to express the interest and sense of identity of the new local communities'. They therefore recommended 'local councils' which would succeed the present county boroughs, boroughs, districts and parishes. They would be concerned with local amenities and (in the case of the larger councils) would play a part in some of the main services for which the new 'unitary' authorities would have the main responsibility. The Commission referred, in particular, to housing, preservation (of buildings, trees, etc.), conservation, local development and highway improvement – all matters 'which may need action on the local scale as the wider one'.

At the other extreme, the Commission were convinced that higher level units were needed to set the strategic framework for the operational authorities. This need would increase with the growth of population, rising mobility, and the greater involvement of local government in economic questions. To meet this they proposed provincial councils (replacing the present economic planning councils) which would settle the broad economic, land use and investment framework for the planning and development policies of the operational units.

These are the main recommendations of the Majority Report. They rest on the argument that town and country are interdependent, that larger authorities are required, and that the interdependence of services is such that the main unit of local government should be all-purpose.

One member of the Commission, Derek Senior, could not accept the last of these three principles. In a weighty minority report (misleadingly termed *Memorandum of Dissent*), he makes a scathing, cogent criticism of this. He accepted the diagnosis but argued that the all-purpose authorities recommended in the Majority Report would fragment planning and development problems; in most cases they would also be too remote for the democratic and responsive administration of the personal services and too unwieldy for the efficient co-ordination of the whole range of local government functions. In his view the Majority took too theoretical an approach to the problem of local government organization in which the requirements in population terms of administrative efficiency and democratic control are analysed in abstraction from the facts of social geography. He rejected the argument that the unitariness of the all-purpose authority has inherent advantages which outweigh all disadvantages. Indeed, the application of this line of thought clearly involves authorities which are too small for planning and too large for personal services. It also involves an ineffectual role for the provincial authority, which cannot be given development powers without destroying the unitary principle. Similarly the local councils cannot be given decision-making powers:

'In short, by calling in the provincial and "local" councils to reduce the deficiencies inherent in their unitary authorities, my colleagues would at best compromise what is most valuable in the concepts of the provincial and "local" councils and at worst turn their one-tier system into a three-tier one with units inappropriate in scale and composition for most purposes at every level.'[24]

It is worth devoting further space to Senior's argument since it highlights fundamental issues in the current debate on the reorganization of local government to cope efficiently with the problems of town and country planning.

A basic argument is that 'if one wants the interests of a region as a whole to prevail through the democratic process, one must create a structure which enables these interests to find effective expression in action'. The first requirement, therefore, is to define areas of community interest – not in terms of the small community to which people feel they 'belong', but 'the *objective* community of interest which binds together the people who participate in a self-contained complex of social and economic activities based on a single centre'. The objective must be to identify areas of interdependence over which effective action can be taken. Indeed, a major reason for the establishment of the Royal Commission was the inadequacy of the present structure to take effective action. Senior gives a striking example from North and Central Lancashire. A 'new city' is currently under consideration for the Leyland-Chorley area:

'We have been plainly warned that social damage of a serious kind would surely result if this project were to be carried out otherwise than in the context of an operative overall plan for the whole region. When its feasibility was established, the Minister of Housing and Local Government appointed a joint team of planning and economic consultants to assess its predictable impact on the Blackburn and Burnley districts, where higher unemployment, poorer housing conditions, lower rateable values and a less salubrious climate have led to emigration and declining standards. Their conclusion was that the Leyland-Chorley development, though vital to the future prosperity of the region as a whole, could do grave and lasting local damage, especially to the Burnley district, unless an overall plan for the whole area from the Pennines to the coast resulted in a great improvement in east-west transport and communications *before* the building of the new city was far advanced. Then – and only then – the people of the Calder Valley towns who found jobs in the new city's factories and offices could conveniently commute from their present homes, and enterprises ancillary to these new industries could be economically sited in those towns. Otherwise the new city would go on draining the life out of the Calder Valley for many years before its benefits could begin to be felt there. With luck, if the Reorganisation Act provides for the establishment of a regional planning *and development* authority for the whole of this area, it may be just in time.

'Meanwhile the Minister has announced that the Lancashire County Council, in concert with the local authorities concerned, is to make a project study of an improved road link between the Calder Valley and the M6; that he himself, in consultation with the local authorities, proposes to employ consultants to prepare pilot schemes of urban renewal in North East Lancashire; and that he will invite the Lancashire County Council together with the Blackburn and Burnley County Borough Councils, in consultation with the Regional Economic Planning Council and Board, to prepare a plan to form the basis of future development, to make the best use of a new Calder Valley road, and to reserve suitable sites for industrial development. Later the Government will discuss with the North East Lancashire local authorities the best way of meeting their needs in the light of the programme for the development of the new city. *All this elaborate ad-hockery and central government intervention would be unnecessary if there were already a single planning and development authority for the whole city region.* If my colleagues have their way, it may yet be all in vain.'[24]

Senior's alternative proposals are for a two-level structure comprising thirty-five regional authorities, responsible for the planning-transportation-development complex of functions (including water supply, sewerage, refuse disposal and other technical services), for capital investment programming and for police, fire and education; and 148 district authorities responsible for the health service, the personal social services, housing management, consumer protection and all other functions involving personal contact with the citizen. Additionally he proposes, at 'grass-roots' level, common councils representing existing parishes and towns or parts of towns small enough to have a real feeling of community, and at the other extreme five provincial councils.

Apart from Senior's fundamentally different set of proposals, two other 'notes of reservation' accompany the Majority Report. Sir Francis Hill and Mr R. C. Wallis outline proposals which would have the effect of increasing the number of unitary authorities from 58 to 63. Mr J. L. Longland, on the other hand, proposed a reduction to 50.

Proposals of the Royal Commission on Local Government for England (outside London)

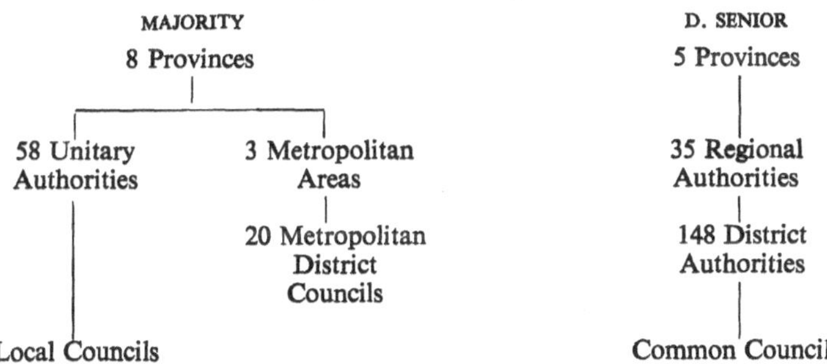

The Royal Commission on Local Government was charged with the task of renewing the structure of local government in relation to existing functions and within the context of the current division of responsibility between local and central government. There is, therefore, little discussion of local-central relationships, though the points are made that 'provincial councils will give the national government new opportunities for decentralizing power and developing new methods of collaboration between central and local government', and that 'the new metropolitan and unitary authorities will be strong enough for Parliament and central government to trust them with increased responsibility and substantially relax the present detailed supervision'.

Senior, on the other hand, devotes a whole chapter to the issue, with the justification that the setting up of the Crowther Commission on the Constitution radically changes the framework of thinking on local government reorganization. We return to this issue in the chapter on regional planning.

WALES

Wales was excluded from the terms of reference of the Redcliffe-Maud Commission on the ground that consideration of the specific problems of the Principality had already reached an advanced stage as a result of the work of the Local Government Commission for Wales (set up under the Local Government Act, 1958) and the further study which had been made of their 1962 Report.[12] Furthermore, the need for early action in Wales was considered to be particularly urgent in view of the very large number of small and inadequate authorities. To quote the 1967 White Paper[28] (which outlined 'for public discussion' the Government's reorganization proposals): 'it was apparent that local government in the Principality could be reorganized on lines that would secure its early strengthening'. (Nevertheless, by the time of writing, no reorganization had commenced!)

The problem of Wales, and particularly of central Wales, is that the counties have very small scattered populations and extremely small resources. The Local Government Commission proposed a reduction in the number of counties from thirteen to seven, the demotion of Merthyr Tydfil from a county borough to a non-county borough, and boundary extensions to Cardiff, Newport and Swansea. These proposals were very strongly opposed particularly by those counties which were, in the process of amalgamation, to be divided.

The current proposals are for five counties formed by amalgamation. If the recommendations are accepted the number of local authorities in Wales would be reduced from 181 to 44.

LONDON

While, over most of the country, reorganization is being considered, in London it has been effected. The London Government Act, 1963, came into operation in 1965. In brief, the Act established a Greater London Council covering an area of about 620 square miles and a population of nearly eight million; and 32 new London Boroughs (plus the unmolested ancient City of London). These replaced the London County Council, 28 Metropolitan Boroughs, the County Council of Middlesex, and the County Boroughs of Croydon, East Ham and West Ham. Considerable parts of Essex, Hertfordshire, Kent and Surrey were transferred to the new Greater London area.

In this area the London Boroughs are the main local authorities but the Greater London Council has important functions in relation to strategic planning and services which need to be planned and administered over a wider area – overall planning, main highways, traffic control, overspill housing and the fire and ambulance services.

The GLC has the responsibility of preparing the strategic Development Plan (now technically a 'structure plan') for the whole of the Greater London area. (This was published in 1969.) It lays down the policies relating to population, housing, employment, transport and, indeed, all major issues which come within the compass of strategic planning. Within this 'strategic framework' the London Borough Councils will each produce their own local development plans (now also structure plans).

The position in London is unique. The relationship between the GLC and the London Borough Councils is not the same as that between a county and a county district. The Boroughs are large authorities with major responsibilities in their areas: indeed, they are the local authorities for their areas. The GLC is the local planning authority for Greater London *as a whole*: the Boroughs are the planning authorities for their areas – though there is a complex web of inter-relationships. In certain areas, such as Covent Garden, and in relation to certain types of development of strategic importance such as transport terminals, university development, major places of public assembly, the GLC itself is the local planning authority. Planning applications for other developments of 'strategic significance' have to be referred by the Borough Councils concerned to the GLC, and there is a wide range of provisions for consultations.

A convenient summary of the situation in relation to the development plan and the 'partnership' of the GLC and the Boroughs is to be found in the *Statement* of the Greater London Development Plan. This underlines the fact that the GLDP is intended to form the 'context' for the Borough Plans which will follow it; but in practice a hard and fast division of functions is neither possible nor desirable. Indeed, it is possible (to say the least) that, when the Borough Plans are prepared within the 'context', issues will emerge that require a revision of this context. The GLDP is therefore essentially a conceptual plan at this stage. It states a set of principles for the future development of Greater London which will have to undergo a 'process of validation' over a number of years.

The *Statement* couches the issues very much in technical terms, but in reality the crucial problems are policy and political ones. The policies and politics of the individual Boroughs are not necessarily consonant with those of the GLC. It is not without good reason that the Redcliffe-Maud Commission (majority) stressed the advantages of the all-purpose authority – 'local government in its simplest, most understandable and potentially most efficient form'. But in some areas (a few, according to the majority; everywhere, according to Senior) there are overriding benefits to be obtained from a two-tier structure. Nowhere is this clearer than in London. There has then to be a 'partnership' or what the GLC inelegantly refer to as an 'iterative process'. But it would be naive to assume that this makes life easy: on the contrary, it underlines the fact that planning has far more to do with politics than with technical issues.

REFERENCES AND FURTHER READING

1 Cullingworth, J. B., *Housing in Greater London*, London School of Economics, Greater London Papers No. 4, 1961.

2 Greater London Council, *Greater London Development Plan: Statement*, GLC, 1969.

3 Local Government Commission for England, *Report No. 1: Report and Proposals for the West Midlands Special Review Area*, HMSO, 1961.

4 Local Government Commission for England, *Report No. 2: Report and Proposals for the West Midlands General Review Area*, HMSO, 1961.

5 Local Government Commission for England, *Report No. 3: Report and Proposals for the East Midlands General Review Area*, HMSO, 1961.

6 Local Government Commission for England, *Report No. 4: Report and Proposals for the South Western General Review Area*, HMSO, 1963.

7 Local Government Commission for England, *Report No. 5: Report and Proposals for the Tyneside Special Review Area*, HMSO, 1963.

8 Local Government Commission for England, *Report No. 6: Report and Proposals for the North Eastern General Review Area*, HMSO, 1963.

9 Local Government Commission for England, *Report No. 7: Report and Proposals for the West Yorkshire Special Review Area*, HMSO, 1964.

10 Local Government Commission for England, *Report No. 8: Report and Proposals for the York and North Midlands General Review Area*, HMSO, 1964.

11 Local Government Commission for England, *Report No. 9: Report and Proposals for Lincolnshire and East Anglia General Review Area*, HMSO, 1965.

12 Local Government Commission for Wales, *Report and Proposals for Wales*, HMSO, 1963.

13 MHLG, *Areas and Status of Local Authorities in England and Wales*, Cmd. 9831, HMSO, 1956.

14 MHLG, *Functions of County Councils and County District Councils in England and Wales*, Cmnd. 161, HMSO, 1957.

15 MHLG, *Local Government Finance (England and Wales)*, Cmnd. 209, HMSO, 1957.
16 MHLG, Circular No. 58/59, *Delegation of Planning Functions*, HMSO, 1959.
17 MHLG, *London Government: Government Proposals for Reorganisation*, Cmnd. 1562, HMSO, 1961.
18 MHLG, *Management Study on Development Control*, HMSO, 1967.
19 Richards, P. G., *Delegation in Local Government*, Allen & Unwin, 1956.
20 Richards, P. G., *The New Local Government System*, Allen & Unwin, 1968.
21 Royal Commission on Local Government in England, *Written Evidence of the Ministry of Housing and Local Government*, HMSO, 1967.
22 Royal Commission on Local Government in England, *Local Government Reform* (Summary of the Report and D. Senior's 'Alternative Conclusions and Recommendations'), Cmnd. 4039, HMSO, 1969.
23 Royal Commission on Local Government in England, *Vol. 1. Report* (Redcliffe-Maud Report), Cmnd. 4040, HMSO, 1969.
24 Royal Commission on Local Government in England, *Vol. 2. Memorandum of Dissent by Mr D. Senior*, Cmnd. 4040—I, HMSO, 1969.
25 Royal Commission on Local Government in England, *Vol. 3. Research Appendices*, Cmnd. 4040—II, HMSO, 1969.
26 Royal Commission on Local Government in Greater London, *Report* (Herbert Report), Cmnd. 1164, HMSO, 1960.
27 Royal Commission on Local Government in Scotland, *Report and Appendices* (Wheatley Report), Cmnd. 4150, HMSO, 1969.
28 Secretary of State for Wales, *Local Government in Wales*, Cmnd. 3340, HMSO, 1967.
29 Seward, G. and Forster, G. H., *The Local Government Act, 1958*, Charles Knight & Co., 1959.
30 Town Planning Institute, 'Planning Administration: The Establishment of Separate Planning Departments – A Statement of Policy by the Town Planning Institute', *Journal of the Town Planning Institute*, Vol. 49, No. 3, March 1963.

Chapter VI

PLANNING AND LAND VALUES

THE UTHWATT REPORT

'It is clear that under a system of well-conceived planning the resolution of competing claims and the allocation of land for the various requirements must proceed on the basis of selecting the most suitable land for the particular purpose, irrespective of the existing values which may attach to the individual parcels of land.'[14] It was the task of the Uthwatt Committee, from whose report this quotation is taken, to devise a scheme which would make this possible. Effective planning necessarily controls, limits, or even completely destroys, the market value of particular pieces of land. Is the owner therefore to be compensated for this loss in value? if so, how is the compensation to be calculated? and is any 'balancing' payment to be extracted from owners whose land appreciates in value as a result of planning measures? This problem of compensation and 'betterment' arises fundamentally 'from the existing legal position with regard to the use of land, which attempts largely to preserve, in a highly developed economy, the purely individualistic approach to land ownership'. This 'individualistic approach', however, has been increasingly modified during the past hundred years. The rights of ownership were restricted in the interests of public health: owners had (by law) to ensure, for example, that their properties were in good sanitary condition, that new buildings conformed to certain building standards, that streets were of a minimum width, and so on. It was accepted that these restrictions were necessary in the interests of the community – *salus populi est suprema lex* – and that private owners should be compelled to comply with them even at cost to themselves. 'All these restrictions, whether carrying a right to compensation or not, are imposed in the public interest, and the essence of the compensation problem as regards the imposition of restrictions appears to be this – at what point does the public interest become such that a private individual ought to be called on to comply, at his own cost, with a restriction or requirement designed to secure that public interest? The history of the imposition of obligations without compensation has been to push that point progressively further on and to add to the list of requirements considered to be essential to the well-being of the community.'* But clearly there is a point beyond which restrictions cannot reasonably be imposed on the grounds of 'good neighbourliness' without payment of compensation – and 'general consideration of regional or national policy require so great a restriction on the landowner's use of his land as to amount to a taking away from him of a proprietary interest in the land'.

This, however, is not the end of the matter. Planning sets out to achieve a selection of the most suitable pieces of land for particular uses. Some land will therefore be zoned for a use which is profitable for the owner, whereas other land will be zoned for a use having a low – or even nil – private value. It is this difficulty of 'development value' which raises the compensation problem in its most acute form. The development value which may legitimately – or hopefully – be expected by owners is in fact spread over a far larger area than is likely to be developed. This *potential* development value is therefore speculative, but until the individual owners are proved to be wrong in their assessments (and how can this be done?) all owners of land having a potential value can make a case for compensation on the assumption that their particular pieces of land would in fact be chosen for development if planning restrictions were not imposed. Yet this '*floating value*' might never have settled on their land, and obviously the aggregate of the values claimed by the individual owners is likely to be greatly in excess of a total valuation of all the pieces of land. As Haar has nicely put it, the situation is akin to that of a sweepstake: a single ticket fetches much more than its mathematically calculated value, for the simple reason that the grand prize may fall on any one holder.[3]

Furthermore, the public control of land use necessarily involves the shifting of land values from certain pieces of land to other pieces: the value of some land is decreased, while that of other land is increased. Planning controls do not destroy land values: in the words of the Uthwatt Committee, 'neither the total demand for development nor its average annual rate is materially affected, if at all, by

* *Uthwatt Report*, [14], p. 20. In a footnote there is reference to a dictum of Wright, J. (1 K.B. 458): 'A mere negative prohibition, though it involves interference with an owner's enjoyment of property, does not, I think, merely because it is obeyed, carry with it at common law any right to compensation. A subject cannot at common law claim compensation merely because he obeys a lawful order of the State'. However, full acceptance of this common law rule would necessarily result in hardship and inconsistent treatment between individuals (e.g. between the owners of land zoned for agriculture and land zoned for building).

planning ordinances'. Nevertheless, the owner of the land on which development is prohibited will claim compensation for the full potential development of his land, irrespective of the fact that that value may shift to another site.

In theory, it is logical to balance the compensation paid to aggrieved owners by collecting a betterment charge on owners who benefit from planning controls. But previous experience with the collection of betterment had not been encouraging. The principle had been first established in an Act of 1662 which authorized the levying of a capital sum or an annual rent in respect of the 'melioration' of the properties following street widenings in London. There were similar provisions in Acts providing for the rebuilding of London after the Great Fire. The principle was revived and extended in the Planning Acts of 1909 and 1932. These allowed a local authority to claim, first 50 per cent, and then (in the later Act) 75 per cent, of the amount by which any property increased in value as the result of the operation of a planning scheme. In fact, these provisions were largely ineffective since it proved extremely difficult to determine with any certainty which properties had increased in value as a result of a scheme (or of works carried out under a scheme) or, where there was a reasonable degree of certainty, how much of the increase in value was directly attributable to the scheme and how much to other factors. The Uthwatt Committee noted that there were only three cases in which betterment had actually been paid under the Planning Acts, and all these were before the 1932 Act introduced a provision for the deferment of payment until the increased value had actually been realized either by sale or lease or by change of use. In short, it had not proved possible to devise an equitable and workable system.

The Uthwatt Committee concluded that the solution to these problems lay in changing the system of land ownership under which land had a development value dependent upon the prospects of its profitable use. They maintained that no new code for the assessment of compensation or the collection of betterment would be adequate if this individualistic system remained. The system itself had inherent 'contradictions provoking a conflict between private and public interest and hindering the proper operation of the planning machinery'. A new system was needed which would avoid these contradictions and which so unified existing rights in land as to 'enable shifts of value to operate within the same ownership'. The logic of this line of reasoning led to a consideration of land nationalization. But this the Committee rejected on the grounds that it would arouse keen political controversy, would involve probably insuperable financial problems, and would necessitate the establishment of a complicated national administrative machinery. In their view the solution to the problem lay in the nationalization not of land itself but of all development rights in undeveloped land.

THE 1947 ACT

Essentially, this is precisely what the 1947 Town and Country Planning Act did. Effectively, development rights and their associated values were nationalized. No development was to take place without permission from the local planning authority. If permission were refused, no compensation would be paid (except in a limited range of special cases). If permission were granted, any resulting increase in land value was to be subject to a development charge. The view was taken that 'owners who lose development value as a result of the passing of the Bill are not on that account entitled to compensation'. This cut through the insoluble problem posed in previous attempts to collect betterment values created by public action. Betterment had been conceived as 'any increase in the value of land (including the buildings thereon) arising from central or local government action, whether positive, e.g. by the execution of public works or improvements, or negative, e.g. by the imposition of restrictions on the other land'. The 1947 Act went further: all betterment was created by the community, and it was unreal and undesirable (as well as virtually impossible) to distinguish between values created, e.g. by particular planning schemes, and those due to other factors such as the general activities of the community or the general level of prosperity.

If rigorous logic had been followed, no payment at all would have been made for the transfer of development values to the State, but this – as the Uthwatt Committee had pointed out – would have resulted in considerable hardship in individual cases. A £300 million fund was established for making 'payments' to owners who could successfully claim that their land had some development value on the 'appointed day' – the day on which the provisions of the Bill which prevented landowners from realizing development values came into force. Considerable discussion took place during the passage of the Bill through Parliament on the sum fixed for compensation and it was strongly opposed on the ground that it was too small. The truth of the matter was that in the absence of relevant reliable information any global sum had to be determined in a somewhat arbitrary way; but in any case it was not intended that everybody should be paid the full value of their claims. Landowners would submit claims to a centralized agency – the Central Land Board – for 'loss of development value', i.e. the difference between the 'unrestricted value' (the market value without the restrictions introduced by the Act) and the 'existing use value' (the value subject to these restrictions). When all the claims had been received and examined, the £300 million would be divided between claimants at whatever proportion of their 1948 value that total would allow. (In the event the estimate of £300 million was not as far out as critics feared. The total of all claims eventually amounted to £380 million.)

The original intention was to have a flexible rate of development charge. In some cases 100 per cent would be levied, but in others a lower rate would be more appropriate in order to encourage development 'on account of economic conditions in the country generally, or in particular areas where unemployment is above the average', or where it was important to secure 'a particular piece of development now, instead of in, say, twenty years'.* However, when the Regulations came to be made, the Government maintained that the policy which had been set out during the passage of the Bill through the House was unworkable. The only explanation given for this was that 'the whole conception is that the value of land is divided into two parts – the value restricted to its existing use and the development value. The market value is the sum of the two. If, by the action of the State, the development value is no longer in the possession of the owner of the land, then all he has left is the existing use value. Moreover, the fund of £300 million is being provided for the purpose of compensating the owner of land for this reduced value . . . therefore the owner of land can have no possible claim to any part of the development value and it is logical and right that the State should, where development takes place, make a charge which represents the amount of the development value.' The whole idea of variable development charges (particularly for the depressed areas) was rejected, and a flat-rate 100 per cent levy introduced.

These provisions – of which only the barest summary has been given here – were very complex, and, together with the inevitable uncertainty as to when compensation would be paid and how much it should be, resulted in a general feeling of uncertainty and discontent which did not augur well for the scheme. The principles, however, were clear. To recapitulate, all development rights and values were vested in the State: no development could take place without permission from the local planning authority and then only on payment of a betterment charge to the Central Land Board. The nationalization of development rights was effected by the 'promised' payment of compensation. As a result landowners only 'owned' the existing-use rights of their land and it thus followed, first, that if permission to develop was refused no compensation was payable, and, secondly, that the price paid by public authorities for the compulsory acquisition

* *H.L. Debates*, Vol. 432, Col. 983, January 29, 1947. See also *H.C. Debates*, Vol. 451, Cols. 294–5, May 26, 1948.

of land would be equal to the existing-use value, i.e. its value excluding any allowance for future development.

THE SCHEME IN OPERATION

The scheme did not work as smoothly as was expected. In their first annual report the Central Land Board 'noted with concern some weeks after the Act came into operation that despite the liability for development charge land was still being widely offered and, still worse, taken at prices including the full development value'. This remained a problem throughout the lifetime of the scheme – though the magnitude of the problem still remains a matter of some controversy. It is certainly true that conditions were such that developers were prepared to pay more than existing-use prices for land; but the conditions were rather extraordinary. As the Board pointed out in their second report:

'The evidence available to the Board of prices paid for land for development suggests that sales at or near existing use value are more the exception than the rule. To a large extent this is due to the severe restriction on building. Building licences are difficult to get and the developer who has been fortunate enough to obtain one is often willing to pay a much inflated price for a piece of land upon which to build. In other words, a "scarcity value" attaches at present to the possession of a licence. The theory that the development charge would leave the developer unwilling or unable to pay more than existing use value for his land is not at present working out in practice, especially since a would-be house-owner who pays building value to the seller of the land, as well as a development charge to the Board, is still paying less in the total cost of his house than he would have to pay for an existing house with vacant possession.'

It was to prevent such problems that the Central Land Board had been given powers of compulsory purchase at the 'correct' price. These powers were used – not as a general means of facilitating the supply of land at existing-use prices, but selectively 'as a warning to owners of land in general'. Furthermore, they were used only where an owner had actually offered his land for sale at a price above existing-use value. Thus, purchases by the Board would have done nothing to facilitate an increase in the total supply of land for development even if they had been much more numerous. But, in fact, their very rarity served only to make the procedure arbitrary in the extreme and, indeed, may have added to the reluctance of owners to offer land for development at all.

The Conservative Government which took office in 1951 was intent on raising the level of construction activity and particularly the rate of private house-building. Though, within the limits of building activity set by the Labour Government, it is unlikely that the development charge procedure seriously affected the supply of land it is probable that the Conservative Government's plans for private building would have been jeopardized by it. This was one factor which led the new Government to consider repealing development charges.

The basic difficulty was that purchasers of land were compelled to pay a premium above the existing-use value in order to persuade an owner to sell: a development charge of 100 per cent therefore constituted a permanent addition to the cost of development. Moreover, the basis of the development charge was uncertain:

'Since it is assessed on the difference between the value of the land without permission to develop and its value for the development permitted, the amount of the charge is inevitably a matter of judgment and valuation – and therefore for negotiation, in the same way as the price of land is a matter for negotiation. In some cases quite small adjustments in the two values during the process of such negotiation will have a very large effect on the amount of development charge finally assessed. This is inherent in the nature of the charge, but the effect is to destroy confidence in its validity. Those who view development charge as a tax on development – and they are in the great majority – look for some definite relation between the amount assessed and the cost of the land or of the development; and their failure to find any makes them very critical of the method of assessment'.[19]

Further problems began to loom ahead as the final date for payments from the £300 million fund (July 1, 1953) drew near. First, the payment of this sum of money over a short period would have a considerable inflationary effect. Secondly, all claimants on the fund would receive payment whether or not they had actually suffered any loss as a result of the 1947 Act. (Some would have already recovered the development value of the land by selling at a high price; others may never have wished to develop their land, and, indeed, might even have bought it for the express purpose of preventing its development.) But the main difficulty was that if compensation were paid out on this 'once for all' basis, 'it would be exceedingly difficult for any future Government ever to make radical changes in the financial provisions, however badly they were working. For all the holders of claims on the fund would have been compensated for loss of development value – those who will be allowed to develop their land as well as those who will not.'

Some amendment of the 1947 Act scheme was clearly necessary, but though there might have been agreement on this, there was no equal agreement on what the amendments should be. There was a real fear that an 'amendment' which satisfied developers would seriously weaken or even wreck the planning machine: the scheme was part of a complex of planning controls which might easily be upset and result in a return to the very problems which the 1947 Act was designed to solve. Various proposals were currently being canvassed, but the most popular was a reduction in the rate of development charge. The intention was to provide an incentive to owners to sell their land at a price which took account of the developer's liability to pay the (reduced) charge. The Government took the view that this was not possible: 'vendors of land, like vendors of any other commodity, will always get the best price that they can, and the development charge, however small, would in effect be passed on, in whole or in part, to the ultimate user of the land'. Furthermore, the Government's objective was not merely one of easing the market in land: they were particularly concerned to encourage more private development, and even a low rate of development charge would act as a brake. On the (implicit) assumption that market prices for land would rise, the time would inevitably come when the charge would begin to greatly exceed the corresponding claim on the £300 million fund. Finally, it was felt that once the rate of development charge was reduced there would be no clear principle as to the level at which it should continue to be levied – 'the process of reduction, once begun, would be difficult to stop'. In short, the Government held that the financial provisions of the 1947 Act were inherently unsatisfactory and could not be sufficiently improved by a mere modification: what was needed was a complete abolition of development charges.

THE 1954 SCHEME

The abolition of development charges was made on the ground that they had proved 'too unreliable an instrument to act as the lynch-pin of a permanent settlement'. But, at the same time, if the main part of the planning system was to remain, some limit to the liability to compensation for planning restrictions was essential. Otherwise effective planning controls would become prohibitively expensive: the cost of compensation for restrictions, if paid at the market value, would be crippling. The solution arrived at was to compensate only 'for loss of development value which accrued in the past up to the point where the 1947 axe fell – but not for loss of development value accruing in the future'.

There were some clear advantages in this scheme: not only was the

State's liability for compensation limited, but it was to be paid only if and when the owner of land suffered from planning restrictions. The compensation would be the 'admitted claim' on the £300 million fund (plus one-seventh for accrued interest on the amount of the claim). But not all admitted claims were to be met, even where loss of development value was caused by refusal of planning permission or by conditions attached to a permission. The 1932 Act had clearly established the principle that compensation should not be paid for restrictions imposed in the interest of 'good neighbourliness' and this principle was extended. No compensation was payable for refusal to allow a change in the use of a building; or for restrictions regarding density, layout, construction, design and so on; or for refusal to permit development which would place an undue burden on the community (e.g. in the provision of services). Some of these matters clearly fall within the 'good neighbour' concept,* while others are based on the principle that compensation is not to be paid merely because maximum exploitation has been prevented so long as development of a reasonably remunerative character is allowed.

The 1954 scheme† did not put anything in place of the development charge: the collection of betterment was now left to the blunt instruments of general taxation. Hence the attempt to 'hold the scales evenly between those who were allowed to develop their land and those who were not' was abandoned, but the use of 1947 development values as a 'permanent basis for compensation' safeguarded the public purse. On the other hand this meted out only a very rough justice to owners. The official view – at this date – was that this was not so:

'It may be suggested that to limit compensation in the way proposed will work unfairly in certain cases. Land which in 1947 had little development value, and therefore no claim or only a small claim on the fund, may at some future date acquire considerable development value. Values will tend to follow the development plans, and land which acquires a high development value will normally be land on which development will be permitted; but there will be exceptions and it may be thought that to limit compensation in these cases will

* The Act did, however, extend this principle drastically: a matter which evoked some opposition. For a fuller discussion see, for example, F. V. Corfield, *Compensation and the Town and Country Planning Act, 1959*, Solicitors' Law Stationery Society, 1959, p. 53 *et seq.*

† There were two Acts. The Town and Country Planning Act, 1953, abolished development charges, while the Town and Country Planning Act, 1954, limited compensation for the loss of development values to those sites for which a claim had been approved, and then only under defined circumstances when an application to develop was actually refused.

inflict hardship on owners who are refused permission to develop or whose land is bought compulsorily. It is important, however, to remember that all transactions in land since 1947 have taken place in the full knowledge that the 1947 development value was the most that anyone would hope to receive by way of compensation from the £300 million fund. Purchasers in future will be able to safeguard themselves by ensuring that permission to develop is forthcoming before they pay more than current existing-use value or, where a claim on the fund passes with the land, current existing-use value plus 1947 development value.'[19]

But this ignored the fact that the new scheme established a dual market in land. Compensation both for planning restrictions (in cases where a claim had been admitted) and for compulsory purchase by public authorities was to be paid on the basis of existing use plus any admitted 1947 development value, but private sales would be at current market prices. The difference between these two values might be very substantial, particularly where development of a far more valuable character than had been anticipated in 1947 took place. Furthermore, with the passage of time land values generally would increase, especially if inflation continued. Whatever theoretical justification there might be for the dual market it would appear progressively unjust. Again, there is a real distinction between the hardships inflicted by a refusal of planning permission (i.e. the loss of the development value of land) and that caused by the loss of the land itself (i.e. compulsory purchase). In the first case the owner retains the existing use value of his land and is worse off only in comparison with owners who have been fortunate in owning land on which development is permitted and who can therefore realize a capital gain. But in the second case compulsory acquisition at less than market price involves an actual loss since the owner is not only deprived of his property, he is also compensated at a price which might be less than he paid for it and would almost certainly be insufficient to purchase a similar parcel of land in the open market.

Finally, though it must be generally accepted that individuals cannot be protected from foolish actions based on an inadequate knowledge of the law, the situation following the 1954 Act was so complex and – because of the inevitable unpredictability of the necessity for compulsory purchase – so risky that it appeared likely (in retrospect at least) that public opinion would demand a further change. There was an omen of this even while the legislation was passing through Parliament. A certain Mr Pilgrim had bought, in 1950, a vacant plot of land adjoining his house. To pay for this he raised a mortgage of £500 on his house. Some years later the Romford Borough Council compulsorily acquired the land at the existing-use value of £65. (No claim had ever been made on the £300 million fund for loss of development value.) Mr Pilgrim committed suicide. Naturally the case attracted a lot of attention and as a result a new provision was introduced in the 1954 Bill to alleviate the position of persons, usually small owners, who suffered loss on compulsory acquisition because there was no established claim on the £300 million fund. This provision permitted the payment of an *ex gratia* supplement in cases of this kind.

To recapitulate, the effect of the complicated network of legislation which was now (1954) in force was basically to create two values for land according to whether it was sold in the open market or acquired by a public authority. In the former case there were no restrictions and thus land changed hands at the full market price. But in the latter case the public authority would pay only the existing (1947) use value plus any agreed claim for loss of 1947 development value. This was a most unsatisfactory outcome. As land prices increased, due partly to planning controls, the gap between existing use and market values widened – particularly in suburban areas near green belt land. The greater the amount of planning control, the greater did the gap become. Thus, owners who were forced to sell their land to public authorities considered themselves to be very badly treated in comparison with those who were able to sell at the enhanced prices resulting in part from planning restrictions on other sites. The inherent uncertainties of future public acquisitions – no plan can be so definite and inflexible as to determine which sites will (or might) be needed in the future for public purposes – made this distinction appear arbitrary and unjust. The abolition of the development charge served to increase the inequity.

The contradictions and anomalies in the 1954 scheme were obvious. It was only a matter of time before public opinion demanded further amending legislation.

THE 1959 ACT: THE RETURN TO MARKET VALUE

Opposition to this state of affairs increased with the growth of private pressures for development following the abolition of building licences. Eventually the Government was forced to take action. The resulting legislation (the Town and Country Planning Act, 1959) restored 'fair market price' as the basis of compensation for compulsory acquisition. This, in the Government's view, was the only practicable way of rectifying the injustices of the dual market for land. An owner now obtained (in theory at least) the same price for his land irrespective of whether he sold it to a private individual or to a public authority.*

These provisions thus removed a source of grievance, but they did nothing towards solving the fundamental problems of compensation and betterment, and the result proved extremely costly to public authorities. If this had been a reflection of basic principles of justice there could have been little cause for complaint, but in fact an examination of the position shows clearly that this was not the case.

In the first place, the 1959 Act (like previous legislation) accepted the principle that development rights should be vested in the State. This followed from the fact that no compensation was payable for the loss of development value in cases where planning permission was refused. But if development rights belong to the State, surely so should the associated development values? Consider, for example, the case of two owners of agricultural land on the periphery of a town, both of whom applied for planning permission to develop for housing purposes – the first being given permission and the second refused on the ground that the site in question was to form part of a green belt. The former benefited from the full market value of his site in residential use, whereas the latter could benefit only from its existing value. No question of compensation arose since the development rights already belonged to the State, but the first owner had these given back to him without payment. There was an obvious injustice here which could have eventually led to a demand that the 'penalized' owner should be compensated.

Secondly, as has already been stressed, the comprehensive nature of our present system of planning control has had a marked effect on values. The use for which planning permission has been, or will be, given is a very important factor in the determination of value. Furthermore, the value of a given site is increased not only by the development permitted on that site, but also by the development not permitted on other sites. In the example given above, for instance, the value of the site for which planning permission for housing development was given might be increased by virtue of the fact that it was refused on the second site.

* There were several qualifications, *inter alia*:

No account was taken of any increase in the value of the site which was brought about by the development scheme for which the land was being acquired.

If the development scheme increased the value of contiguous land belonging to the same owner, this increase was set off against the compensation payable on the land to be acquired. (No account was taken of any decrease in the value of land attributable to the threat of compulsory acquisition.)

THE LAND COMMISSION ACT, 1967

Mounting criticism of the inadequacy of the 1959 Act led to a number of proposals for a tax on betterment, by way either of a capital gains tax or of a betterment levy. The Labour Government which was returned to power in 1964 introduced both. The 1967 Finance Act introduced a capital gains tax and the 1967 Land Commission Act introduced a new betterment levy. Broadly, the distinguishing principle is that capital gains tax is charged on increases in the current use value of land only, while betterment levy is charged on increases in development value.

The legislation is extremely complex and only a brief summary is attempted here.

The rationale underlying the Land Commission Act was set out in a 1965 White Paper[18]:

'In the Government's view it is wrong that planning decisions about land use should so often result in the realizing of unearned increments by the owners of the land to which they apply, and that desirable development should be frustrated by owners withholding their land in the hope of higher prices. The two main objectives of the Government's land policy are, therefore:

(i) to secure that the right land is available at the right time for the implementation of national, regional and local plans;

(ii) to secure that a substantial part of the development value created by the community returns to the community and that the burden of the cost of land for essential purposes is reduced.'

To enable these two objectives to be achieved a Land Commission has been established (with headquarters located at Newcastle upon Tyne – in line with the dispersal of offices policy). The Commission can buy land either by agreement or compulsorily, and it has been given very wide powers for this purpose. The second objective is met by the introduction of a betterment levy on development value. This is necessary not only to secure that a substantial part of the development 'returns to the community', but also to prevent a two-price system as existed under the 1954 Act. The levy is deducted from the price paid by the Commission on its own purchases and is paid by owners when they sell land privately. A landowner thus receives the same net amount for his land whether he sells it privately, to the Land Commission or to another public authority.

This in essence is the system introduced by the Act, but the complications involved in applying this system extend over 102 sections and sixteen schedules. Several features must, however, be explained more fully.

COMPULSORY PURCHASE

Though the Commission can buy by agreement they have to have effective powers of compulsory purchase 'if they are to ensure that the right land is made available at the right time'. There are two reasons for this. First, though the levy is at a rate (initially 40 per cent) thought to be adequate to leave enough of the development value to provide 'a reasonable incentive', some owners of land may still be unwilling to sell. Secondly, though the net price obtained by the owner of land should be the same irrespective of whether the body to whom he sells it is private or public, some owners may be unwilling to sell to the Land Commission. This reluctance may be all the greater on the part of those who, speculating on the return of a Conservative government, have noted the present Opposition's repeated statement that the Land Commission has 'no place in a free society' and the promise that 'the next Conservative Government will sweep it away into the junkheap where it belongs'. (This is not, of course, a point which is made in the White Paper!)

The Act provides two sets of compulsory powers. One is the normal powers available to local authorities, with the usual machinery for appeals and a public inquiry. Under these powers the Commission have to disclose the purpose for which they require the land. These powers can be used for purchasing land scheduled for development in a development plan, or for land permitted for development.

Of particular importance is the provision whereby land can be acquired by means of a *vesting declaration*. The advantages of a vesting declaration is that the Commission obtains a good title to the land (without investigation of the title) and can dispose of it for development as soon as the declaration takes effect. By this means the delays of the normal conveyancing procedure are avoided. Furthermore, 'the settlement of compensation can proceed independently of the vesting and the Commission will be able in most cases to pay out more quickly by accepting, without full investigation, the title that the owner of the interest claims he holds and by relying upon their ability to sue for recovery of overpayment and to prosecute in the unlikely event of a false claim'. (Local authorities now have the same powers under the Town and Country Planning Act, 1968.)

The second set of compulsory powers do not become operative until the 'second appointed day' which may be any time within five years of the 'first appointed day' (April 6, 1967). These powers will be brought into effect only if it appears 'that it is necessary in the public interest to enable the Commission to obtain authority for the compulsory acquisition of land by a simplified procedure'. They provide for a rapid procedure under which objectors would have no right to state their case at a public inquiry, and the Commission need not disclose the purpose for which the land is required. The purpose here is to deal quickly and effectively with landowners who are holding up development.

MANAGEMENT AND DISPOSAL OF LAND

It was intended that the Commission would often be acquiring land in advance of need. They have, therefore, been given wide powers of managing and disposing of land; but they can also develop land themselves. Land can be sold or leased to public or private bodies for any purpose – even if the purpose is different from the one for which the land was purchased. Land which is sold can be made subject to restrictions and future development value can be reserved to the Commission. Such land disposals are known as 'crownhold'.

Normally the Commission must dispose of land at the best price they can obtain, but there is one important exception. This is the 'concessionary crownhold disposition' which can be made for land which is to be developed *for housing purposes.* Here the Commission can dispose of land at less than the market price. All such housing land is subject to crownhold restrictions or covenants. In the case of owner-occupiers the Commission has the right of pre-emption on terms which ensure that the amount of the concession (and future increases in development value) accrue to them. Concessionary crownholds are also given to 'bodies which can effectively supervise the assignment of such houses', such as housing associations.

THE BETTERMENT LEVY

The levy differs from the development charge of the 1947 Act in two important ways. First, it does not take all the development value. The Act does not specify what the rate is to be, but it has been made clear that the initial rate of 40 per cent will be increased to 45 per cent and then to 50 per cent 'at reasonably short intervals'. Thereafter, 'the question of increasing the rate further will be examined as acquisitions by the Commission, and thus their ability to provide land for development, increase'.

The second difference from the development charge is that though the levy will normally be paid by the seller, if 'when the land comes to be developed, it still has some development value on which levy has not been taken in previous sales, that residual value will be subject to levy at the time of development'. Thus (ignoring a few complications and qualifications), if a piece of land is worth £500 in its existing use but is sold for £3,500 with planning permission, the levy is applied to the difference, i.e. £3,000 – the levy, at the initial rate, is £1,200. If, however, the land were sold (at existing-use value plus a 'hope' value that planning permission might be obtained) at £1,000, while the full development value was £3,500, the levy would be paid by both seller and purchaser: £200 by the former and £1,000 by the latter.

Certain bodies are exempt from the levy – for instance, local authorities, new-town development corporations, the Housing Corporation and housing societies.

The proceeds of the levy are expected to amount to £80 million in a full year. This is to be paid into a Land Acquisition and Management Fund. The intention was expressed in the White Paper that part of the proceeds would be passed on to local authorities. It is not yet clear how this will be done.

THE FIRST TWO YEARS OF THE LAND COMMISSION

Land for Development

The Commission's first task was to assess the availability of, and demand for, land for house-building, particularly in the areas of greatest pressure. In their first annual report, they pointed to the difficulties in some areas particularly in the South East and the West Midlands where the available land was limited to only a few years' supply. Most of this land could not, in fact, be made available for early development. Much of it was in small parcels; some was not suitable for development at all because of physical difficulties; and, of the remainder, a great deal was already in the hands of builders. Thus there was little that could be acquired and developed immediately by those other builders who had an urgent need for land. All this highlighted the need for more land to be allocated by planning authorities for development.

The Land Commission have to work within the framework of the planning system. Though a Crown body, they do not operate as such and thus are subject to the same planning control as private developers. The intention was that the Commission would work harmoniously with local planning authorities and form an important addition to the planning machinery. As the Commission have pointed out, though Britain has perhaps the most sophisticated planning system of any country, it is one designed to control land use rather than to promote the development of land. The Commission's role is to ensure that land allocated for development is in fact developed – by channelling it to those who will develop it. They can use their powers of compulsory acquisition to amalgamate land which is in separate ownerships and acquire land whose owners cannot be traced. They can purchase land from owners who refuse to sell for development or from builders who wish to retain it for future development.

In their first report, the Commission gently referred to the importance of their role in acting 'as a spur to those local planning authorities whose plans have not kept up with the demand for various kinds of development'. Though they stated their hope that planning authorities would allocate sufficient land, they warned that in some cases they might have to take the initiative and, if local authorities refused planning permission, go to appeal. In their second report their line was much stronger. They pointed out that, in the pressure areas, they had had only modest success in achieving a steady flow of land on to the market. This was largely because these are areas in which planning policies are aimed at containing urban growth and preserving open country.

In spite of exhortation by the Minister, local authorities, particularly in the Outer Metropolitan Area, have been releasing land at a rate which is considerably below requirements. The Commission are therefore beginning to act independently of local authorities and seeking land suitable for development: this will be made the subject of applications for planning permission at the same time as draft compulsory purchase orders are published. The Commission state explicitly that they expect in some cases that it will be necessary to seek planning decisions from the Minister on appeal.

This is a new role for the Commission and one which is important if adequate land is to be available. But it is not one which will endear them to the local authorities who are seeking to prevent development!

During 1968-9, the Commission purchased 946 acres of land for development. Of these, 274 acres were bought for resale to public authorities and 672 for sale to builders. A further 5,217 acres had been approved for acquisition, and 21,000 acres were under consideration at the end of the year.

There has so far been little reference to the problem of 'land hoarding', except in relation to Scotland where it has been found that much of the land suitable for housing development is in the hands of a small number of building firms. Since the Commission have a specific remit in Scotland to make land available for a greatly increased programme of private enterprise house-building, they are taking action to bring some of this land on to the market.

Owners of land can, of course, appeal against a compulsory purchase order. Three Ministerial decisions on public local inquiries announced in 1969 can be given by way of illustration.

A builder at Killearn, near Glasgow, was in the opinion of the Commission not developing his holdings of land quickly enough. The Commission issued a draft CPO on 52 acres, and a local inquiry was held. The Secretary of State for Scotland decided against the Order.

An inquiry concerning a 50-acre site in Chelmsford followed

objections to a draft CPO which was issued by the Commission because the owners refused to sell land which had been zoned for housing. The Minister of Housing and Local Government confirmed the order in respect of 47 of the 50 acres.

In Stoke-on-Trent an inquiry was held into a proposal to acquire a narrow strip of land separating two factories owned by an engineering firm. The firm were anxious to link up their factories, but were unable to negotiate the purchase of the land. A CPO was confirmed.

Much of the Commission's purchases are, however, carried out by agreement. It should be noted that the statistics of land acquired do not wholly reflect the scale and impact of the Commission's activities. The knowledge that the Land Commission is searching for land and that they have compulsory powers which they are prepared to use is often sufficient to bring land on to the market. The Commission have estimated that the amount of land brought forward as a result of their activities has been at least as much as they have purchased.

Betterment Levy

Betterment levy is payable on the development value of land realized on or after April 6, 1967. The Land Commission Act provided for certain transitional exemptions and, more important, exemptions for any development started before the operative date. Naturally (and legitimately) a very large number of developments were 'started' to forestall liability to the levy. The Commission estimate that the effect of all these factors has been to exempt from levy about two years' supply of building land.

As a consequence the levy got off to a slow start: indeed, even slower than had been expected. In the first year the number of assessments issued was 3,449, resulting in a total levy charge of £1,646,300. In the second year the number rose to 15,390 and the total levy to around £15 million.

A number of modifications in betterment levy were made in the Finance Act, 1969, and by regulation. These aim at exempting small transactions (which are disproportionately expensive to deal with) and at reducing hardship, particularly for owner-occupiers.

It is still too early to predict the likely total proceeds from the levy when the transitional arrangements lapse, but the original estimate of £80 million a year may be on the high side.

Land Management

It is also too early to assess the financial success of the Commission's land operations. The price paid by the Commission is market value less the amount of any betterment levy which the vendor would have to pay to the Commission if he were selling to any other purchaser. The Commission sell land normally at full market value.

By the end of the year 1968-9, 946 acres of land had been purchased and six acres sold. The land which was sold had cost £33,927 and realized £37,063, a surplus of £3,136. Since the Commission's financial policy is to turn over their stock of land as quickly as possible (thus enabling further land to be purchased while keeping borrowing to a minimum), land disposals will accelerate rapidly. However, the Commission have a further responsibility which runs counter to that of making the best use of capital: they must ensure that land is released in an 'orderly' manner. It may be necessary for them to hold land until basic services, such as roads and services, can be provided or until sufficient progress has been made in providing essential local authority services such as schools.

This issue of 'orderly development' is of importance for both developers and local authorities. What success the Commission will have remains to be seen. But the essential device is a surprisingly simple and attractive one: the unique power of the Commission to buy land net of betterment value and retain the resulting financial advantage in their land acquisition and management fund.

REFERENCES AND FURTHER READING

1 Ashworth, W., *The Genesis of Modern British Town Planning*, Routledge, 1954.
2 Corfield, F. V., *Compensation and the Town and Country Planning Act 1959*, Solicitors' Law Stationery Society, 1959.
3 Haar, C. M., *Land Planning Law in a Free Society*, Harvard University Press, 1951.
4 Hall, P. (Ed.), *Land Values*, Sweet & Maxwell, 1965.
5 Harris, B. and Nutley, W. G., *Betterment Levy and the Land Commission*, Butterworth, 1967 (with a supplementary 'Service Volume').
6 Heap, D., *Encyclopaedia of Betterment Levy and Land Commission Law and Practice*, Sweet & Maxwell, 1967 (in loose-leaf form with regular supplements).
7 Heap, D., *Introducing the Land Commission Act*, Sweet & Maxwell, 1967.
8 Land Commission, *Annual Reports*, HMSO.
9 Land Commission, *Statements and Memoranda; Extra-Statutory Concessions* (reproduced in Heap, D., *Encyclopaedia of Betterment Levy and Land Commission Law and Practice*, Sweet & Maxwell).
10 MHLG, *Betterment Levy; An Explanatory Memorandum on Part III of the Land Commission Act 1967*, HMSO, 1967.
11 MHLG, *Modifications in Betterment Levy*, Cmnd. 4001, HMSO, 1969.
12 Ministry of Local Government and Planning, *Town and Country Planning 1943-1951 Progress Report*, HMSO, Cmd. 8204, 1951.
13 Parker, H. R., *Paying for Urban Development*, Fabian Society, 1959.
14 *Report of the Expert Committee on Compensation and Betterment* (Uthwatt Report), Cmd. 6386, HMSO, 1942.
15 Seward, G. and Stewart Smith, W. R., *The Land Commission Act 1967*, Knight, 1967.
16 Turvey, R., *The Economics of Real Property*, Allen & Unwin, 1957.

17 Wells, Sir Henry, 'Land for Housing', *Housing Review*, Vol. 17, No. 6, November-December 1968, pp. 174-7.

18 White Paper, *The Land Commission*, Cmnd. 2771, HMSO, 1965.

19 White Paper, *Town and Country Planning Act 1947; Amendment of Financial Provisions*, Cmd. 8699, HMSO, 1952.

Chapter VII

AMENITY

THE CONCEPT OF AMENITY

'Amenity' is one of the key concepts in British town and country planning; 'it underlines all modern planning administration and is necessarily one of the Ministry's main preoccupations'.[39] Yet it appears only four times* in the 1947 Act (and the consolidated 1962 Act), and nowhere in the legislation is it defined. The Act merely states that 'if it appears to a local planning authority that it is expedient in the interests of amenity', they may take certain action – in relation, for example, to unsightly neglected waste land or to the preservation of trees. It is also one of the factors that may need to be taken into account in controlling advertisements and in determining whether a discontinuance order should be made. It is a term widely used in planning refusals and appeals; indeed the phrase 'injurious to the interests of amenity' has become part of the stock-in-trade jargon of the planning world. But like the proverbial elephant, amenity is easier to recognize than to define – with the important difference that, though all would be agreed that an elephant is such, there is considerable scope for disagreement on the degree and importance of amenities: which amenities should be preserved, in what way they should be preserved, and how much expense (public or private) is justified. The problem is relatively straightforward in so far as trees are concerned, as is apparent from the excellent book *Trees in Town and City* produced by the Ministry in 1958.[22] It is much more acute in connection with electricity pylons – yet the Central Electricity Generating Board is specifically charged not only with maintaining an efficient and co-ordinated supply of electricity but also with the preservation of amenity. Here the question is not merely one of sensitivity but also of the enormous cost of preserving amenities: the cost of a 275 kV overhead line is £25,000 a mile compared with £400,000 a mile for

* Town and Country Planning Act, 1962, Sections 28, 29, 34 and 36.

underground cables. Apart from the apparently insoluble problems of cost, there is the problem of determining how much control the public will accept. Poor architecture, ill-conceived schemes, 'mock-Tudor' frontages may upset the planning officer, but how much regulation of this type of 'amenity-injury' will be publicly acceptable? And how far can negative controls succeed in raising public standards? Here emphasis has been laid on design bulletins, design awards and such ventures as those of the Civic Trust – a body whose object is 'to promote beauty and fight ugliness in town, village and countryside'.[12] Nevertheless, local authorities have power not only to prevent developments which would clash with amenity (e.g. the siting of a repair garage in a residential area) but also to reject badly designed developments which are not intrinsically harmful. Indeed 'outline planning permission' for a proposal is often given on the condition that detailed plans and appearance meet the approval of the authority.

Thus, though amenity may be an elusive quality, it is one which has constantly to be borne in mind and decided upon by planning practitioners. But amenity is more than good design. As Lord Holford has put it:

'. . . amenity is not a single quality, it is a whole catalogue of values. It includes the beauty that an artist sees and an architect designs for; it is the pleasant and familiar scene that history has evolved; in certain circumstances it is even utility – the right thing in the right place – shelter, warmth, light, clean air, domestic service . . . and comfort stations.'[18]

This extensive concept of amenity underlines its important role in British town and country planning. Its all-embracing yet vague character makes it at one and the same time crucial and vulnerable. To particularize, the Ministry has stated:

'The following are cases in which the claim of amenity is fairly clear, though the decision on each must turn on the balance of conflicting interests: the disturbance of a residential area caused by noise from a saw mill or a repair garage, by the smell or flies from pig sties, by dust or smoke from industry, or by the general bustle created by the establishment of a business; the spoiling of a stretch of country by ugly houses or perhaps by any houses at all; the erection anywhere of a badly designed or badly sited building, unsightly in itself or unneighbourly; the alteration or destruction of a particularly charming or interesting building; any development likely to concentrate traffic in places where there is not enough room to take it comfortably; failure to provide enough shops, schools and open space to serve the neighbourhood; the felling of trees even though mature, with no provision for replanting; advertisement hoardings in unsuitable places. Anything ugly, dirty, noisy, crowded, destructive, intrusive or uncomfortable, may "injure the interests of amenity" and, therefore, be of concern to the planning authority.'[39]

This goes far towards encompassing a major part of 'planning': and another passage in the same Ministry report goes even further: 'The new towns are themselves essays in amenity, and in the re-planning of damaged and blighted areas of existing towns, and in the framing of development plans for country and town alike, the fundamental requirements are those of amenity – pleasant and convenient living conditions, a decent amount of open space and proper facilities for recreation.' There is a striking similarity between these official pronouncements and the arguments put forward a half-century earlier by those who campaigned for the introduction of town planning.

In recent years, however, there has been a marked sharpening of interest in amenity, caused partly by the rapid rate of development, and an awareness of the inadequacy of the planning system automatically to preserve and enhance amenity. Perhaps the most striking statement is to be found in the 1968 Countryside Act which requires every Minister, Government Department and public body to have regard to the desirability of conserving the natural beauty and amenity of the countryside in all their functions relating to land. Lawyers may rightly point out that this does not constitute, of itself, an effective restriction on any statutory power or discretion, but it is an important statement of policy and one which the statutory and voluntary guardians of amenity will seize upon whenever it is infringed. There is more to planning than law.

The preservation and development of amenity thus form a basic objective of planning policy. From this point of view, amenity can hardly be discussed separately. Nevertheless, there are certain matters where planning controls are specifically, and almost exclusively, concerned with amenity. The control of advertisements is a prime example of this.

CONTROL OF ADVERTISEMENTS

The need to control advertisements has been long recognized. Indeed, the first Advertisements Regulation Act of 1907 antedated by two years the first Town Planning Act. But even when amended and extended (in 1925 and 1932) the control was quite inadequate. Not only were the powers permissive, they were also limited. For instance, under the 1932 Act the right of appeal (on the ground that an advertisement did not injure the amenities of the area) was to the magistrates court – hardly an appropriate body for such a purpose. The 1947 Act set out to remedy the deficiencies. There are, however, particular difficulties in establishing a legal code for the control of advertisements. Advertisements may range in size from a small window-notice to a massive hoarding; they range in purpose from a bus-stop sign to a demand to buy a certain make of detergent; they could be situated alongside a cathedral, in a busy shopping street or in a particularly beautiful rural setting; they might be pleasant or obnoxious to look at; they might be temporary or permanent; and so on. The task of devising a code which would take all the relevant factors into account and, at the same time, achieve a balance between the conflicting interests of legitimate advertising or notification and 'amenity' presents real problems. Advertisers themselves frequently complain that decisions in apparently similar cases have not been consistent with each other. The official Ministry view is that no case is exactly like another and hard and fast rules cannot be applied: each case has to be considered on its individual merits in the light of the tests of amenity and – the other factor taken into account – public safety.

The control of advertisements is exercised by Ministerial Regulations. The Minister has very wide powers of making regulations 'for restricting or regulating the display of advertisements so far as appears to the Minister to be expedient in the interests of amenity or public safety'. The question of 'public safety' is rather simpler than that of amenity – though there is still ample scope for disagreement: the relevant issue is whether an advertisement is likely to cause danger to road users (and also to 'persons using railways, inland waterways, coastal waters and airfields'). Examples are advertisements which obstruct the line of sight at a corner or bend, or obstruct the view of a traffic sign or signal, and illuminated advertisements which are likely to dazzle or confuse road users or are likely to be mistaken for traffic lights.

The definition of an advertisement is not quite as complicated as that of 'development', but it is very wide: 'advertisement means any word, letter, model, sign, placard, board, notice, device or representation, whether illuminated or not, in the nature of and employed wholly or in part for the purposes of advertisement or direction. . . .' Four classes of advertisement are 'excepted' from all control – those on enclosed land, inside a building, on a vehicle and those incorporated in and forming part of a building. As one might expect, there are some interesting refinements of these categories, which can be ignored for the present purposes (though we might note, in passing, that a vehicle must be kept moving, or to use the more exact legal language, must be normally employed as a moving vehicle on a highway or railway – and the same applies to vessels). With these exceptions, no advertisement may be displayed without 'consent'. However, certain categories of advertisement can be displayed without 'express consent'; so long as the local authority takes no action they are 'deemed' to have received consent. These include advertisements by local authorities, statutory and public undertakers (e.g. bus-stop signs and timetables); advertisements 'relating to premises on which they are displayed' (e.g. hotel and inn signs; professional or trade plates); certain advertisements of a temporary nature (e.g. 'To Let' signs); advertisements on business premises (e.g. advertisements relating to the sale of goods); election notices, statutory advertisements and traffic signs. Then there is the very important and wide class of 'existing' advertisements, i.e. those which existed on August 1, 1948, as well as a category which at first sight seems a most curious one – advertisements which continue to be displayed after expiry of an express permission. This last group needs some explanation: all new advertisements – except those referred to above – require express planning consent from the local authority. This is given for a maximum period of five years. (If the period is less than five years it ranks as a conditional consent.) After that period consent is 'deemed' to have been given unless the local authority invoke the 'challenge' procedure. A local authority can 'challenge' any advertisement (with certain exceptions, e.g. election notices and traffic signs) for which express or deemed consent is required. This means that the authority can serve notice that an application for express permission must be made within a specified period; this application can be refused and the advertisement must then be removed. There is the normal right of appeal to the Minister. To summarize (with some loss of accuracy), smaller advertisements used for everyday business purposes can usually be displayed without express consent; express consent is needed for larger advertisements, such as those displayed on hoardings. But any advertisement (with a few exceptions) can be 'challenged' by a local authority.

This is not, however, all there is to advertisement control. In some areas, e.g. national parks or near a cathedral, it may be desirable to virtually prohibit all advertisements of the poster type and to seriously restrict other advertisements including those normally displayed by the ordinary trader. Accordingly, local planning authorities have power to define 'Areas of Special Control' where 'special protection on grounds of amenity' is thought desirable. Within an Area of Special Control the general rule is that no advertisement may be displayed; such advertisements as are given express consent are considered as exceptions to this general rule.

TABLE VII.1

Decisions on advertisement applications, 1967[37]

	Challenge	*New proposals*	*Total decisions*
Within Areas of Special Control:			
Consent granted	107	1,230	1,337
Consent refused	289	649	938
Outside Areas of Special Control:			
Consent granted	119	31,355	31,474
Consent refused	472	6,288	6,760
Total	987	39,522	40,509

Not surprisingly, the control of advertisements has raised some difficult problems. The matter has been put rather nicely by Lord Luke (a spokesman for the advertising industry): 'Local authorities are concerned to preserve visual amenities. Advertisers want to foster the material amenity of providing the public with the widest possible choice of goods at the most economical prices.'[3] Local planning authorities appear to agree that the controls work reasonably well, though independent critics have argued that they are complicated and so lenient as to be ineffective, while the advertisement industry often complains of the unreasonable and unrealistic attitude of some local authorities. Controversy has particularly centred on 'clutter' – excessive, ill-sited, crowded and badly arranged advertisement displays. Local authorities have pressed for stronger powers to deal with clutter, but the Government have preferred to give the industry (which maintains that clutter cannot be controlled by regulations) the opportunity of dealing with the problem themselves. The industry set up a Consultative Committee and, in 1960, issued a 'Code of Standards for Advertising on Business Premises'. They argue that the objective of reducing clutter can be best achieved by trade associations bringing pressure to bear on their members.

They point out that between 1962 and 1969 some 330,000 advertisements were removed or resited voluntarily at a cost approaching £1 million. Long-drawn-out discussions between the Ministry, the advertising industry and the local authority associations have not so far reached any agreement on the need for legislative changes.

One of the difficulties which would follow from greater controls would be an increase in the number of appeals. Indeed, it has been proposed that advertisement appeals should be abolished. At one stage during the passage through Parliament of the Bill which became the 1968 Planning Act, it was announced that the Government had decided to do this. The proposal was, however, withdrawn and an alternative system, suggested by the Outdoor Advertising Council, is under consideration.

This has proved a very difficult field in which to obtain unanimity, but the effectiveness of the controls and agreements is very apparent to the European (and, still more, the American) visitor.

CONSERVATION

Britain has a remarkable wealth of historic buildings, but changing economic and social conditions often turn this legacy into a liability. The cost of maintenance, the financial attraction of redevelopment, the need for urban renewal, the roads programme and similar factors often threaten buildings which are of architectural or historic interest. This is a field in which voluntary organizations have been particularly active – as witness the work of the National Trust, the Ancient Monuments Society, the Society for the Protection of Ancient Buildings, the Victorian Society and others. As is so often the case, voluntary effort preceded State action. The Society for the Protection of Ancient Buildings was founded in 1877. The National Trust (or to use its full name, the National Trust for Places of Historic Interest or Natural Beauty) was founded in 1895. Though the first State action came in 1882 with the Ancient Monuments Act, this was important chiefly because it acknowledged the interest of the State in the preservation of ancient monuments. Such preservation as was achieved under this Act (and under similar Acts passed in the following thirty years) resulted from the goodwill and co-operation of private owners. It was not until 1913 that powers were provided to compulsorily prevent the damage or destruction of monuments. Strictly speaking, the Ancient Monuments Acts are outside the legal realm of town and country planning, but their objects and scope demand that they be considered within the same context. The responsible Government Department is the Ministry of Public Building and Works, which also has charge of a number of historic buildings belonging to the Crown. The term 'ancient monument' is defined very widely and could include almost any building or structure made or occupied by man at any time: the Ministry is responsible for the care and preservation of prehistoric settlements, Roman walls, Norman castles and Gothic abbeys. It is advised by three Ancient Monuments Boards for England, Scotland and Wales, who recommend monuments whose preservation is of national importance. Such monuments are 'scheduled': obligations are thereby imposed on owners and occupiers. The owner of a scheduled monument must give the Ministry three months' notice if he wishes to repair, alter, demolish or, indeed, do any work affecting it.

There are over 12,000 protected monuments in Britain. In cases where a monument is in danger of destruction or damage, an Interim Preservation Notice (lasting for a maximum period of twenty-one months) or a more permanent Preservation Order can be made, which prohibits any work without the written consent of the Minister. The Ministry can become the 'guardian' of a monument whereby it becomes permanently responsible for preservation, maintenance and management, or they can acquire monuments. In total, over 700 monuments are in the charge of the Ministry of Public Building and Works.

Under the Historic Buildings and Ancient Monuments Act, 1953, the MHLG has power to make grants for the preservation of 'buildings of outstanding historic or architectural interest' – and of their contents and adjoining land. It can also purchase such buildings or accept them as gifts. Three Historic Buildings Councils (for England, Scotland and Wales) were set up as advisory bodies. The 1953 Act was passed primarily to deal with the problem of preserving houses or buildings which were inhabited or 'capable of occupation' – these were not covered by the earlier legislation. Over a thousand grants totalling over £6 million had been made by the end of 1966.

LISTED BUILDINGS

Under planning legislation, the Ministry of Housing maintains lists of buildings of 'special architectural or historic interest'. There are two objectives here. First, 'listing' is intended to provide guidance to local planning authorities in carrying out their planning functions. For example, in planning redevelopment, local authorities will take into account listed buildings in the area. Buildings in a slum clearance area may be preserved with the aid not only of grants from the Historic Buildings Council but also with house improvement grants available under the Housing Acts. Secondly, and more directly effective, when a building is listed no demolition or alteration which would materially alter it can be undertaken by the owner without the approval of the local authority. This is technically termed 'listed building consent'.

Applications for listed building consent have to be advertised and any representation must be taken into account by the local authority before they reach their decision. Where demolition is involved, the local authority has to notify the appropriate local amenity society, and a number of other bodies, namely the Ancient Monuments Society, the Council for British Archaeology, the Georgian Group, the Society for the Protection of Ancient Buildings, the Victorian Society, as well as the Royal Commission on Historical Monuments. Again any representations have to be taken into account when the application is being considered.

If, after all this, the local authority are 'disposed to grant consent' for the demolition (and, in certain cases, the alteration) of a listed building, they have to refer the application to the Minister so that he can decide whether to 'call in' the proposal and deal with it himself.

As a recent annual report of the Ministry laconically put it, 'this new procedure will make it easier both for the local planning authorities and for the Minister to control proposals affecting historic buildings'.

All these provisions apply to listed buildings (of which there were, at the end of 1968, 115,000), but the Minister has power to list a building at any time and local authorities can serve a 'building preservation notice' on an unlisted building; this has the effect of protecting the building for six months, thus giving time for considering whether or not it should be listed.

With a listed building the presumption is in favour of preservation. Indeed 'listing' is in essence a collective preservation order. It is an offence to demolish or to alter or extend a listed building unless listed building consent has been obtained. This is different from the general position in relation to planning permission where an offence arises only after the enforcement procedure has been invoked. Fines for illegal works to listed buildings are related to the financial benefit expected by the offender.

The legislation also provides a deterrent against deliberate neglect of historic buildings. This was one way in which astute owners could circumvent the earlier statutory provisions: a building could be neglected to such an extent that demolition was unavoidable, thus giving the owner the possibility of reaping the development value of the site. In such cases the local authority can now compulsorily acquire the building at a low price, technically known as 'minimum compensation'. If the Minister approves, the compensation is assessed on the assumption that neither planning permission nor listed building consent would be given for any works to the building except those for restoring it to, and maintaining it in, a proper state of repair; in short, all development value is excluded.

The strength of these powers (and others not detailed here) reflect the concern which is felt at the loss of historic buildings. They are not, however, all of this penal nature. Indeed, ministerial guidance has emphasized the need for a positive and comprehensive approach. Grants are available under the Local Authorities (Historic Buildings) Act, 1962, the Historic Buildings and Ancient Monuments Act, 1953, and under the Housing Acts. Local authorities can also purchase properties by agreement, possibly with grant-aid from the Ministry under the 1953 Act. Furthermore, an owner of a building who is refused 'listed building consent' can, in certain circumstances, serve a notice on the local authority requiring them to purchase the property. This is known as a *listed building purchase notice*. The issue to be decided here is whether the land has become 'incapable of reasonably beneficial use'. It is not sufficient to show that it is of less use to the owner in its present state than if developed.*

More important is the emphasis on areas, as distinct from individual buildings, of architectural or historic interest. This was introduced by the Civic Amenities Act, 1967 (promoted as a private member's Bill by Duncan Sandys, President of the Civic Trust, and passed with Government backing). This gave statutory recognition for the first time to the area concept and made it a *duty* of local planning authorities 'to determine which parts of their areas are areas of special architectural or historic interest, the character of which it is desirable to preserve or enhance' and to designate such areas as *conservation areas*. When a conservation area has been designated, the Act requires special attention to be paid in all planning decisions to the preservation or enhancement of its character and appearance.

Given a framework of this kind, there is considerable scope for voluntary action in 'preserving or enhancing' the character of an area. Great impetus to the formation and effectiveness of local civic and amenity societies has been given by the Civic Trust. When the Trust was founded in 1957 there were only 200 such societies in Great Britain; by April 1969 there were 670 registered with the Trust.

The Trust now publishes a large number of pamphlets (a few of which are listed at the end of this chapter), and provides assistance and advice to local societies. Its regular *Progress in Creating Conservation Areas* provides not only a complete list of conservation areas, but also detailed reports and maps on individual schemes. (By November 1969 the number of conservation areas in Great Britain had reached 665.)

* The provisions apply also to conditional listed building consent and revocation or modification of consent. For further discussion see p. 106 *et seq* above.

Mention should also be made of the Historic Buildings Bureau and the Preservation Policy Group. The former is a small Government agency which has the function of bringing together buyers and sellers of those historic buildings which qualify for inclusion in the statutory lists and need special help to find a market. The Preservation Policy Group was set up in 1966 'to co-ordinate the special studies of historic towns and consider the results, to consider what changes are desirable in current legal, financial and administrative arrangements for preservation, including the planning and development aspects, and to make recommendations'. The Group assisted in framing proposals which are now incorporated in the 1968 Town and Country Planning Act (and which are summarized above). The four studies – of Bath, Chester, Chichester and York – have now been published.[29, 30, 31, 32]

ECCLESIASTICAL BUILDINGS

Ecclesiastical buildings are exempt from the provisions of the Ancient Monuments Act and the Planning Acts. This exemption dates back to 1912 when Archbishop Davidson successfully argued that the Church has its own system of law for protecting churches. Until very recently a corollary of this was that churches of outstanding architectural or historic interest were not eligible for grants on the recommendation of the Historic Buildings Councils. The Redundant Churches and Other Religious Buildings Bill, 1969, however, provides for grants (initially up to £200,000) for the preservation of selected buildings which are no longer used as places of worship. Exchequer aid is to be channelled through the Redundant Churches Fund set up by the Church of England under the Pastoral Measure, 1968. An equal contribution to the Fund is to be made by the Church Commissioners.

These measures apply only to Church of England buildings. However, redundant places of worship of other denominations can now be transferred to the Minister of Housing and Local Government or the Secretary of State for Wales if he wishes to acquire them for preservation under the Historic Buildings and Ancient Monuments Act, 1953.

PRESERVATION OF TREES AND WOODLANDS

'Trees are an indispensable raw material, but they are no less necessary as an adornment of town and country, and they are also a great joy in themselves. "Trees", said R. L. Stevenson, "are the most civil society." It is this aspect of trees which has led to the introduction into most recent Planning Acts of special provisions by which trees may be preserved, though without prejudice to good forestry and good farming.'[39]

Trees are clearly – so far as town and country planning is concerned – a matter of amenity. Indeed, the powers which local authorities have with regard to trees can be exercised only if it is 'expedient in the interests of amenity'. Where the local authority are satisfied that it is 'expedient', they can make a *tree preservation order* – applicable to trees, groups of trees, or woodlands. Such an order can prohibit the cutting down, topping or lopping of trees except with the consent of the local planning authority. Mere preservation, however, leads eventually to decay and thus defeats its object. To prevent this a local authority can make replanting obligatory when they give permission for trees to be felled. The aim is to avoid any clash between good forestry and the claims of amenity. But the timber of woodlands always has a claim to be treated as a commercial crop, and though the making of a Tree Preservation Order does not necessarily involve the owner in any financial loss (isolated trees or groups of trees are usually planted expressly as an amenity), there are occasions when it does. Yet though woodlands are primarily a timber crop from which the owner is entitled to benefit, two principles have been laid down which qualify this. First, 'the national interest demands that woodlands should be managed in accordance with the principles of good forestry', and secondly, where they are of amenity value, the owner has 'a public duty to act with reasonable regard for amenity aspects'. It follows that a refusal to permit felling or the imposition of conditions on operations which are either contrary to the principles of good forestry or destructive of amenity ought not to carry any compensation rights. But where there is a clash between these two principles compensation is payable. Thus in a case where the 'principles of good forestry' dictate that felling should take place, but this would result in too great a sacrifice of amenity, the owner can claim compensation for the loss which he suffers. Normally a compromise is reached whereby the felling is deferred or phased. An early case reported in the *Progress Report* of the Ministry of Town and Country Planning is illustrative:

'In the Conway Valley a large estate had changed hands and, as often happens in such cases, an application was made for a licence to fell the trees, which are a particularly beautiful feature of the landscape, visible from many directions and from a considerable distance. The local planning authority were consulted and made a tree preservation order which was confirmed. A subsequent application to the local planning authority for permission to fell some 750 trees, stated to be mature, was refused on the grounds that any felling would be injurious to amenity. In granting permission, on appeal, for the felling of 174 specified trees, the Minister observed that felling likely to cause serious injury to the woodland character of the area could not be justified unless the future welfare of the woodlands or other urgent public need made such a course unavoidable. He was satisfied, however, that felling to the extent specified in his decision would not only be harmless to amenity but would also benefit the woods since it would help the growth of young trees. "Merely to forbid the felling of any trees however old and rotten they may become, is to doom the wood to death. This would be to betray our trusteeship for future generations both of trees and of mankind." '[39]

The commercial felling of timber is subject to licence from the Forestry Commission and special arrangements exist for consultation between the Commission, the MHLG and the local planning authority.

Planning powers go considerably further than simply enabling local authorities to preserve trees. The National Parks and Access to the Countryside Act, 1949 enabled planning approvals to be given subject to the condition that trees are planted and local authorities themselves have power to plant trees on any land in their area. With the increasing vulnerability of trees and woodlands to urban development and the needs of modern farming, wider powers and more Exchequer aid have been provided by the Civic Amenities Act, 1967, the Countryside Act, 1968, and the Town and Country Planning Act, 1968. Local planning authorities are now *required* to ensure that conditions (preferably reinforced by tree preservation orders) are imposed for the protection of existing trees and for the planting of new ones. This, together with the Ministry's continuous emphasis on the importance of trees, has led to a substantial increase in the number of tree preservation orders being made. In 1964, 662 orders were submitted to the Ministry for confirmation; in 1967 there were 737, and in 1968, over 1,200.

Prior to the Civic Amenities Act, tree preservation orders had to be confirmed by the Minister. The Act introduced 'provisional tree preservation orders' which take immediate effect. Following the Town and Country Planning Act, 1968, ministerial confirmation is needed only where there is an objection to the order.

The Countryside Act has widened the compensation provisions to cover cases where an owner is required to replant in the interests, not of commercial forestry, but of amenity. It also empowered the Forestry Commission to plant and manage trees in the interests of amenity and to acquire land for this purpose. Previously the Commission's powers were limited to growing trees for timber. Also noteworthy is the provision of an Exchequer grant for local authorities (and in certain circumstances individuals and societies) who plant trees for amenity purposes anywhere in the countryside and acquire land for the purpose. These new provisions reflect the increasing importance attached to the amenity value of trees.

The scope for positive action is illustrated by a 1957 report of the Worcestershire County Planning Officer[48] which notes that upwards of 25 per cent of the planning applications received each year involve some consideration of existing trees or the planting of new ones. In one year over sixty proposals for development were approved subject to tree planting conditions. In this county an expert Forestry Officer has been appointed and his services are available both to public and private developers. Much more can be done by agreement and negotiation – together with expert assistance – than by mere regulation.

The planting of trees on highways has a forty-year history. The 1925 Roads Improvement Act gave local authorities powers to acquire land on the side of highways 'for the purposes of planting and amenity'. Lack of technical expertise led to some unhappy results and the Road Beautifying Association was established in 1928 to rectify this. Though a voluntary body, this Association did notable work, for example on the Kingston and Dorking by-passes, the Dorking-Leatherhead road, the Denham-Rickmansworth section of the North Orbital Road, the Basingstoke and Romsey by-passes, the Woodbridge and Colchester by-pass and the Market Harborough by-pass. Following the 1937 Trunk Roads Act, the Association was officially appointed as adviser on trunk road planting to the Ministry of Transport. This work is now carried out directly by the Ministry, with advice from an expert Advisory Committee on the Landscape Treatment of Trunk Roads, but the Association's services are still retained by a number of local authorities, and among its recent achievements is the tree belt screening for the Esso refinery extension at Fawley on Southampton Water. The Ministry of Transport has a 'countryside planting programme', and in 1967–8 over half a million trees and shrubs were planted near trunk roads and motorways.[40]

Like so many aspects of amenity, trees are the particular concern of voluntary bodies. The Men of Trees is one such body – founded in 1923 by Richard St Barbe Baker. Several branches exist in this country and there are many overseas. But the need for action on the part of public authorities is becoming increasingly recognized. A Ministry Circular of 1956 exhorted local authorities who were undertaking slum clearance or redevelopment not to fail 'to seize this unique opportunity to introduce more trees into their areas', and a handsome book published by the Ministry in 1958 (*Trees in Town and City*) maintained that 'hardly a street could not be improved, if someone would give thought to planting the right trees in the right places'. One of the Ministry's series of Design Bulletins (*Landscaping for Flats*) dealt with planting in the wider context of landscaping: 'No single factor has a greater effect on the appearance of a housing estate than the presence – or absence – of trees'. The problem is only in part one of costs; it is much more one of sensitivity and thoughtfulness. To a large extent the basic issues are the same as those involved in good design: a subject to which we now turn.

PLANNING AND GOOD DESIGN

Good design is an elusive quality which cannot easily be defined. As Lord Holford has said, 'Design cannot be taught by correspondence; words are inadequate, and being inadequate may then become misleading, or even dangerous. For the competent designer a handbook on design is unnecessary, and for the incompetent it is almost useless as a medium of instruction.'[21] Yet local authorities have to pass judgment on the design merits of thousands of planning proposals each year, and pressure is mounting from governmental, official and professional bodies for higher design standards to be imposed. The principles of good design and their execution lie outside the scope of this book; here reference can be made only to the powers and practices of local authorities, and some of the particular problems which arise. It needs to be stressed, however, that good design is not basically a matter of cost, but of the combined skills and sensitivity of the architect, the client and the builder.

Planning authorities have a clear legal power to grant planning permission subject to conditions relating to design and appearance. Planning permission is frequently given for a proposed development on the basis of an 'outline application', and subject to the condition that the detailed plans meet with their approval: if the detailed plans are unsatisfactory they can be rejected. There is a difficult problem here which basically stems from the fact that it is not the function of the planning authority to provide developers with good designs, and the amendment of a poor design may produce a compromise result almost as unsatisfactory as the original. Furthermore, the impossibility of laying down generally applicable principles (except that of employing a 'good' architect!) makes the task of the local planning authority a difficult one. A well-staffed and organized authority will spend considerable time with developers discussing sketch-plans – but not all authorities are well staffed or organized and the importance which is placed on this aspect of planning control varies greatly between authorities. Some have prepared notes for the guidance of developers, and there are various publications of the MHLG and of voluntary bodies which have the same objective. Major developments are often referred to the Royal Fine Art Commission for their opinion.

Yet some local authorities are still apparently under the impression that the Ministry will allow appeals against planning refusals based solely on design grounds. This is not so – as the various Ministers have emphatically declared, and as can be deduced from the published decisions on planning appeals. Perhaps the best statement of policy on this question is to be found in the June 1969 *Bulletin of Selected Planning Appeals*:

'One of the objects of planning is to prevent bad design and to encourage good. But unfortunately it is not possible to lay down rules defining what is good and what is bad; and much may in any event turn on the site. Moreover, opinions, even expert opinions, can often differ.

'It is therefore difficult to offer useful advice to intending developers other than the obvious advice that they should take trouble to ensure that the designs submitted are good. If they are in doubt how to ensure this, the authority may be able to help them if they ask for advice before starting on plans.

'Two questions can arise on design. The first is whether the design is bad in itself: fussy or ill proportioned, or downright ugly. The second is whether, even if the design is not bad in itself, it would be on the particular site: right out of scale with close neighbours (which does not mean that it need be similar to neighbouring designs), an urban design in a rural setting, or a jarring design or the wrong materials in a harmonious scene.

'It is obviously desirable that in operating control over designs authorities should be guided by the advice of a qualified architect; and if a district council have not got this, the county council may be able to assist them. Authorities should always be prepared to arrange for this architectural adviser to discuss proposals with developers, whether at the outset on a request for advice or when plans have been submitted about which they are doubtful.

'Planning control should not be used to stifle initiative and experiment in design; a design is not bad because it is new and different

–it may be very good. Designs should be rejected only if the objection is clear and definite and can be explained. It is not enough to say that a design will "injure the amenities" or "conflict with adjoining development"; it must be explained why it will do so.

'In general, planning control of design should be exercised with great restraint. But where a design is plainly shoddy or badly proportioned or out of place, the authority should not hesitate to ask for something better.'

But the written word cannot have the required impact – on either the developer or the local planning authority; hence the superiority of the well-illustrated *Design Bulletins* and *Housing Manuals* issued by the Ministry. Also important – though probably of limited impact – are the Design Awards made by the Ministry on the recommendations of regional panels of judges appointed jointly by the Minister and the Royal Institute of British Architects.

One particular problem in this field is that of 'modern' designs. Local authorities, like building societies, often prefer the safe and conventional, and are none too happy about avant-garde architecture. An early case (summarized in the July 1950 issue of the *Bulletin of Selected Appeal Decisions*) which attracted a great deal of interest was as follows:

'*Erection of dwelling-house disapproved on grounds of architectural design:* The appellant – an architect – wished to build a dwelling-house for his own occupation on a ¼ acre plot of land in a borough on the outskirts of London. Permission was refused on the ground that the external appearance of the building was out of harmony with the development of the locality.

'The house was of modern design. The appellant's original design included a copper roof which was almost flat, but to meet the wishes of the Council he had altered this to a tile roof of 30 degrees pitch. He had also agreed to site the building further back behind a group of trees following the contour of the land. He represented that a house of modern design with a similar roof had been approved on an adjoining site after the first design showing a flat copper roof had been altered; that his latest design offended no architectural principles; and that planning control of external appearance of buildings was not intended to apply to cases such as this.

'The Council stated that the house was unlike the ordinary development in the locality and they objected to its general appearance for that reason.

'The Minister said that the merits of an architectural design must always be a matter of opinion. He considered that the refusal of planning permission for the erection of buildings on grounds of design alone was not justified unless there was some evidence to substantiate the claim that the building, when erected, would have a seriously detrimental effect on the visual amenities of the neighbourhood. There was no such evidence in this case. The development in the immediate neighbourhood was very varied in character and of no architectural merit. It included houses of the speculative builders' type with occasional imitation half-timber work, a large rambling house in depressing grey stucco with casement windows and a tile roof of 45 degrees to 50 degrees pitch and a Victorian building of yellow stock brick with a low pitch slate roof and sash windows. The appellant had revised his design more than once to meet the wishes of the Council and the Minister saw no reason to regard the development as in any way objectionable. He allowed the appeal.'

Normally, planning permission and appeals excite little public interest even when the proposals are of particular importance. In part this may be because of the inadequate publicity given to development proposals, and the restrictions to which 'third parties' are subject – a matter which is discussed in the final chapter. To a very limited extent the Royal Fine Art Commission are able to fill this gap. Appointed under Royal Warrant in 1924, their functions are to advise Government Departments and other public bodies when requested to do so and when the Commission think that their advice would be useful. They can also offer advice if they think that a project may affect amenities of public or national importance. In practice this means that anyone can raise a question of 'public amenity or artistic importance' with them: it is for the Commission to decide whether the question is of sufficient importance to warrant their attention. Any advice, however, has to be given to a public body.

The Commission can call witnesses before them and inspect sites. Present members include Sir Colin Anderson (Chairman), Sir John Betjeman, Sir Hugh Casson, Sir Frederick Gibberd, Lord Holford, Lord Llewelyn-Davies, Sir Leslie Martin, John Piper and Sir Basil Spence. The outspoken reports of the Commission have referred to a very wide range of developments, from the colour of telephone kiosks to the siting of power stations in National Parks. The work of the Commission is not fully reported and, indeed, a totally misleading impression can be gained from its periodic reports[43] which concentrate on the more important developments referred to them on which they are not satisfied with the final outcome. Thus the 1957 Report, for example, refers to their misgivings on high buildings adjacent to the Royal Parks; their objections to the Park Lane carriageway in Hyde Park; their regret that planning permission had been given for the development of a site in Lincolns Inn Fields; their concern over the unimaginative designs for barrack blocks and other Army buildings, and the damage to amenities caused by the use of rural land by Service Departments; their alarm at the outcrop of ribbon development, the very low standard of speculative housing and the need for more architectural advice to local planning authorities.

Increasingly the work of the Commission is concerned with broad issues of 'public amenity or artistic importance'. In recent years they have devoted a major part of their time to the problems arising from 'the all-pervading demands of traffic in towns, over-dense building on urban sites and the lack of co-ordinated planning – even of public services'.

The Commission's nineteenth report provides a useful outline of their history, the scope of their work and their procedure.

It is difficult to assess what impact the Commission have*: certainly it is by no means as great as the Commission would wish. They can only advise, and, if their advice is rejected, report accordingly. Where an authority 'is not prepared to accept the Commission's general recommendations, whether on account of undertakings already given or for other reasons', the Commission are faced with the difficult choice between withdrawing their interest entirely and trying to improve in detail a scheme of which it fundamentally disapproves. 'In many cases the Commission feels that its duty to the public requires the second course, but by adopting it, it runs the risk of being made partially responsible in the eyes of the public for the final result.'†

There are other amenity and preservation societies which act as watch-dogs, such as the Councils for the Preservation of Rural England and Wales, the Georgian Society, the Victorian Society, and so on. Of particular note is the Civic Trust founded in 1957 on the initiative of Mr Duncan Sandys to promote high standards of architecture and civic planning and to encourage a wider interest in the appearance of towns and villages.

All these bodies do useful work, but their impact is limited. The fundamental problem, as repeatedly stressed by such bodies as the

* 'There is absolutely no means of compelling the building promoter to take its advice. But despite its constitutional weaknesses, the Commission is a much more valuable guardian of good architecture than the secrecy of its proceedings allows generally to be known.' E. Carter, *The Future of London*, Penguin Books, 1962, pp. 176–7.

† The quotations are from *Tenth Report of the Royal Fine Art Commission, 1950 and 1951*, Cmd. 8697, HMSO 1952, p. 6.

Council for the Preservation of Rural England and the Royal Institute of British Architects, is to educate public opinion – and the lay members of local planning committees. Though more adequate planning powers would assist, there is no substitute for this. The Minister has power to provide by order that appeals against decisions of local planning authorities on matters of design and appearance should be referred to an independent tribunal and to himself. This power has never been used: but even if it were it would not affect poor designs which are passed by local authorities and on which there is consequently no appeal.

Of more significance are the sixty-eight architectural advisory panels originally set up in the 1920s. These panels, which considered 14,000 planning applications in 1967, give advice to local planning authorities and district councils exercising delegated powers. In the words of the panels' Central Committee, the lay members of local authorities should not only 'strive to raise general standards of design, they should do this without frustrating creative work: they are, however, unlikely to succeed without competent advice and assistance from the architectural profession. The panels can assist all authorities regardless of size but they are of particular value to those authorities who do not themselves employ qualified architects.'[6] Over 600 architects serve on these panels. They undoubtedly contribute to the improvement of standards of design but, of course, they can operate only where they are welcomed.

HIGH BUILDINGS

For centuries towns have been developed with low buildings, and intrusions into the skyline were reserved for religious, military, and cultural buildings.[19] The first competitors were the chimneys, the mills and the factories of the Industrial Revolution – the symbols of new power. But a general movement upwards was held back by constructional and technical limitations, as well as by the shock of dismay at what Pevsner has called the unredeemable horror of the fourteen-storey Queen Anne's Mansions, built in 1878. The advent of steel and reinforced concrete frames, the lift and new methods of fire-fighting* opened up enormous possibilities for high buildings, thus giving scope for architectural freedom and for intensive and

* Before the fire-fighting methods devised for New York skyscrapers, the traditional maximum length of the fireman's ladder was only 100 feet. Buildings above this height were generally prohibited for fire-safety reasons. The tower of London University (210 feet) was reluctantly approved by the London County Council only on condition that the upper floors were not occupied! See A. Ling.[19]

profitable development of expensive sites. The increasing profitability of high-density redevelopment, together with the smallness of many redevelopment sites, have led to a situation where, to quote the sixteenth report of the Royal Fine Art Commission, 'the dominating consideration in the instructions given to the architect is all too often simply the desire for the largest area of lettable floor space consistent with planning procedure on small and restricted sites; . . . this is no way to produce fine urban architecture'. In the Commission's view the drabness and mediocrity of many of the buildings recently constructed in city centres spring from the restricted site and opportunities available to the architect. This is essentially a problem of the assembly of land, techniques of comprehensive development and the adequacy of planning powers. Even if individual high buildings are of architectural merit there still remains the problem of their siting. The Royal Fine Art Commission have repeatedly complained of the siting of high buildings on the fringes of city parks (where there is the particular temptation of easy 'angles of light' and the fine view afforded to the occupiers) and the intrusion of giant blocks of flats or offices in small town squares. The problem has attracted most attention in London.* Two types of control are exercised in Greater London. The first is 'Plot Ratio Control',† by which the amount of floor space is determined in relation to the area of the site. A single-storey building covering the whole of a site would have a plot ratio of 1 : 1, as would a two-storey building covering a half of the site, or a three-storey building covering a third of the site. The system makes for flexibility and effectively prohibits the canyon building of Manhattan. It can be used in conjunction with planning standards relating to daylighting, car-parking, etc., none of which it supersedes.

Aesthetic control cannot be operated in a similar fashion and the situation in London is now further complicated by the division of responsibility between the GLC and the London Boroughs. Proposals for buildings over 150 feet in the central area, and 125 feet elsewhere in Greater London, have to be referred to the GLC for

* But see T. Sharp's report on Cambridge,[45] where he recommends the prohibition of tower blocks everywhere in the City and a maximum permitted height of five storeys.

† See *A Plan to Combat Congestion in Central London*, London County Council, 1957. Plot ratio control was introduced in 1948, replacing the control by means of height zoning, angular limits, and a system of percentage of site covered by buildings at different levels of the building. It has the advantage of allowing a greater flexibility in design, and of allowing an advance estimate to be made of the floor area which can be permitted on any given site. The system was originally outlined in Ministry of Town and Country Planning, *The Redevelopment of Central Areas*, 1947, where it is referred to as the Floor Space Index.

direction. The GLC have produced (as part of the Greater London Development Plan) a report which sets out the basis for a threefold classification of land in London, together with a map which shows in broad terms the areas to which the three categories might apply.[16] This non-statutory map is a guide for the London Boroughs; the definition of areas is a matter for local development plans.

The three categories are:

(i) Areas in which high buildings are inappropriate.
(ii) Areas which are particularly sensitive to the impact of high buildings.
(iii) Areas in which a more flexible or positive approach is possible.

The GLC policy (to be applied within their area of competence) is set out on page 190.

Height is, of course, a relative term. The GLC study defines a high building as 'one which significantly exceeds the height of its surroundings, and includes all types of structures including masts, pylons, cooling towers, chimneys, etc.'.

The new policy is an attempt to overcome the inadequacies of earlier approaches (which were detailed in previous editions of this book). Whether the Royal Fine Art Commission will have further criticism to make remains to be seen. The problem is an extremely difficult one.

This discussion highlights some of the problems inherent in the British planning system, and indeed, in any attempt to control development in a society where there is a predominantly individualistic pattern of land ownership. There is a definite limit to the area over which controls can be effectively, usefully and equitably operated – and this is particularly so in relation to amenity and aesthetics. To the economist probably the most striking aspect of this summary of the problem in relation to high buildings is the complete absence of any reference to economics. Critics of the Greater London Council seem to assume not only that the Council has extraordinary legal powers and financial resources (e.g. to make high buildings materialize at will) but also that it can largely ignore the economics of high buildings on particular sites.

The limit to controls is not, however, only economic: there is the further question of how far it is justifiable to exercise controls in the interests of amenity and aesthetics.* Sometimes there is a clear public responsibility: there would be no doubt as to what decision

* For a passionate argument against high building see T. Sharp, *Town and Townscape*, John Murray, 1968.

TABLE VII.2 *GLC policy on high buildings*

	Category (i) *Areas in which High Buildings are inappropriate*	Category (ii) *Areas which are particularly sensitive to the impact of High Buildings*	Category (iii) *Areas in which a more flexible or positive approach is possible*
General Indication of Areas	(*a*) Within or with a visual relationship to famous areas of Special Character (e.g. Whitehall, Trafalgar Square, the Tower of London, Hampton Court). (*b*) Within or with a visual relationship to other areas of high environmental quality or unified design (e.g. Blackheath and Greenwich Park, the central Royal Parks). (*c*) Situations in which high buildings would spoil traditional or famous views (e.g. Houses of Parliament, St Paul's Cathedral, Buckingham Palace). (*d*) Major high points and ridges (e.g. Sydenham Hill, Harrow-on-the-Hill, Shooter's Hill).	(*a*) Areas of visual significance such as other high points and ridges not covered in category (i) (e.g. Hainault, Alexandra Palace ridges). (*b*) Areas of rural character (e.g. Barnes Common, Epping Forest, parts of the Green Belt). (*c*) Certain Thames-side areas. (*d*) Other areas of Metropolitan Importance. (*e*) Areas of Architectural or Historic Interest.	Areas not covered by the other categories.
General Policy	Normally proposals for high buildings within these areas would be refused. Exceptions would be rare.	The indication of these areas has been related to the policy for Areas of Metropolitan Importance. It may be necessary to consider some areas as potential ones in which high buildings would be inappropriate. It must be open to the Council and other local planning authorities to add others as experience and knowledge are gained.	Decisions within this category must be related to the character of the area and its density. Depending upon experience and future pressure this category may need refinement.
Criteria to be used in judging proposals	Not applicable.	That a development conforming with the general height of surrounding buildings would have serious disadvantages and that the freedom of layout resulting from a high building would enable major public improvements and amenities to be achieved. That the proposal would not harm the essential character of the surrounding area. That the high building would identify and emphasize a point of civic or visual significance both locally and in relation to the urban scene over the whole area from which it will be visible.	That the building would preferably identify and emphasize a point of visual significance.

Applicable to both Category (ii) and Category (iii)

That the proposed building, from wherever it is seen, would not mar the skyline nor intrude to the detriment of any famous or pleasant view.
That the proposal would be very carefully related to its surroundings, both existing and proposed, and especially to any other high buildings or prominent features in the vicinity.
That the site is sufficiently large and comprehensive to secure a complete and well-designed setting of lower buildings and/or landscaped open space.
That the amenities and development possibilities of surrounding sites and buildings would not be impaired.
That in view of the inevitable prominence of a high building it should be of outstanding architectural quality.
That due account is taken of the effects of wind turbulence in the siting of any high building and that every effort has been made to contain or eliminate such turbulence.

ought to be taken on an application to erect a 300-foot-high slab block in Parliament Square; but a large number of cases are by no means as simple as this, and on many issues the final judgment must be a subjective one. This raises the further question of how much society is prepared to pay for amenity and beauty – the same question which arises with power stations and pylons in national parks. No piece of administrative machinery will ever abolish these fundamental issues.

REFERENCES AND FURTHER READING

1 Advertising Association, *Advertising Outdoors*, 1962.
2 Advertising Association, *How Advertising Disciplines Itself*, 1962.
3 Advertising Industry Consultative Committee, *Code of Standards for Advertising on Business Premises*, 1960.
4 Ancient Monuments Boards for England, Wales and Scotland, *Annual Reports* (published in one volume), HMSO.
5 Carter, E., *The Future of London*, Penguin Books, 1962.
6 Central Committee for the Architectural Advisory Panels, *The Architectural Advisory Panels*, 1969.
7 Civic Trust, *Magdalen Street, Norwich*, 1959.
8 Civic Trust, *Conservation Areas: Preserving the Architectural and Historic Scene*, 1967.
9 Civic Trust, *Street Improvement Schemes*, 1967.
10 Civic Trust, *The Civic Society Movement*, 1967.
11 Civic Trust, *The Civic Trust Trees Campaign*, 1967.
12 Civic Trust, *The Trust in Planning*, 1967.
13 Countryside Commission, *Annual Reports*, HMSO.
14 Crowe, S., *The Landscape of Roads*, Architectural Press, 1960.
15 Fedden, R., *The Continuing Purpose: A History of the National Trust, its Aims and Work*, Longmans, 1968.
16 Greater London Development Plan, *Statement*, and *Report of Studies* (Chapter 8: 'The Metropolitan Scene'), GLC, 1969.
17 Historic Building Councils for England, Wales and Scotland, *Annual Reports*, (published separately), HMSO.
18 Holford, Sir William, *Preserving Amenities*, Central Electricity Generating Board, 1959.
19 Ling, A., 'Skyscrapers and their Siting in Cities', *Town Planning Review*, Vol. 34, No. 1, April 1963.
20 London County Council, *A Plan to Combat Congestion in Central London*, LCC, 1957.
21 MHLG, *Design in Town and Village*, HMSO, 1953.
22 MHLG, *Trees in Town and City*, HMSO, 1958.
23 MHLG, *Bulletin of Selected Planning Appeals*, No. 1–13, HMSO, 1947–58; *Selected Planning Appeals (Second Series)*, No. 1–5, 1959–63, HMSO.
24 MHLG, *New Houses in the Country*, HMSO, 1960.

25 MHLG, Circular No. 51/63, *Development near Buildings of Special Architectural or Historic Interest*, HMSO, 1963.
26 MHLG, *Landscaping of Flats*, Design Bulletin No. 5, HMSO, 1963.
27 MHLG, Circular No. 53/67, *Civic Amenities Act 1967 – Parts I and II*, HMSO, 1967.
28 MHLG, *Historic Towns: Preservation and Change*, HMSO, 1967.
29 MHLG, *Bath: A Study in Conservation*, HMSO, 1968.
30 MHLG, *Chester: A Study in Conservation*, HMSO, 1968.
31 MHLG, *Chichester: A Study in Conservation*, HMSO, 1968.
32 MHLG, *York: A Study in Conservation*, HMSO, 1968.
33 MHLG, Circular No. 61/68, *Town and Country Planning Act, 1968–Part V: Historic Buildings and Conservation*, HMSO, 1968.
34 MHLG, *Preservation of Historic Buildings and Areas*, Development Control Policy Note No. 7, HMSO, 1969.
35 MHLG, *Protecting our Historic Buildings: A Guide to the Legislation*, 1969. Obtainable *gratis* from MHLG.
36 MHLG, Circular No. 1/69, *Town and Country Planning (Tree Preservation Order) Regulations 1969*, HMSO, 1969.
37 MHLG, *Handbook of Statistics, 1968*, HMSO, 1969.
38 Ministry of Town and Country Planning, *The Redevelopment of Central Areas*, HMSO, 1947.
39 Ministry of Town and Country Planning, *Town and Country Planning Progress Report, 1943–1951*, Cmd. 8204, HMSO, 1951. (Chapter X, 'Amenity').
40 Ministry of Transport, *Roads in England: Report by the Ministry of Transport for the Year Ended 31st March 1968*, H.C. Paper No. 1, November 1968.
41 Nottinghamshire County Planning Department, *Newark: Action for Conservation*, Notts. C.C., 1968.
42 Royal Commission on Historical Monuments, *Monuments Threatened or Destroyed*, HMSO, 1963.
43 Royal Fine Art Commission, Periodic Reports (*Twentieth Report*, Cmnd. 3905, HMSO, 1969).
44 Ryan, P., *The National Trust*, Dent, 1969.
45 Sharp, T., 'Dreaming Spires and Teeming Towers', *Town Planning Review*, Vol. 33, No. 4, January 1963.
46 Sharp, T., *Town and Townscape*, John Murray, 1968.
47 Ward, P. (ed.), *Conservation and Development in Historic Towns and Cities*, Oriel Press, 1968.
48 Worcestershire County Planning Department, *Trees in Worcestershire*, Worcestershire County Council, 1957.
49 Worskett, R., *The Character of Towns: An Approach to Conservation*, Architectural Press, 1969.

Chapter VIII

DERELICT LAND AND MINERAL WORKINGS

THE DEFINITION OF DERELICT LAND

'Derelict' land – defined as 'land so damaged by industrial or other development that it is likely to remain out of use unless subjected to special treatment' – is commonly thought of as a legacy of the Industrial Revolution. Certainly there is an appalling legacy: in 1967 there were, in England and Wales, 112,428 acres of derelict land. What is not usually realized is the scale of continuing dereliction. Some 6,000 acres are used each year for surface mineral working of which some 4,000 are for sand and gravel extractions. Additionally 500 acres are used for the tipping of colliery spoil and a further 500 acres become derelict from other causes. The Ministry's 1963 brochure, *New Life for Dead Lands: Derelict Areas Reclaimed*, put the total at about 150,000 acres. Of this, some 60,000 acres consisted of spoil heaps, 60,000 acres of excavations and 'holes in the ground', and 30,000 acres of other types of dereliction. This makes the 1967 figure of 112,428 acres an apparently significant improvement, though it is clear that the figures have to be treated with caution.

Indeed, the statistics are inadequate to allow an adequate picture to be drawn of the rate at which land is being currently consumed. Thus a railway closure, or the closure of a coal mine with large heaps of spoil means that land ceases to be in use and so technically becomes derelict. In recent years there has been a gross annual increase of from 3,000 to 6,000 acres of derelict land, offset in part by nearly 2,000 acres a year of reclamation by local authorities. This does not, of course, signify that land is being currently *consumed* on this scale. The statistics reflect the bringing into account of pre-planning control activities, often at the point of time when the user of the land ceases operation.

Nevertheless, there can be little doubt that the problem is being contained rather than solved. This is borne out by the figures in

Table VIII.1 which have been obtained from the Ministry of Housing and Local Government. These relate to England only.

TABLE VIII.1

Derelict land and reclamation, England, 1964 – 67

	Total derelict land (acres)	*Land reclaimed/landscaped* (acres)
1964	84,900	2,076
1965	90,986	2,061
1966	92,876	1,641
1967	92,643	1,639

Much derelict land (particularly waste tips and abandoned industrial land) is concentrated in relatively small parts of the older industrial areas of the North, the Midlands and South Wales. It is this 'random incidence' (to use a phrase of the Hunt Committee) which hinders a more rapid rate of reclamation. Quite small local authorities with small resources of money, staff or expertise may find themselves faced with large problems. Even larger authorities may be faced with a formidable problem. Stoke-on-Trent, for example, has no less than 1,681 of its 23,000 acres derelict. The Hunt Committee called for a national programme and the establishment of a derelict land reclamation agency.[10]

RECLAMATION

Great advances in reclamation techniques have been made since the 'thirties. Slow and costly 'pick and shovel' methods have now given way to modern earth-moving machines which can move mountains of material at relatively low cost. Techniques of 'making soil' have been refined and it is now possible to make grass and trees grow in the most uncongenial conditions. Furthermore, rising land values and the need for sites for open space, playing fields and all types of urban development have added an impetus to reclamation, particularly in or near urban areas. But local authorities have no statutory duty to reclaim derelict land or to improve its appearance. Their powers are purely permissive and, as is so often the case, much depends on the energy of individual local authorities. Some have paid scant attention to the problems, whereas others have appointed staff to deal with them and have worked to a planned programme. The Ministry maintain that probably two-thirds of existing derelict land could either be reclaimed or improved in appearance by landscaping – 'what is wanted is a determination by the local authority concerned to deal with all the land that might be treated within a given time'.*

There are various powers available to local authorities quite apart from their normal powers to provide housing, open space and schools. Under these general powers they can acquire derelict land and reclaim it during the normal course of development. Derelict land can also be acquired under the wider powers provided by the Planning Acts; these enable local authorities to undertake any work for which powers are not already available. Finally, the National Parks and Access to the Countryside Act gives specific powers for the acquisition of derelict land and the restoration and improvement of such land whether or not it is owned by the local authority. There is thus no shortage of powers. The question of finance is, however, different. Costs of reclamation vary widely, but the average is around £1,300 per acre in England and rather more in Wales. It would cost around £100 million to reclaim the 70,000 acres in England and Wales which are thought to justify treatment.

Government grants are available at three different rates. In development areas, the rate is 85 per cent, provided that 'it appears to the Board of Trade' that the clearance of the land 'is expedient with a view to contributing to the development of industry'. This grant is given under the Industrial Development Act of 1966. The Local Government Act of the same year provided a 50 per cent grant for other areas. In National Parks and Areas of Outstanding Natural Beauty, however, the grant is at the rate of 75 per cent. Additionally, there is Exchequer assistance through the resources element of the rate support grant. (The 'resources element' – similar to the earlier rate deficiency grant – is payable to any authority with rate resources lower than the national average in proportion to their population.) Following the Hunt Committee Report,[10] the Government announced its intention of paying 75 per cent grant in many of the areas where there are serious amounts of dereliction.

Considerable progress has been made by a number of local authorities. Lancashire County Council, for example, has an annual programme of tree planting on derelict land: between 1951 and 1968 more than 1½ million trees were planted on 85 sites covering 850 acres. A programme of reclamation on colliery waste sites is also under way; examples of these with illustrations (which are far more eloquent than words) are given in the Ministry's brochure on *New Life for Dead Lands*.[14] More exciting is the use of flashes or

* *New Life for Dead Lands*, p. 3. The remaining third 'has perhaps less claim for immediate attention because it is remote from urban or village communities and has not become a source of nuisance or concern to the public'.

wet gravel pits for sailing – for instance, Pennington Flash in Lancashire and the disused gravel workings at Horbury in the West Riding. Where land can be made attractive for housing the increased site values can quickly recoup the cost of reclamation – as in the Wallbrook housing scheme at Coseley in Staffordshire.

The problem remains, however, of keeping pace with new dereliction. It has been reported that in Lancashire there had been an 'addition of 4,000 acres to Lancashire's derelict acreage in ten years . . . over 14,000 Lancashire acres were in current use for mineral extraction and tipping; . . . these activities accounted for two acres in every five taken each year for development of all kinds; . . . in the present administrative and financial circumstances the County Council could not hope to keep pace with the spread of dereliction'.[5] At first sight this seems incomprehensible; surely the planning machine is adequately geared to control these operations, at least to the extent of ensuring that any dereliction is cleared up when the operations are finished? Here it is necessary to examine the scope and character of planning controls over mineral workings.

CONTROL OF MINERAL WORKING *

The reconciliation between economic and amenity interests in mineral working is an obvious matter for planning authorities. It would, however, be misleading to give the impression that the function of planning authorities is simply to fight a continual battle for the preservation of amenity. Planning is concerned with competing pressures on land and with the resolution of conflicting demands. Amenity is only one of the factors to be taken into account. Thus it is a general policy to ensure that mineral working is carried on 'with proper regard for the appearance and other amenities of the area', and that when the working is finished the land should (wherever practicable) not be left derelict but 'restored or otherwise treated with a view of bringing it back to some form of beneficial use'. At the extreme – where mineral working would involve 'too great injury to the comfort and living conditions of the people in the area or to amenities generally' – mineral working can be limited or even prevented. Here a balance has to be struck between the economic need for minerals and the interests of amenity, and it is relevant

* Provisions relating to the control of mineral workings are scattered about several Acts and numerous regulations and circulars. A useful comprehensive summary is given in the Ministry's memorandum *The Control of Mineral Working* (revised edition 1960) though this is now outdated by the Town and Country Planning Act, 1968. (Unless otherwise indicated, quotations are taken from this source.)

(and indeed essential) to consider whether economic needs can be satisfactorily met from other sources with less damage to amenity.

There is, however, the equally important matter of safeguarding mineral deposits. Planning authorities have the positive function of ensuring that mineral deposits are not unnecessarily sterilized by surface development but are kept available for exploitation.

These are the broad policy matters with which planning authorities are concerned. The necessary powers are provided in the Planning Acts. Briefly these are for the making of the essential survey of resources and potentialities, the allocation of land in development plans, and the control (by means of planning permission) of mineral workings.

The survey required for the development plan is not, of course, simply a geological one. The planning authority has to assess the amount of land required for mineral working, and this demands an assessment of the future demand likely to be made on production in their area.

Mineral undertakers have long-standing powers to obtain rights over land containing mineral deposits. These were extended by regulations made under the Town and Country Planning Act of 1947. With the range of powers available mineral workings cannot, without good cause, be prevented by private landowners.

Powers to control mineral workings stem from the definition of 'development', which includes 'the carrying out of . . . mining . . . operations in, on, over or under land'. Further, the tipping of waste constitutes development (i.e. a material change of use) if, generally speaking, the area or height is extended. Special provisions apply to the National Coal Board's operations, which can be ignored for the moment. Apart from this, all mineral workings, ancillary buildings, depositing of waste, and the construction of means of access to sites require planning permission. Because of the national need for minerals, planning authorities have been strongly advised by the Ministry to pay attention to economic considerations: 'A fundamental concern of planning policy must be to ensure a free flow of mineral products at economic cost.' The long-term planning that is required for mineral exploitation means that planning permissions have generally been given for a working with a long life – commonly not less than fifteen years, and on occasion up to sixty years. Before reaching a decision on an application, it is often necessary for the planning authority to consult a number of interested parties: the Ministry of Agriculture, the Forestry Commission, the statutory water undertakers, a river or conservancy board, the Ministry of Transport, and perhaps the Countryside

Commission, the Nature Conservancy and the Inspector of Ancient Monuments. The representations of these bodies can lead to the making of conditions or the reinforcement of conditions which the planning authority wishes to impose in the interest of amenity. Conditions can be imposed, for example, requiring a phased programme of work in order to minimize the disturbance to agriculture, or a planned programme of working and restoration can be required. Conditions relating to restoration are among the most important. A mineral undertaker cannot, however, be required to put the land to any specific use after extraction has been completed, but, *where practicable,* he can be required to leave it in a condition comparable to that in which he found it. Unfortunately restoration is not always practicable. 'The extent to which reclamation is possible will depend first on the physical nature of the quarry. About one-third of the land used for quarrying represents the wet working of gravel; about one-third deep quarries working into a hillside or deep holes in the ground or a combination of both; one-sixth shallow quarries; and the remaining sixth workings in which a thin seam is extracted from beneath thick overburden. Wet gravel pits and other excavations which become waterlogged can be reclaimed only when suitable extraneous filling material is available at an economic cost; they sometimes have value for fishing, yachting or other recreational purposes, possibly after some landscape treatment has been carried out. Other deep holes can generally be put to use only when filling material is available. Waste material – including any overburden – can sometimes be used to reclaim part of the quarry or to raise the general level sufficiently for use to be made of the whole. (But the cost of such operations can often make this impracticable.) Shallow quarries and some hillside quarries where the floor is not much below the level of the adjoining land can often be brought back to use readily without the necessity of filling. Quarries working thin seams beneath thick overburden can also be readily reclaimed, the most numerous of this class being ironstone quarries.'*

* It is a happy circumstance when the problem of filling in holes can be solved at the same time as that of disposing of waste material. Each year some 100 million cubic yards of refuse weighing 13 million tons are disposed of by local authorities (see J. C. Wylie, *Progress in Refuse Disposal,* Council for the Preservation of Rural England, Sheffield and Peak District Branch, 1962). The Central Electricity Generating Board has to dispose of over five million tons of pulverized fuel ash each year (E. G. Barber, *Win Back The Acres,* Central Electricity Generating Board, 1963, p. 8). Sand or gravel pits and quarries are ideal repositories for such materials. Unfortunately the geographic distribution of suitable sites does not match the distribution of the supply of suitable filling material, and the cost of long-distance transportation can be prohibitive.

TABLE VIII.2

Production of coal and certain other minerals, Great Britain, 1938–68

	Coal		Iron Ore and Ironstone	Chalk	Clay, shale, etc.	Gravel and sand	Igneous Rocks	Limestone
	Deep-mined Million tons	*Opencast* Million tons	000 tons	000 tons	000 tons	000 tons	000 tons	000 tons
1938	227·0	—	11,859	10,406	26,822	22,198	11,900	18,905
1947	186·7	10·2	11,091	9,820	18,035	29,896	10,050	18,514
1954	213·6	10·0	15,557	15,624	28,950	53,486	13,217	29,356
1960	186·0	7·6	17,087	15,505	30,814	73,376	16,265	40,079
1964	186·8	6·8	16,326	18,263	34,129	102,973	22,948	57,078
1967	165·0	7·1	12,739	18,070	37,070	107,765	33,732	76,162
1968 (provisional estimates)	157·2	6·9	13,715	18,640	39,040	105,901	35,611	82,816

Source: Ministry of Power, *Digest of Energy Statistics 1968 and 1969*, and *Statistical Digest* for earlier years.

THE IRONSTONE RESTORATION FUND

Of particular interest in this connection is the Ironstone Restoration Fund. This was established under the Mineral Workings Act, 1951, to assist in the financing of reclamation in the Midlands ironstone field where working was by opencast methods. Generally, ironstone operators and landowners make a contribution to the Fund totalling 2¼d. for each ton of ironstone extracted by opencast working. The Exchequer contributes a further ¾d. a ton. Payments are made from the Fund for old derelict workings and for new workings where the cost of restoration exceeds a standard rate of £110 per acre. By the end of March 1968, the Fund had paid (or would pay) £255,000 for the restoration of land left derelict before 1950; £1,250,000 for the restoration of subsequent workings in accordance with the conditions attached to planning permissions; £130,000 for approved works not required by conditions but deemed necessary for amenity or agricultural purposes; £438,000 for work authorized by the Ministry of Agriculture to bring restored land into a good state of cultivation and fertility; and £28,000 for the afforestation of worked ironstone land.

The principle underlying this scheme – that land exploitation carries with it a duty to shoulder at least part of the costs of restoration – would at first sight seem capable of extension. A similar principle – that exploitation involves costs to others which should be borne at least in part by the exploiters – is accepted in the Cheshire brine pumping subsidence scheme. The Brine Pumping (Compensation for Subsidence) Act, 1891, provided for payments to certain owners of property damaged by subsidence, from the proceeds of a levy of up to 3d a ton of white salt produced within the Northwich area. The Cheshire Brine Pumping (Compensation for Subsidence) Act, 1952, brought the scheme in line with modern operating conditions and considerably extended the area over which it operated. The procedure is thus basically the same as with ironstone restoration – a levy on all operators related to their production. For a nationalized industry the principle can be extended further, as in the Coal Mining (Subsidence) Acts of 1950 and 1957. These place on the National Coal Board the responsibility for making good any damage caused by subsidence resulting from coal mining – or the working of coal and other minerals simultaneously. Under the 1950 Act grants were paid by the Treasury to the Board in respect of additional expenditure which the Act imposed on them, but this arrangement was not repeated in the 1957 Act. Thus the Board carries the whole financial responsibility for subsidence damage.

Restoration can be a difficult and expensive operation. It follows that (as with subsidence) there is a case for 'pooling' in order that, for example, the costs of achieving some socially desirable restoration does not involve prohibitive expense for a particular operator. Some costs can, however, legitimately be placed squarely on individual operators. This is the case with improving the appearance of mineral workings by tree and shrub planting. Planning permission for mineral operations can be made conditional on adequate screening being provided.

COAL

Planning control over the operations of the National Coal Board is subject to special provisions. Briefly, the continued working of mines begun before July 1, 1948 is 'permitted development', and therefore does not require specific planning approval. The same applies to the continuance of waste tipping. Furthermore, there is a general permission for any development in connection with coal industry activities (as defined in section 63 of the Coal Industry Nationalization Act, 1946) and carried out in the immediate vicinity of a pithead.* However, certain restrictions can be imposed (on the

* This constitutes 'permitted development' under the General Development Order (see chapter IV, p. 93 *et seq.*). However, under the same Order, a Directive can be made withdrawing a particular development from this class. In one reported case this power was used to limit mining in order to reduce serious subsidence dangers. See Ministry of Housing and Local Government, *Selected Planning Appeals*, Bulletin No. XI, 1952 (XI/19) and Bulletin No. XII, 1957 (XII/37 and 38).

erection of buildings) in the interest of amenity. Mining operations on new sites require planning permission in the ordinary way.

Only 4 per cent of coal output in Britain comes from opencast workings – a very much lower proportion than in other countries. One of the reasons for the low proportion is that, despite its profitability, opencast working arouses considerable opposition – from farmers, local authorities, local inhabitants, amenity organizations and even miners.* Clearly the visual impact of opencast working is far greater than that of deep mining, yet the loss of amenity is temporary and full restoration is practicable and usual; indeed, there can be a resultant improvement in amenity.

Opencast coal working began during the war under emergency legislation. It continued under this legislation until 1958 and, though usually constituting 'development', was therefore outside the scope of planning control. The Opencast Coal Act, 1958, laid down a special method of control operated by the Minister of Power. Notices must be served on the local authorities concerned and, if they raise objections, the Minister must hold a public local inquiry. The Minister of Power can direct that planning permission for the operations concerned 'be deemed to be granted'. His direction may include conditions of the sort commonly applied to planning permissions, and must include conditions to secure the restoration of the site. Where the land is in agricultural use it is normally obligatory for the conditions to provide for the restoration of the land so that it is fit for agricultural use.

The problem of reconciling economic needs with those of amenity admits of no simple solution in a small highly industrialized country; and the indications are that the problem will become more rather than less acute. This is partly because of the increasing need for minerals and partly because of the increasing claims of a population which is steadily growing. Planning controls have achieved a considerable improvement both in resolving conflicts in the light of the relative importance of the claims and in the restoration of mineral workings. The techniques now available for reclamation, screening and landscaping hold considerable promise for the success of an accelerated programme. What is needed is a positive planning approach. Relatively few local authorities have embarked on extensive programmes of reclamation or improvement. As with so many aspects of positive planning (as distinct from regulatory

* See R. T. Arguile, 'Some Notes on Opencast Coal Mining', *Journal of the Town Planning Institute*, Vol. XLVIII, June 1962, pp. 170–1. Opencast mining has shown a profit each year since 1953; between 1963 and 1968 the average profit was 18s. 3d. before charging interest and 17s. after charging interest. (See *Annual Reports* of the National Coal Board.)

controls) the weak link is often the competence of local authorities. Unfortunately, the areas with the largest problems are often the least able to afford the relatively small expense involved or – more important – the necessary staff. The reorganization of local government could set the scene for a major advance on this front.

NEW LEGISLATION

Major new legislation is under discussion on the working of minerals and land reclamation.

The first was announced in June 1969 and is intended to ease the problems faced by mining companies searching for and exploiting mineral deposits. It is believed that this will significantly reduce imports (over £2,000 million of minerals – excluding gold – were imported in 1968).

At present mining companies are sometimes hampered because they are unable to trace the owners of mineral rights or cannot make satisfactory agreements with owners. Under the proposals, the appropriate Minister would licence operators to explore for minerals and would be empowered to acquire mineral rights compulsorily for subsequent use by the operator in cases where it was in the national interest that they be exploited.

Consultations are proceeding with interested organizations, mining and chemical companies, property owning associations, farmers' representatives and bodies such as the National Trust and the Council for the Preservation of Rural England.

Less advanced are discussions on the establishment of a national land reclamation agency. This was recommended by the Hunt Committee, but was initially unfavourably received since it was seen in terms of a reduction in the powers of local authorities. The Chairman of the National Coal Board (Lord Robens) has, however, stressed that a national agency would work in conjunction with, and assist, local authorities. The proposal is that the agency would be based on the Open Cast Executive of the National Coal Board (which has had wide experience in this field).

REFERENCES AND FURTHER READING

1 Arguile, R. T., 'Some Notes on Opencast Coal Mining', *Journal of the Town Planning Institute*, Vol. XLVIII, June 1962, pp. 170–1.
2 Arvil, R., *Man and Environment*, Penguin Books, Revised Edition, 1969.
3 Barber, E. G., *Win Back the Acres*, Central Electricity Generating Board, 1963.
4 Barr, J., *Derelict Britain*, Penguin Books, 1969.
5 Casson, J., 'The Impact of Industry on the Countryside' (Conference Report), *Architects Journal*, October 25, 1961.
6 Civic Trust, *Derelict Land*, 1964.
7 Crowe, S., *Tomorrow's Landscape*, Architectural Press, 1956.
8 Durham County Council, *Derelict Land in the North East*, 1965.
9 Hilton, K. J., *The Lower Swansea Valley Project*, Longmans, 1967.
10 *The Intermediate Areas* (Hunt Report), Cmnd. 3998, HMSO, 1969, especially pp. 135–41.
11 MHLG, *Derelict Land and its Reclamation*, Technical Memorandum No. 7, MHLG, 1956. (Out of print.)
12 MHLG, *The Control of Mineral Working*, HMSO, Revised Edition, 1960.
13 MHLG, Circular No. 30/60, *Local Employment Act, 1960: Rehabilitation of Derelict, Neglected or Unsightly Land*, HMSO, 1960.
14 MHLG, *New Life for Dead Lands: Derelict Acres Reclaimed*, HMSO, 1963.
15 MHLG, Circular No. 17/67, *Rehabilitation of Derelict, Neglected or Unsightly Land: Industrial Development Act, 1966 and Local Government Act, 1966*, HMSO, 1967.
16 National Coal Board, *Annual Reports*, HMSO.
17 North West Economic Planning Council, *Derelict Land in the North West*, 1969 (published by the Council, Sunley Building, Piccadilly Plaza, Manchester M1 4BE).
18 Oxenham, J., *Reclaiming Derelict Land*, Faber, 1966.
19 Seventh Report from the Estimates Committee, Session 1962/63,

Administration of the Local Employment Act, 1960, H. C. Paper 229, HMSO, 1963.

20 Wylie, J. C., *Progress in Refuse Disposal*, Council for the Preservation of Rural England, Sheffield and Peak District Branch, 1962.

Chapter IX

PLANNING FOR LEISURE

The subject – and the problem – of planning for leisure is a large one. It encompasses national parks, access to the countryside, nature reserves, camping, caravanning, rambling and youth hostelling, waterways, parks and many other aspects of recreation. It involves difficult questions of amenity – if only because too many people can easily destroy the amenities they seek. Some aspects of preservation have been discussed in Chapter VII; here we shall be concerned with some of the major issues not merely of preserving and safeguarding amenities but of catering in a positive way for the increasing demand for leisure from a population which itself may experience an increase of over a third by the end of the century.

NATIONAL PARKS AND ACCESS TO THE COUNTRYSIDE

The demand for public access to the countryside has a long history,[25] stretching from the early nineteenth-century fight against enclosures, James Bryce's abortive 1884 Access to Mountains Bill, and the attenuated Access to Mountains Act of 1939, to the promise offered by the National Parks and Access to the Countryside Act of 1949 – an Act which, among other things, poetically provides powers for 'preserving and enhancing natural beauty'. Many battles have been fought by voluntary bodies such as the Commons, Open Spaces and Footpaths Preservation Society and the Council for the Preservation of Rural England (whose annual reports clearly indicate that their continued activity is still all too necessary), but they worked largely in a legislative vacuum until the Second World War. By the end of the 'twenties the campaign for public access to the countryside became concentrated on the need for national parks such as had been established in Europe and North America, but though an official National Park Committee reported (in 1931) in favour of a national policy, no Government action was taken. The mood engendered by the Second World War augured a better reception for the Scott Committee's emphatic statement that 'the establishment of National Parks in Britain is long overdue'.[47] The Scott Committee had very wide terms of reference* and for the first time an overall view was taken of questions of public rights of way and rights of access to the open country, and the establishment of national parks and nature reserves within the context of a national policy for the preservation and planning of the countryside. Government acceptance of the necessity for establishing national parks was announced in the series of debates on post-war reconstruction which took place during 1942 and 1943, and the White Paper on *The Control of Land Use* referred to the establishment of national parks as part of a comprehensive programme of post-war reconstruction and land use planning. Not only was the principle accepted but, probably of equal importance, there was now a central government department with clear responsibility for such matters as national parks. There followed a series of reports on national parks, nature conservation, footpaths, and access to the countryside.

THE DOWER AND HOBHOUSE REPORTS

The Dower Report[40] was a personal report to the Minister of Town and Country Planning by John Dower, published 'for information and as a basis for discussion'. A national park was defined as 'an extensive area of beautiful and relatively wild country, in which, for the nation's benefit and by appropriate national decision and action:

(*a*) the characteristic landscape beauty is strictly preserved;
(*b*) access and facilities for public open-air enjoyment are amply provided;
(*c*) wild life and buildings and places of architectural and historic interest are suitably protected; while
(*d*) established farming is effectively maintained'.

This conception of a national park was accepted by the Hobhouse Committee[42] who also agreed with Dower's proposal for a special National Parks Commission – 'a body of high standing, expert qualification, substantial independence and permanent constitution, which will uphold, and be regarded by the public as upholding, the

* The terms of reference were: 'to consider the conditions which should govern building and other constructional development in country areas consistently with the maintenance of agriculture, and in particular the factors affecting the location of industry, having regard to economic operation, part-time and seasonal employment, the well-being of rural communities and the preservation of rural amenities'. The Committee maintained that in order to see the problems of the countryside in perspective it was necessary to interpret these terms widely. Thus rural amenities were 'a *national* heritage' and hence 'there must be facility of access for all'. This line of reasoning led them to recommend national parks, nature reservations, and so on.

landscape, agricultural and recreational values whose dominance is the essential purpose of National Parks'. This Commission would select the areas for national parks and would employ in each park administrative and technical staff, headed by an Assistant Commissioner. These local executive bodies would act on behalf of the Commission and the local planning authority for each park. Management was to be under the control of an *ad hoc* Park Committee consisting of a chairman and fourteen members appointed by the Commission, together with fourteen members appointed by the local authorities in whose areas the park was situated. The whole cost of administering the parks was to be borne by the Exchequer.

This administrative organization was devised in accordance with the conception of *national* parks as envisaged in both the Dower and Hobhouse Reports. Since the legislation departed substantially from these recommendations, it is worth outlining the reasoning to be found in these Reports. National parks were to be administered for the benefit of the nation: this apparent tautology had the implication that planning in park areas should not be carried out by the ordinary local government bodies with the Commission acting as an adviser and supplier of grants. Such a system would 'tend to separate and oppose, rather than to unite and fuse, the national and local points of view and requirements; it would multiply delays by inserting an additional rung in the planning ladder; and by dividing responsibility, it would encourage inefficient administration and patchy compromise plans. . . . If National Parks are provided *for* the nation they should clearly be provided by the nation. . . . Their distinct costs should be met from national funds.'

To appreciate the force of this line of reasoning it is necessary to realize that national parks were not envisaged as rural museums. The new administration was viewed not merely as a machine for operating controls but also as a means for implementing 'a progressive policy of management, designed to develop the latent resources of the national parks for healthy enjoyment and open-air recreation to the advantage of the whole nation'. Among the management functions listed in the two reports were the acquisition of land for specific purposes (the Hobhouse Committee envisaged a tenth of the area of national parks coming into the Commission's hands during the first ten years of the operations); the removal or improvement of disfigurements or 'inappropriate' development (e.g. the surface restoration of abandoned mineral workings); the prevention of litter and of damage to crops, walls, trees, etc. ,the collection and disposal of rubbish, and the carrying out of repair works; skilled management to foster natural rejuvenation of trees, and a programme of steady and discriminating tree planting; assisting local highway authorities in the provision of parking places, viewpoints and other subsidiary roadworks needed for the benefit of visitors; the provision (often through voluntary bodies) of holiday accommodation – quiet hostels for elderly people, holiday camps or guest-houses for families, camps and hostels for younger people, camping and caravanning sites; the establishment of National Park Centres for field studies; the development of facilities for fishing, riding, small-boat sailing; and so on. A capital expenditure of £9,250,000 was proposed over the first ten-year period, with recurrent expenditure rising to £750,000 a year.*

THE NATIONAL PARKS AND ACCESS TO THE COUNTRYSIDE ACT, 1949

The Government, however, took the view that the newly constituted planning authorities (under the 1947 Act) should be given the responsibility for national parks: these authorities were only just beginning to function and it was unreasonable at this stage to suggest that they were incapable of meeting this responsibility. A National Parks Commission was to be established but its functions were to be mainly advisory. As might be expected, criticism was centred on this issue. It was suggested that county councils would be concerned primarily with local interests and would not be keen to incur expenditure for the benefit of visitors. One speaker commented that the proposed Commission bore about the same relationship to that recommended by the Dower and Hobhouse Reports as a baby's comforter bore to a real feeding-bottle: 'it may be superficial resemblance, attract and soothe the innocent, but it stops short and there is nothing behind it'.†

The Government, however, were not to be shaken. Probably they felt that they had already taken sufficient powers away from local government and that it was politically inadvisable to create another *ad hoc* executive body. Be that as it may, the new functions were laid on the shoulders of local authorities. The National Parks Commission had a predominantly advisory role. (The past tense is used since the National Parks Commission was replaced by the Countryside Commission in 1968.) It had a general duty to advise the Minister on matters affecting the natural beauty of the countryside – primarily but not exclusively in national parks and other 'areas of outstanding

* These figures include expenditure on 'Conservation Areas'. See below, p. 213 *et seq.*

† W. S. Morrison in the Second Reading Debates, *H.C. Debates*, Vol. 463, col. 1491. Argument by analogy always carried the risk that the opposite party will turn it to its own advantage. So it was in this case: the Minister replied that a comforter is not used to comfort the baby – 'it is used to preserve the amenities of the neighbourhood; so is the National Parks Commission!' (op. cit., col. 1657).

TABLE IX.1

National Parks in England and Wales

	Date designation confirmed	*Area (sq. miles)*	*Local authority areas*	*Administrative arrangement*
Peak District	1951	542	Derbyshire CC Staffordshire CC Cheshire CC West Riding CC Sheffield CBC	Joint Board
Lake District	1951	866	Cumberland CC Lancashire CC Westmorland CC	Joint Board
Snowdonia	1951	845	Caernarvonshire CC Denbighshire CC Merioneth CC	Joint Advisory Committee*
Dartmoor	1951	365	Devon CC	Committee of the County Council
Pembrokeshire Coast	1952	225	Pembrokeshire CC	Committee of the County Council
North York Moors	1952	553	North Riding CC	Committee of the County Council
Yorkshire Dales	1954	680	North Riding CC West Riding CC	Joint Advisory Committee*
Exmoor	1954	265	Devon CC Somerset CC	Joint Advisory Committee*
Northumberland	1956	398	Northumberland CC	Committee of the County Council
Brecon Beacons	1957	519	Breconshire CC Carmarthenshire CC Monmouthshire CC	Joint Advisory Committee*
		5,258		

* There are separate Park Planning Committees in each of the constituent counties.

natural beauty'. Its main executive function was to select, after consultation with the local authorities concerned, the areas where it considered that national parks should be established. It also had a general responsibility for considering what action was required in the parks in order that these objects might be fulfilled, but could only make recommendations to planning authorities and 'representations' to the Government.

Having decided that executive functions should be the responsibility of local authorities, the problem immediately arose as to what should be done in cases where a park lay in the area of more than one local authority. The Act provided that in such cases a joint planning board was to be the normal organization, though exceptionally a joint advisory committee might be established as an alternative. In fact, due to the strenuous opposition of local authorities (who were particularly anxious about the financial implications) only two joint Boards were set up. Four parks have Joint Advisory Committees as well as separate Park Planning Committees in each of the constituent local authorities. The remaining four parks lie wholly within the area of one local authority and are administered by a single local authority committee.

Whatever the form of administration, one-third of the members are nominated by the Commission. The intention is to ensure that there is always a number of people serving on the planning authority who are known for their interest in the national parks movement as distinct from purely local problems.

A full account of the work of the National Parks Commission (and its successor, the Countryside Commission) is given in their annual reports. Here only a few significant points can be raised.

A problem which has particularly exercised the attention of the Commission and the Park Authorities is that of development by Government Departments and statutory undertakers. Fears that this would prove a major problem were voiced during the debates on the Bill. Indeed, it was pointed out that 'the demands of these bodies would be more difficult to resist than those of private developers since the Government would in effect be not only the judge but also the defendant. The catalogue of what Lord Strang, former Chairman of the Commission, has called 'alien intrusions' is a formidable one, and includes new defence installations in the North Yorkshire moors and on the Pembrokeshire Coast; masts for the GPO, the Air Ministry, the Ministry of Aviation, for defence or for communications or for air navigation: masts for the police and other services and for transport undertakings; a nuclear electricity generating station and a pumped storage installation in Snowdonia with the accompanying network of transmission lines on pylons for the supergrid; overhead distribution lines in every part of the country; two oil refineries and an oil terminal on Milford Haven astride the eastern boundary of the Pembrokeshire Coast Park; recurrent and increasing demands for water in almost every national park, culminating in the great controversy aroused by the claims of the Manchester Corporation upon Ullswater and Bannisdale. The problem is an intractable one. By their very nature national parks are ideally suitable for military training; they contain valuable mineral deposits; some of them can provide unrivalled water resources; the development programme of the Central Electricity Generating

Board (to meet a demand for electricity which is doubling every ten years) involves a wide and high-powered transmission network and thus more and bigger pylons which cannot be hidden in the landscape and which cannot be obviated – except at enormous cost – by placing cables underground. These are all symptoms of the enormous pressures on land exerted by an increasingly affluent society in a densely populated country.

It would, however, be misleading to give the impression that the Commission have had no success. Much more effort is now being expended to make 'inevitable' developments as unharmful as possible. Statutory undertakers such as the Central Electricity Generating Board are now legally required to plan their operations with regard to amenity and to employ landscape architects; and public companies can be obliged or persuaded to do likewise. The nuclear power station in Snowdonia and the development by the petroleum companies at Milford Haven can be instanced.

This conflict between utility and beauty arises in a less spectacular but more intense form in connection with the livelihood and living conditions of the people who inhabit the parks. National parks in this country are not vast reserves of the kind found in Africa or America. They are areas of designated land in which ordinary rural life, rural industry and afforestation continue normally. The people living in these areas rightly demand modern amenities such as electricity and telephones, good-quality housing and – obviously – employment. These 'amenities' may clash with those sought by visitors, but the inhabitants cannot be expected to forgo these 'alien intrusions'. Nor should they be expected to shoulder the financial burdens involved in placing cables underground, in using expensive materials in new buildings for the sake of pleasant appearance,* or in repairing damage caused by visitors.

* During the passage of the National Parks Bill the Government resisted several amendments designed to provide compensation for extra expenditure resulting from higher planning standards or in connection with, for example, the placing of cables underground. The justification was twofold. First, compensation for 'loss of value' resulting from conditional planning approval was already provided for. Secondly, 'the whole principle of the 1947 Act is that a planning authority can impose high standards of conditions on development, and is not subject to compensation demands other than the £300 million which we have set aside for the purpose. That sum has bought out development rights. Against that, we impose development charges when development rights are restored, and these development charges are assessed on the value of those rights. That means that if an onerous condition is imposed on a person who wishes to develop, the size of a development charge should be by so much the less' (*H.C. Standing Committee Debates*, June 1, 1949, col. 592). The first point has not proved applicable and the second is no longer relevant. (For a fuller discussion see Chapter VI above.)

The biggest conflict, however, is that between the twin purposes of the Act: to preserve amenities and to promote the enjoyment of the public. The Pembrokeshire Coast Park Planning Committee has stressed that there is a conflict between the desire to extend the enjoyment of a thing of beauty and the danger that if this opportunity is offered too widely and without proper care the result will be the destruction of the beautiful thing itself. The same concern is increasingly being expressed throughout the parks. The Lake District Planning Board has warned that tourism in the Lake District is, by sheer weight of numbers, killing what it seeks to enjoy. Similar fears have been expressed by voluntary bodies. Thus, the Friends of the Lake District argue that the park 'is gradually being destroyed by too many people' and the Ramblers' Association maintain that 'there is a grave danger that the more popular national parks will be overwhelmed by the sheer number of vehicles crowding into them'.[56]

There is no easy solution to this; but clearly there comes a time when restrictions have to be imposed. Developments to foster public enjoyment – such as road improvements and caravan sites – have to be curtailed in order to prevent too many people frustrating their own purposes. Thus a proposal to hold water speed-record attempts on Ullswater and Coniston Water was rejected partly on the ground of direct nuisance and noise, but also because 100,000 people might be attracted to the area.[31] The situation can be met in part by the scheduling and public acquisition of certain areas in each park as a reserve, to be kept free of all developments. An expansion of facilities for parking, camping, accommodation and the like is, nevertheless, necessary. Both these require a more positive approach than has been evidenced since the passing of the 1949 Act. A change in policy was heralded by the 1966 White Paper, *Leisure in the Countryside*. This is discussed, together with the 1968 Countryside Act, later in this chapter.

AREAS OF OUTSTANDING NATURAL BEAUTY

Both the Dower and the Hobhouse Reports proposed that, in addition to national parks, certain areas of outstanding landscape beauty should be subject to special protection. These areas did not (at that time) require the positive management which it was assumed would characterize national parks, but 'their contribution to the wider enjoyment of the countryside is so important that special measures should be taken to preserve their natural beauty and interest'. The Hobhouse Committee proposed that these 'Conservation Areas' should be the responsibility of local planning authorities, but would receive expert assistance and financial aid from the National Parks

Commission. Advisory Committees (with a majority of local authority members) would be set up to ensure that they would be comprehensively treated as a single unit. A total of fifty-two Conservation Areas, covering 9,835 acres was recommended – including, for example, the Breckland and much of central Wales, long stretches of the coast, the Cotswolds, most of the Downland, the Chilterns and Bodmin Moor.

The 1949 Act did not contain any special provisions for the care of Conservation Areas, the power under the Planning Acts being considered adequate for the purpose. It did, however, give the National Parks Commission power to designate *Areas of Outstanding Natural Beauty* and provided for Exchequer grants on the same basis as for national parks. So far, twenty-five Areas have been designated and the Commission are having discussions with local authorities concerning a further eight.

TABLE IX.2

Areas of Outstanding Natural Beauty

	Date designation confirmed	*Area (square miles)*
Gower	1956	73
Quantock Hills	1957	38
Lleyn	1957	60
Surrey Hills	1958	160
Northumberland Coast	1958	50
Cannock Chase	1958	26
Dorset	1959	400
Shropshire Hills	1959	300
Malvern Hills	1959	40
Cornwall	1959	360
North Devon	1960	66
South Devon	1960	128
East Hampshire	1962	151
East Devon	1963	103
Isle of Wight	1963	73
Forest of Bowland	1964	310
Chichester Harbour	1964	29
Solway Coast	1964	41
Chilterns	1965	309
Sussex Downs	1966	379
Cotswolds	1966	582
Anglesey	1967	83
South Hampshire Coast	1967	30
Norfolk Coast	1968	174
Kent Downs	1968	326
		4,291

Generally, Areas of Outstanding Natural Beauty are smaller than National Parks. They are the responsibility of local planning authorities who have powers for the 'preservation and enhancement of natural beauty' similar to those of park planning authorities. Unfortunately, despite the Exchequer grant-aid which is available for 'improvement' schemes, local planning authorities are often reluctant to make use of their powers. This is due partly to their unwillingness to incur the necessary expenditure and partly to the fact that they simply do not think in terms of catering for the holiday-maker. Some authorities, however, have followed more enlightened policies. Recent examples quoted in the annual reports of the National Parks Commission and the Countryside Commission include reclamation of a former RAF camp in Cannock Chase, a discontinuance order on a scrap-dump near Old Sodbury, the purchase of land for public access at Durlston Head, Swanage (which is on the route of the South-West Peninsula Coastal Footpath), and increased public access in the Surrey Hills. Nevertheless, there is a good reason to lament with the Commission that progress has been very slow.

THE COASTLINE

About a third of the coastline of England and Wales is included in National Parks and Areas of Outstanding Natural Beauty. Additionally, development plans indicate 'Areas of High Landscape Value' and 'Areas of Scientific Interest' – national nature reserves or sites of special scientific interest notified to local planning authorities by the Nature Conservancy. Then there are coastal areas owned or protected by the National Trust. Nevertheless, the pressures on the coastline are proving increasingly difficult to cope with. Growing numbers of people are attracted to the coast for holidays, for recreation and for retirement. Furthermore, there are economic pressures for major industrial development in certain parts, particularly on some of the estuaries: Milford Haven and Southampton Water are cases in point.

The problem is a difficult one which cannot be satisfactorily met simply by restrictive measures: it requires a positive policy of planning for leisure. A welcome move in the right direction was started in 1963 with a Ministry circular *Coastal Preservation and Development* to local planning authorities with coastal boundaries. This argued that because the coast is of exceptional value and subject to heavy pressures for development it merits special study and control. Authorities with coastal boundaries were, therefore, asked to make a study of their coastal areas in consultation with the National Parks Commission and, for scientific advice, the Nature Conservancy. The objectives were to:

(*a*) ascertain which parts need safeguarding so that the natural attractions may be enjoyed to the full;
(*b*) decide locations where facilities for holidaymakers and other development should be concentrated;
(*c*) take steps to restore lost amenities as far as possible and create new ones;
(*d*) take account of the potential impact of proposals on areas of scientific interest.

TABLE IX.3

The coasts of England and Wales, 1966–7

Total coastline	2,742 miles
Total 'coastal belt'	1,494,653 acres

A. *Developed coastal frontage*

	Existing miles	*Proposed* miles	*Total* miles	*Total* as % of coastal frontage
Substantial built-up areas	402	23	425	15·5
Industrial and commercial uses	134	23	157	5·7
Camping and caravan sites	80	25	105	3·8
Total	616	71	687	25·0

B. *Protective ownerships*

	Miles No.	*Miles* %	*Acres* No.	*Acres* %
National Trust	152	5·5	25,799	1·7
Forestry Commission	18	0·6	12,005	0·8
National Nature Reserves	59	2·2	12,004	0·8
Local Nature Reserves	24	0·9	4,355	0·3
Local Authority	110	4·0	25,095	1·7
Others (commons, golf courses, etc.)	51	1·9	17,292	1·2
Total	414	15·1	96,550	6·5

C. *Other protective classifications*

	Miles No.	*Miles* %	*Acres* No.	*Acres* %
National Parks	266	9·7	115,303	7·7
Confirmed Areas of Outstanding Natural Beauty	781	28·5	342,511	22·9
Sites of Special Scientific Interest	465	16·9	86,707	5·8
Total	1,512	55·1	544,521	36·4

D. *Defence and other Government land*

	Miles No.	*Miles* %	*Acres* No.	*Acres* %
Total	134	4·9	50,331	3·4

E. *Policies of protection*

	Miles No.	*Miles* %	*Acres* No.	*Acres* %
Policies of protection in Development Plan	943	34·4	423,831	28·4
Other policies of protection	773	28·2	360,624	24·1
Total	1,716	62·6	784,455	52·5

Source: Countryside Commission, *The Coasts of England and Wales; Measurements of Use, Protection and Development*, HMSO, 1968.

Notes to Table:

The acreages are those of the 'coastal belt', defined as all land within a line drawn one mile inland from the coast.

Since these figures were collated, three additional Areas of Outstanding Natural Beauty have been confirmed: South Hampshire Coast, Norfolk Coast and Kent Downs.

The 'other protective classifications' (part C of the Table) are, in the main, additional to the 'protective ownerships' (part B), but there is some possible overlap.

Detailed notes on the figures are to be found in the Commission's report.

The circular was followed in 1965 by a letter expressing the deep concern of the Planning Ministers about the worsening situation and the inadequacy of the measures being taken to prevent the spread of development on the coast. Maritime local planning authorities were exhorted to speed up plans and policies. A series of regional conferences on 'Coastal Preservation and Development' were announced. These were held in 1966 and 1967 and resulted in a series of regional reports.[17] Indeed, it is a pity that the number of reports which have been published on this issue in recent years is not a reflection of the action which is under way. Nevertheless, there is little doubt that public (and local government) concern has been aroused. This, together with the National Trust's 'Enterprise Neptune', holds out some promise of safeguarding considerable stretches of the coast.

'Enterprise Neptune' was launched in 1965 and aimed at raising £2 million to enable the Trust to extend their protection over the finest coastlands that still remained unspoilt. The Trust conducted a survey which showed that of the 3,000-mile coastline of England, Wales and Northern Ireland one-third was 'already beyond redemption' and that only some 900 miles remained of outstanding quality. Before they had launched Enterprise Neptune the Trust had gradually acquired 175 miles of coast. By the end of 1968, through that campaign, they had brought under their protection, by purchase, gift and the acquisition of protective covenants, a further 94 miles and were actively negotiating for another 55 miles. When these negotiations are completed the total length of coast protected by the Trust will exceed 330 miles – more than one-third of the finest coastline remaining.

PUBLIC RIGHTS OF WAY

The origin of a large number of footpaths is obscure. As a result, innumerable disputes have arisen over public rights of way. Before the 1949 Act these disputes could be settled only by a case-by-case procedure, often with the evidence of 'oldest inhabitants' playing a leading role. The unsatisfactory nature of the situation was underlined by the Scott, Dower and Hobhouse Reports, as well as by the Special Committee on Footpaths and Access to the Countryside.[43] All were agreed that a complete survey of rights of way was essential, together with the introduction of a simple procedure for resolving the legal status of rights of way which were in dispute. The National Parks Act provided for both.

Responsibility for making the survey of paths rests with county councils. Obviously footpaths are far more important in the countryside than in urban areas and for this reason county boroughs are not obliged to undertake a survey, but they can do so if they feel that one is needed (twenty-nine have in fact adopted the survey provisions of the Act). Urban areas within administrative counties can be excluded from a survey if the Minister agrees. Maps are prepared in three stages: draft, provisional and definitive. A *draft map* shows the paths over which the council, as a result of its survey, decides that there are reasonable grounds for believing that a public right of way exists. When this is published 'representations' can be made for certain paths to be excluded or new ones added. There is a right of appeal to the Minister. This procedure provides an opportunity not only for objections from landowners, but also for organizations and individuals concerned with the preservation of rights of way to present their case for paths which are not included in the map. After all objections and appeals have been settled, a *provisional map* is published incorporating all the changes which have been decided. At this stage landowners can contest a path by appealing to Quarter Sessions for a declaration as to the existence or non-existence of rights of way. Subject to certain rights of appeal to the High Court, these declarations are final. When all the disputed cases have been dealt with by Quarter Sessions, a *definitive map* is published: this provides conclusive evidence of the existence of all rights of way shown on it – though there is provision for revision.

The preparation of this 'Doomsday Book of Footpaths' has proved a laborious and lengthy process. Much of the work has fallen on parish councils who naturally have a much more intimate and detailed knowledge of local history and local conditions than a district or county council. The Act actually specifies that parish councils are to be consulted – the only reference in the whole field of planning legislation to these bodies. Parish councils, however, have negligible financial resources and have to rely entirely on the assistance of volunteers. Indeed, the Ministry have stated that a great deal of the survey work can be carried out by volunteers, and some county councils have made formal requests for assistance to voluntary bodies. To meet this demand several of these bodies have formed a Central Rights of Way Committee. This Committee gives advice and assistance to surveying authorities on all footpath questions, and promotes and co-ordinates the organization of voluntary effort.

Under the Act, the normal completion date for the preparation of draft maps was to be December 1952; in fact, it was not until June 1960 that all draft maps had been published, and at the end of 1960 definitive maps had been published for only fourteen whole counties and parts of three other counties. The reason lies in the fact that so much of the burden is placed on voluntary bodies – a matter on which there has been considerable controversy. But though slow, the work is proceeding, and (to lapse into the official language of the Ministry's Annual Reports) 'once done, the job will be done for all time, and is very well worth doing!'

A Footpaths Committee, under the Chairmanship of Sir Arthur Gosling, was appointed in 1967 'to consider how far the present system of footpaths, bridleways and other comparable rights of way in England and Wales and the arrangements for the recording, closure, diversion, creation and maintenance of such routes are suitable for present and potential needs in the countryside and to make recommendations'.

Its report was published in 1968,[39] and the majority of the recommendations have been implemented in the Countryside Act, 1968, and the Town and Country Planning Act, 1968. These include placing a duty on landowners to maintain stiles and gates and requiring highway authorities to make a contribution towards the cost, providing for pedal cyclists to use bridleways, and placing a duty on highway authorities to signpost footpaths and bridleways where they leave a metalled road. A special review must be made of roads used as public paths so that public rights over them will be clear.

LONG-DISTANCE FOOTPATHS

Though work on the footpaths survey has been disappointingly slow, considerable progress has been made with what are officially termed 'long-distance routes'. These hikers' highways now extend over a thousand miles and include the 250-mile long Pennine Way and the 168-mile Offa's Dyke. The designation of these routes has been equally laborious, but they have had the attention and backing of the National Parks Commission – which has official responsibility for

TABLE IX.4

Long-distance footpaths

	Date approved	*Length* (miles)
Pennine Way	1951	250
Pembrokeshire Coast Path	1953	167
Offa's Dyke Path	1955	168
South Downs Way	1963	80
South West Peninsula Coast Path:		
North Cornwall	1952	135
South Cornwall	1954	133
South Devon	1959	93
Somerset and North Devon	1961	82
Dorset	1963	72
Yorkshire Coast and North York Moors	1965	93
		1,273

their establishment. The Commission are the initiating body: they make the proposals, discuss them with the local authorities concerned and present a report to the Minister. This shows the route together with existing public rights of way, and may contain proposals for the improvement of paths and the provision of new ones; ferries; and accommodation, meals and refreshments. However, though eligible for Exchequer grant, the implementation of approved proposals rests with District Councils. The Commission can negotiate, persuade and offer assistance, but they can go no further. Furthermore, since the completion of the statutory survey of rights of way by local authorities has (in the words of the Commission) been so woefully slow, the legal status of footpaths is often uncertain. This – and particularly the slow progress made with the creation of new rights of way – has held back the completion of approved long-distance routes.

Only on the Pennine Way are rights of way complete, though three others were (in 1968) near completion: the Yorkshire Coast and North York Moors Path, the Pembrokeshire Coast Path and the Dorset Path.

The Commission put to the Gosling Committee a number of proposals (which are detailed in their 18th Annual Report) for the development of recreational possibilities of the public path network in a modern context. These included the institution of regional walking routes, ring and radial footpaths for towns and other local footpath systems, to be supported by grants from national funds. The Gosling Report eschewed such exciting ideas and the ideas found no favour at the time of the Countryside Bill. The Commission, however, have not given up: in their 1968 Annual Report they say that 'bearing in mind our widened responsibilities under the 1968 Act we intend to elaborate and pursue our ideas on these topics'.

ACCESS TO OPEN COUNTRY

The question of footpaths is only one aspect of the much wider issue of public access to the open countryside. The Hobhouse Committee wanted the public to have an automatic right of access over all uncultivated land – whether mountain, moor, heath, down, cliff, beach or shore, and including suitable stretches of inland water. This the Government did not feel able to accept. It was argued that legislative intervention was quite unnecessary over wide areas since *de facto* access was already granted. What was required was machinery for providing access where it was needed: and, in equity, the onus of establishing the need (and the claim that it should be met) should be placed on those who sought additional facilities – rather than the onus of establishing that there ought not to be access being placed on landowners. This approach had an additional practical and administrative advantage: to grant a general right of access would involve dealing with a large number of objections, whereas if local authorities simply decided to which areas new access provisions should apply the number of objections would be far more manageable. Accordingly, the Act empowers local planning authorities to provide rights of access either by making agreements with owners, or failing that, by making 'access orders'. Agreements and orders are subject to ministerial confirmation, and compensation for any consequent depreciation in the value of land is payable. The effect of an access agreement or order is to give the public the right to go on access land 'for the purpose of open-air recreation' – which does not include playing organized games – without being treated as trespassers. The public must, however, comply with any particular restrictions laid down in the agreement and with certain generally applicable restrictions designed to prevent damage to and interference with farming. In some cases it was envisaged that public acquisition might be desirable, and either the local planning authority or the Minister can purchase 'open country', if necessary by compulsion.

When the Bill was passing through Parliament fears were expressed by the open-air societies that if local authorities were left to provide access only as and when they thought it necessary, they would hesitate to act in fear of the many opposing interests that would undoubtedly be aroused. It was argued that a general requirement was necessary compelling local planning authorities to survey the open country in their areas and to take the action necessary to secure additional access: this would not only ensure that local planning authorities made use of their new powers, but would also be likely to make landowners more prepared to enter agreements since they would know from the result of the general survey the probable total extent of the access requirements. The amendment was introduced which requires local planning authorities to make a general survey (by December 16, 1951) and to report to the Minister (normally within one year of the completion of the survey) what action has been taken. Rights of Access Maps are required and these must be made public. Anyone who feels that the authority have not done enough can make representations to the Minister, who can direct the authority to make additional access orders or, in default, make them himself.

Little information is available on the operation of these provisions, but it was not until 1960 (nine years later) that all authorities completed the survey. The 1957 Report of the Ministry noted that fifty county councils and one park planning board had decided that no action was needed under the Act to secure increased facilities for access. Only seven had submitted maps showing the extent of open country in their areas and the action which had been taken to secure public access. Figures published by the Countryside Commission reveal that 61,347 acres of land in National Parks and Areas of Outstanding Natural Beauty were, in 1968, subject to access agreements or have been acquired by local planning authorities.

The 1968 Countryside Act contains important new provisions relating to access. The definition of 'open country' is widened to include woodlands, rivers or canals and land immediately adjacent to these waterways. This is part of the more purposive approach to recreational planning which is further discussed later in this chapter.

FORESTRY

Forestry is relevant in several ways to the subject matter of this book. In the first place it makes major claims on land: Forestry Commission plantations cover over a million acres in England and Wales, and private forestry covers another 1,810,000 acres – a total of over

2¾ million acres.* However, an adequate discussion of the land needs for forestry and of forestry policy would take us too far afield† Here attention is concentrated on two issues: access to forestry land and the conflict between amenity and forestry.

'It is almost a truism that in these small islands it is necessary to reconcile the claims of amenity and economic utilization; if they are kept in watertight compartments there will not be enough land to go round.' So stated the Forestry Commissioners in their 1943 report on *Post-War Forest Policy*. It is in recognition of this fact that the Forestry Commissioners have evolved a positive policy for providing access facilities in State Forests. The policy was first worked out in the New Forest and Dean Forest, the only two of the many Royal Forests which have survived substantially intact from Norman times. Today there are seven Forest Parks of which two are in England and Wales. Additionally there is New Forest, in Hampshire, which though not a Forest Park, can be regarded as such, since it provides equivalent access and recreational facilities.

Some of the land within the boundaries of Forest Parks is too rocky, peaty or exposed for economic afforestation: this 'unplantable' land may form as much as three-quarters of mountainous areas. The object of the Forest Parks is to make this land available to the public for recreation and, at the same time, to provide cheap and convenient camping sites. Each of the parks contains properly equipped camping sites which were used by over 750,000 people in 1968.

Both within and outside the Forest Parks it is the Commission's policy 'to open their plantations to the public wherever this can be done without undue risk of damage, for example through fire, and without prejudicing the legitimate interests of lessors, sporting tenants and neighbours'.

Nevertheless, as the Council for Wales and Monmouthshire have recently stressed in their *Report on the Welsh Holiday Industry*,[16] it is important to recognize that this is not a statutory duty of the Forestry Commission. Nor is it part 'of a comprehensive conscious policy for the visitor based on carefully long-term objectives accompanied by appropriate powers and finance. . . . The Commission must continue to give overwhelming weight to its statutory duty of caring for the trees, and anything it does for the visitor will be an afterthought.' The Council have recommended that the Forestry Commission be

* See the statistics given in the *Forty-eighth Annual Report of the Forestry Commissioners, 1966–67*, H.C. Paper 311, 1968. The private forestry figures include 670,000 acres in Dedication and Approved Woodlands Schemes. The forestry area of Scotland totals 1,880,000 acres.

† See the *Annual Reports* of the Forestry Commissioners and the Report by them on *Post-War Forest Policy*, Cmd. 6447, 1943.

charged with direct responsibility (though subordinate to its present function) to plan and develop its properties in order to provide for the community at large the opportunities for enjoying natural surroundings.

TABLE IX.5

Forest parks in Great Britain

Forest Park	*Situation*	*Area* (acres)
Dean	Gloucestershire and Monmouth	35,000
Snowdonia	Snowdonia National Park	23,700
Border	Mainly Northumberland	126,000[a]
Glen Trool	Galloway	130,127
Queen Elizabeth (Ben Lomond, Loch Ard and the Trossachs)	Perthshire – Stirlingshire	50,000
Argyll	Argyll	63,000
Glen More	Inverness-shire	12,500
New Forest[b]	Hampshire	67,000

[a] Neighbouring woodlands owned by the Forestry Commission (including some within the Northumberland National Park) bring the total area in this region up to 178,000 acres – the largest expanse of forest in the British Isles.

[b] Though not a Forest Park, the New Forest provides similar access and recreational facilities. It is administered under special Acts of Parliament.

It is unfortunate that the Forest Park achievements and the positive policies of the Forestry Commission in relation to access and recreation appear to attract less public attention than their afforestation programme. Much of this must inevitably take place in national parks and areas of outstanding natural beauty – which, it must be remembered, cover over 9,000 of the 58,000 square miles of England and Wales. Afforestation is a necessary economic activity which, together with agriculture, must remain the dominating form of activity over large parts of the national parks. Quite apart from national needs these activities are, in any case, necessary if the inhabitants of these areas are to have employment. Nevertheless, a conflict of interests can occur, particularly when afforestation leads to a complete change in the character of wild and remote areas. The Forestry Commission always consults with the Countryside Commission who make proposals concerning the type and extent of planting. Critics of the Forestry Commission accuse them of blanketing whole hillsides with one species: unfortunately this 'may sometimes be inevitable, but normally scientific forestry and an eye to landscape dictate a much more varied tree cover'. In fact, the Forestry Commission makes a strenuous effort to strike a balance between amenity and utility: witness is borne to this fact by the cases outlined in the annual reports of the Countryside Commission. In the face of a strong amenity case they may even withdraw a proposal completely. Where agreement cannot be reached, the matter is referred for adjudication to the Ministers of Agriculture and Housing.

More difficult are private afforestation proposals. The Countryside Commission have strongly argued the case for some form of control, but as with advertisements clutter, the Government have preferred to encourage a voluntary scheme. (Agriculture and forestry do not constitute 'development' and therefore do not require planning permission.) Such an agreement has now been worked out between Timber Growers' Organization, the County Landowners' Association, the Forestry Commission and the Countryside Commission. This provides for private proposals to be informally submitted to Park Planning Authorities for comment and discussion. A survey – which must of necessity take a considerable time – is to be undertaken in each national park, with a view to dividing land in the parks as far as possible into three categories:

(*a*) areas where there is a strong presumption that afforestation would be acceptable;
(*b*) areas where, although there is a presumption against afforestation, proposals might be acceptable; and
(*c*) areas where there is a strong presumption against afforestation.

The scheme is, of course, purely voluntary and there is no power for enforcement. It is still early to assess its effectiveness, though one Park Authority – the North York Moors Committee – have declared that it is inadequate.*

At first sight it is somewhat paradoxical that an opposite problem arises in connection with the preservation of woodlands in national parks. The woodlands in question are, however, 'amenity woodlands' which add to the beauty of the landscape. Reference has already been made in Chapter VII to Tree Preservation Orders. These have been widely used in national parks, but in some cases what is required is public acquisition. Planning authorities – including park planning authorities – can acquire amenity woodlands and replant derelict areas. Exchequer assistance is available for such acquisitions, but no grant is payable for management. This, together with the fact that only one park authority has a forestry department, has effectively prevented the use of these powers. Only the Peak Planning Board have used the powers widely. The Minister has been pressed to use his own powers of acquisition, which would enable him to contribute towards maintenance and management costs, but this he has refused to do, on

* See *Thirteenth Report of the National Parks Commission, 1962*, H.C. Paper 34, 1962, pp. 37–8, where the reaction of other park authorities is outlined.

the ground that the proper procedure is acquisition by the planning authorities.

NATURE CONSERVATION

The concept of wild life 'sanctuaries' or nature reserves is one of long standing, and, indeed, antedates the modern idea of national parks. In other countries some national parks are in fact primarily sanctuaries for the preservation of big game and other wild life, as well as for the protection of outstanding physiological features and areas of outstanding geological interest. British national parks are somewhat different in concept: the emphasis is on the preservation of amenity and providing facilities for public access and enjoyment. The concept of nature conservation, on the other hand, is primarily a scientific one concerned particularly with research on problems underlying the management of natural sites and of vegetation and animal populations. Nevertheless, as the Huxley Report on *Conservation of Nature in England and Wales*[41] pointed out, there is no fundamental conflict between these two sets of interests: 'Their special requirements may differ, and the case for each may be presented with too limited a vision: but since both have the same fundamental idea of conserving the rich variety of our countryside and sea-coasts and of increasing the general enjoyment and understanding of nature, their ultimate objectives are not divergent, still less antagonistic'. However, to ensure that recreational, economic and scientific interests are all fairly met does present some difficulties. Several reports dealing with the various problems were published shortly after the war.[40, 41, 42] The outcome was the establishment of the Nature Conservancy, constituted by a Royal Charter in March 1949 and given additional powers by the National Parks and Access to the Countryside Act. (The Conservancy is now a component body of the Natural Environment Research Council.) The Conservancy's main duties are to give scientific advice, to establish and manage nature reserves and to organize and develop research. It is the question of nature reserves which has particular relevance to the subject of this book. The Conservancy have powers to acquire land or to enter into agreements with owners in order that nature reserves may be established. In agreement cases the owner remains in full possession and has responsibility for management, but he agrees to manage in accordance with the advice of the Conservancy so as to preserve the scientific interest of the particular area. Local planning authorities can also – in consultation with the Conservancy – set up Local Nature Reserves. The 'declaration' of a Reserve does not of itself confer any public right of access whatsoever. Furthermore, the powers to make access agreements or orders in 'open country' are clearly not applicable to Reserves: to make such an order over a Nature Reserve would be a contradiction in terms. This does not mean, however, that access to Reserves is generally prohibited. It is the policy of the Conservancy to allow as much access as is compatible with proper scientific management. About a half of the land in National Nature Reserves is generally open to the public without any restriction; the remainder is open only by permit.

The Conservancy have had long-term programmes for establishing Reserves. By September 1963, 105 Reserves covering 218,000 acres had been established. By 1968, the number of Reserves had increased to 124 and the acreage to 257,000. The achievements of the Nature Conservancy can be attributed to three basic features. First there is the question of finance: responsibility lies clearly with the Central Government. There is no question of expenditure on National Nature Reserves having to compete with other local projects; nor is there any question of local authority representatives having to cope with the conflict between expenditure on truly local needs and expenditure for the benefit of others. Furthermore, the Conservancy have a considerable budget: £1,326,000 in 1968. As a result of this scale of financial assistance the Conservancy are able to maintain a staff of over 500. Finally, the Nature Conservancy have an approved long-term programme of action. The advantages which follow from this central administration, finance and initiative are obvious. By comparison, only fifteen Local Nature Reserves have been established. As the former Director General, E. M. Nicholson, has stated, 'from considerable experience our conclusion is that it is useless to try from the centre to convert local authorities to the idea that they ought to form and maintain local Reserves'.[59]

TABLE IX.6

Acreage of National Nature Reserves, 1968

	Owned	*Leased*	*Nature Reserve Agreement*	*Total (woodland acreage in brackets)*	*Number of National Nature Reserves*
England	15,065	19,473	22,476	54,014 (4,390)	60
Scotland	48,824	5,290	128,421	182,535 (5,026)	37
Wales	2,472	6,371	8,847	17,690 (1,169)	27
Total acreage	66,361	31,134	159,744	257,239	124
Total woodland acreage				(10,585)	

THE EMERGENCE OF POSITIVE PLANNING FOR LEISURE

During the 'sixties there has developed an increasing awareness on the part of Government that a much more positive approach is needed to the provision of facilities for leisure, recreation and sport. This can be seen in a wide range of fields (stretching beyond the confines of this book) – from the 'arts' to waterways, from sports provision to tourism, and from urban parks to caravanning.

Reports, White Papers and legislation now constitute an impressive library. Several new agencies have been established: some, such as the Sports Council, with wide advisory responsibilities; some, such as the British Tourist Authority and the three Tourist Boards (for England, Scotland and Wales), with responsibilities for the provision of amenities and facilities; others, such as the Lee Valley Regional Park Authority, with specific regional development and management responsibilities. A number of existing bodies have been given new responsibilities: the Waterways Board for example and, of particular importance, the National Parks Commission which has now become the Countryside Commission.

Much of all this is, as yet, only full of promise. It is too early to assess the impact. But clearly there has been a major move towards a positive approach on a significant scale.

All that can be attempted here is a rapid summary of a selected number of new developments – two major surveys and recent legislative changes.

The Government Social Survey

In 1965-6 the Government Social Survey carried out, for the Department of Education and Science, a national survey on 'the present pattern of participation in outdoor and physical recreation and the frequency and manner of use of public open spaces, among people living in the urban areas of England and Wales'. The report, published in 1969, was written by K. K. Sillitoe and, mercifully, has the shorter title of *Planning for Leisure*.[60] This, together with the *Pilot National Recreation Survey* of the British Travel Association and the University of Keele (written by H. B. Rodgers),[57] provides the most comprehensive data yet available on how people spend their leisure. The Social Survey Report is massive: it runs to 300 pages and includes around 150 tables. It includes analyses by age, sex, socio-economic group, social class, educational background and car ownership.

Though the survey was primarily concerned with outdoor and physical recreation, this was set within the context of the total use of leisure time. Moralists may be depressed with the confirmation of television being the most popular and most time-consuming leisure pastime. No individual outdoor activity took up a large proportion of the available leisure time of the sample as a whole, but when combined together they represented a very significant part of the leisure life of the population – about a quarter for men and nearly a fifth for women.

One of the most important conclusions of the study is the effect of car ownership on excursions to the country and seaside and on participation in sports and games. Car owners, not surprisingly, make many more excursions. But they also tend to engage in more sports and games: and this applies to all age groups. The sample was, unfortunately, too small to distinguish the effects of car ownership from income within each age group. But (and here it is worth quoting from the Report):

'whether the underlying cause is primarily a higher income or the increased mobility conferred by car ownership, this data strongly suggests that with future increases in affluence/car ownership we should expect to see an appreciable rise in rates of participation in

TABLE IX.7

Chief leisure activities, urban population, England and Wales, 1965–66

Activity	*Men 19–22 single* %	*Men 31–45 married with children* %	*Men 61+ retired* %	*All Men* %	*Men with car* %	*Men without car* %
Television	11	29	21	23	19	27
Reading	3	4	8	5	4	7
Crafts and hobbies	7	4	4	4	4	4
Decorating and house/vehicle maintenance	6	10	2	8	9	7
Gardening	2	12	18	12	12	12
Social activities	2	2	5	3	3	3
Drinking	6	3	2	3	3	3
Cinema and theatre	4	n.a.	n.a.	1	1	1
Non-physical games and clubs	5	6	3	5	5	5
Physical recreation (incl. dancing)						
(i) participant	27	10	3	11	13	7
(ii) spectator	1	2	3	3	3	3
Excursions	8	8	4	7	11	3
Park visits and walks	2	3	11	5	3	7
Anything else	12	5	10	7	6	8
No answer or 'don't know'	4	2	6	3	4	3

Source: K. K. Sillitoe, *Planning for Leisure*, Government Social Survey, HMSO, 1969.

sports and games, especially amongst people aged 23 years and over. This leads to the interesting conclusion that *there will probably in the future be a reduction in the existing disparity in rates of participation by age*; especially if the decline in activity amongst very young people that is likely to be associated with earlier marriages, also occurs in conjunction with the rise in incomes and car ownership.'

The GLC Surveys

More restricted, but more focused, are the Open Space Surveys carried out by the Greater London Council. The following paragraphs, taken from the *Report of Studies*[29] published by the GLC in connection with the new Greater London Development Plan, summarize some of the main results.

'(*a*) Large number of visits: 70 per cent of the population of Inner London aged 15 and over had visited an open space at least once in the month preceding interview. This included 39 per cent who had made a visit in the last week. The average weekly visit rate was 1·09 visits per adult of the population as a whole.

(*b*) Differences between weekday and weekend use: weekday visits were at least as numerous as weekend visits. Some 70 per cent of all visits in one week occurred between Monday and Friday. Weekend visits were of greater duration, over longer distances, to larger parks and were family rather than individual visits.

(*c*) High proportion of pedestrian visits: 78 per cent of all journeys in the last week were on foot. Even at weekends there was a large proportion of pedestrian visits (68 per cent). Among car owners, over three-quarters of journeys in a week were on foot. It should, however, be noted that these surveys took place in Inner London, where both travel and car parking difficulties probably made more people decide to walk.

(*d*) Large proportion of short journeys: short journeys of less than 0·5 miles formed 58 per cent of all trips to parks. More people travelled this distance during the week (63 per cent) than at weekends (47 per cent). Most pedestrian journeys were under a mile, while journeys by car and public transport tended to be over a mile in length.

(*e*) Use of large parks: 47 per cent of visits in the previous week and 68 per cent of visits made between one and four weeks before interview ('monthly' visits) were to parks of 50 acres and over. (Parks of this size made up 7 per cent of the total number and 84 per cent of the total acreage of parks in and adjacent to the former County of London.) At distances over a mile most visits were to spaces of more than 50 acres.

(*f*) Visit duration: the length of visit showed a direct relationship to distance travelled, size of park visited and type of activity engaged in during the visit.

(*g*) Emphasis on passive recreation: 86 per cent of visits in one week involved activities such as sitting, walking and enjoying the view. Only a minority engaged in specialized activities such as sports (6 per cent), children's games (12 per cent) or entertainment (3 per cent).

Detailed analysis of the survey took into account *inter alia* age, sex, marital status, possession of a car, and proximity of different kinds of open space. Three factors could be distinguished which, either directly or indirectly, are basic to future open space planning:

(*a*) Different 'demand groups' can be distinguished within the population: apart from socio-economic variations, the principal factors underlying differences in habits and attitudes were found to be due to age, sex and family characteristics. The population can be divided into the following 'demand groups':
   (i) mothers with young children;
   (ii) children between 4 and 12/13 years of age;
   (iii) young people between 12/13 and 19 years of age;
   (iv) the 20-34 age-group (including family groups and sportsmen in addition to mothers with young children);
   (v) the 35-64 age-group;
   (vi) men and women aged over 64;
   (vii) 'lunch hour workers.

   These groups differ in the time they have available for visits, in their mobility and in the extent to which their needs are specialized or general.

(*b*) The demand for general recreation in parks is of two basic types: there are two main ways in which parks are used, for general recreation (amenity/landscape features, children's play areas and entertainment facilities) and for sports. The survey results are primarily concerned with general recreation, which includes two broad forms of demand based largely on differences in time available for the visit and on additional constraints such as age or lack of mobility:
   (i) Local: a short distance/short duration/high frequency type of use.
   (ii) Urban or sub-regional: a longer duration/longer distance/lower frequency type of use in which the visitor is more selective in the type and size of park visited. The choice of park is very much wider for those travelling by car or

public transport than for pedestrians. The latter are, however, prepared to travel at least 0·75 mile to find facilities of the right kind for this purpose.

(*c*) A park's catchment area is related to its acreage, and to a lesser extent, to its facilities: the significance of this for open space planning is considerable. It means that the functions of a park are limited by its size and that this limitation can be expressed quantitatively. The average size of catchment area suggested by the survey for three broad size-ranges of park is set out below:

Size of park (acres)	*Average radius of catchment area*
2–49	up to 0·25 mile
50–149	up to 0·75 mile
150 and over	2–5 miles

It will be noted from these figures that a wide range of park sizes have a 'pull' over a similar distance. Detailed analysis has shown that certain sizes of park were relatively ineffective in satisfying certain levels of demand, so that for example a park of 49 acres was performing the same (local) function as one of 5 acres, whereas a slightly larger park would serve a quite different purpose over a much wider catchment area.'

The survey results were used to design a hierarchy of public open space for Greater London. This is illustrated in Table IX.8. Further details can be found in the GLC Reports [28, 29]

COUNTRY PARKS

Hitherto, national recreational policy has been largely concerned with national parks, 'areas of outstanding natural beauty', and the coast. The GLC studies underline the need for a positive policy in relation to metropolitan, regional and country parks. One such park is being developed in the Lee Valley under special legislation. The Lee Valley Regional Park Authority was established in January 1967 with members appointed by fifteen local authorities and with powers to precept on the GLC and the County Councils of Essex and Hertfordshire. This particular area (amounting to nearly 10,000 acres) is, in the official words of the MHLG 'badly disfigured and unattractive'. It is in fact largely derelict and has been for many years. (It is now a quarter of a century since Abercrombie's *Greater London Plan* envisaged the valley as 'an opportunity for a great piece of regenerative planning'.) It has been graphically described (by the Civic Trust) as 'London's kitchen garden, its well, its privy and its workshop . . .

TABLE IX.8

Proposed hierarchy of public open space in Greater London

Type	*Main function*	*Approximate size*	*Distance from home*	*Characteristics*
(*a*) Metropolitan park	Weekend and occasional visits by car or public transport	150 acres	2 miles, or more where the park is appreciably larger	Either (i) natural heathland, downland, commons, woodlands, etc.; or (ii) formal parks providing for both active and passive recreation, e.g. boating, entertainments, etc. (May contain playing fields, but at least 100 acres for other pursuits. Adequate car parking essential.)
(*b*) District park	Weekend and occasional visits on foot	50 acres	¾ mile	Containing playing fields, but at least 30 acres for other pursuits (as in local parks) and some car parking.
(*c*) Local park	For pedestrian visitors including nearby workers	5 acres	¼ mile	Providing for court games, children's play, sitting-out areas, landscaped environment; and playing fields if the parks are large enough.
(*d*) Small local park	Pedestrian visits especially by old people, children, and workers at mid-day; particularly valuable in high-density areas	Under 5 acres	¼ mile or less	Gardens, sitting-out areas and/or children's playgrounds.

London's back door'. The Lee Valley Regional Park Master Plan proposes a very wide range of facilities for recreation and education including twelve major multi-purpose recreation centres as well as four major centres for youth activity, water sports, motor sports and industrial archaeology. These are to be linked by river, canal, parkland and a park road (with tolls), footpaths and bridleways.

The Lee Valley project is an ambitious scheme. It is an exercise in 'regeneration' as well as in recreational planning. It is perhaps unique. But the concept of a major 'out-of-door' recreational facility has attracted considerable discussion in recent years and is now embodied as part of contemporary wisdom in the 1968 Countryside Act. As the 1966 White Paper, *Leisure in the Countryside*, explained, 'country parks' can achieve several desirable objectives at one and the same time. Country parks 'would make it easier for town-dwellers to enjoy their leisure in the open, without travelling too far and adding to congestion on the roads; they would ease the pressure on the more remote and solitary places; and they would reduce the risk of damage to the countryside – aesthetic as well as physical – which often comes about when people simply settle down for an hour or a day where it suits them, somewhere "in the country" – to the inconvenience and indeed expense of the countryman who lives and works there'.

The Countryside Act defines a country park as 'a park or pleasure ground for the purpose of providing or improving opportunities for the enjoyment of the countryside by the public'. This is a rather broad (not to say vague) definition – a matter of some importance, since the Act also provides for Exchequer aid (of 75 per cent) of 'approved expenditure' on country parks: for land acquisition; for landscaping, car parks, lavatories and roads; litter removal; warden services; and major items of renewal and repair.

The Countryside Commission have 'amplified' the statutory definition. Their provisional definition is 'an area of land or land and water normally not less than 25 acres in extent designed to offer to the public, with or without charge, opportunity for varied recreational activities in the countryside'.[49] They have also 'suggested' that to be recognized by the Commission (a necessary step en route to Exchequer aid) a country park must be:

(*a*) readily accessible for motor vehicles and pedestrians;
(*b*) provided with an adequate range of facilities, including, as a minimum, parking facilities, lavatories and a supervisory service;
(*c*) operated as a single unit and managed by a statutory body or private agency or a combination of both.

All this is still under discussion and, when settled, will be spelt out in publications of the Commission.

Picnic places
The Countryside Act also provides new powers for local authorities in relation to picnic sites. The White Paper explained that these sites 'will be places in the countryside and on the coast where a country park would not be justified, but something better than a lay-by is needed by the family who want to stop for a few hours, perhaps to picnic, perhaps to explore footpaths, or simply to sit and enjoy the view and the fresh air'. Accordingly, local authorities are empowered to provide and manage picnic sites. The Commission have published a brochure of advice.[20] An Exchequer grant is now available for the development of picnic sites.

THE COUNTRYSIDE COMMISSION

As already stated, the Countryside Commission have replaced the National Parks Commission. The change of name signifies an extension of function. Responsibilities in relation to National Parks and Areas of Outstanding Natural Beauty remain; but to these are added the duty 'to review, encourage, assist, concert or promote the provision and improvement of facilities for the enjoyment of the countryside generally, and to conserve and enhance the natural beauty and amenity of the countryside, and to secure public access for the purpose of open air recreation'.

The Commission have an important specific duty to undertake and commission research. To assist in this and to bring together the many bodies concerned (in varying degrees) with recreation a Countryside Recreation Research Advisory Group (CRRAG) has been set up and is chaired and serviced by the Commission. The members include representatives of the British Travel Association (now the British Tourist Authority), the British Waterways Board, the Nature Conservancy, the Sports Council, the Forestry Commission and the Water Resources Board.

The Group maintains a comprehensive central record of research studies in the field of countryside recreation and conservation. A *Research Register*[21] has been published. Further publications are in hand on the techniques of surveying visitors to the countryside, the collection and improvement of recreational statistics, and the notation for mapping countryside resources.

A particularly interesting power given to the Commission under the Countryside Act is that of the right to initiate experimental projects involving some new element of countryside planning, and designed to illustrate their appropriateness to the area in which they are carried out or to similar areas. In 1968 a number of projects were being planned: an experimental day-visitor centre in Pembrokeshire; a mountain land-management experiment; and a project on methods of charging at car parks.

RIVERS AND CANALS

Leisure in the Countryside promised that the Government would seek to evolve, in conjunction with the river authorities, public bodies and others concerned, comprehensive plans for developing the use for recreation of the country's waterways, natural or artificial. A major problem of canals, highlighted in the British Waterways Board's report on *The Facts About The Waterways*, is that the minimum cost of keeping non-commercial routes open is at least £600,000 a year. To keep them open for pleasure cruising would add a further £340,000.

Following extensive discussions with the various interested parties and the publication, in 1967, of a White Paper, *British Waterways: Recreation and Amenity*, the 1968 Transport Act provides a 'new charter for the waterways'. The Board's waterways are classified into:

(i) Commercial Waterways: to be principally available for the commercial carriage of freight;
(ii) Cruising Waterways: to be principally available for cruising, fishing and other recreational purposes; and
(iii) the remainder.

The effect of the new arrangements is that over 1,400 miles of waterways will remain open for pleasure cruising. The Board's annual deficits (on all operations) are borne by the Exchequer. It was originally proposed that the financial position in relation to cruising waterways would be reviewed after five years. However, the Government were persuaded that such a formal review would create uncertainty and discourage private commercial investment and development (e.g. in the building of marinas or the provision of cruising craft for hire). Instead, an Inland Waterways Amenity Advisory Council has been established, one of whose functions will be to consider proposals for the closure of individual waterways 'if this becomes necessary in the national interest'. The Council's functions are, however, not narrowly circumscribed; they include:

(*a*) to advise the Board and the Minister on any proposals to add to or reduce the Cruising Waterways;
(*b*) to consider any matter affecting the use or development for amenity or recreational purposes, including fishing, of the Cruising Waterways, and any matter with respect to the provision of services or facilities for those purposes on the Cruising Water-

ways or the Commercial Waterways and, where they think it desirable, to make recommendations on such matters to the Board or to the Minister after consulting the Board; and

(*c*) to be consulted by the Minister on certain proposed Orders to be made by the Minister.

The Board's 1968 Report referred to the 'splendid upsurge of interest shown by public authorities, firms, clubs and organizations who are now able to see a secure future for the development of leisure facilities on and alongside the waterways'. The Board's revenue from all the various amenity uses amounted to £191,000 in 1968 (as compared with £162,000 in 1967). Over 12,000 craft licences were issued in 1968 (an increase of 12·6 per cent over the 1967 figure).

Much of the Board's 'amenity' work is undertaken in co-operation with other bodies. Of particular interest is the Birmingham city centre redevelopment scheme, at the junction of the Birmingham Canal and the Birmingham and Fazeley Canal, where old industrial buildings are being replaced by multi-storey housing set in landscaped gardens. Included in the layout is a new canalside public house, a restaurant and a canalside walk. Some typical old canal cottages are being restored. Most of this work is being carried out by Birmingham Corporation, but the Board are to improve their land and installations facing the site, to dredge the canal adjoining the development, and to provide overnight and permanent moorings and facilities for canal cruisers. Other examples of co-operative schemes are given in the Board's Annual Reports.

TOURISM

In 1967, 30 million Britons took holidays away from home and some 4 million overseas visitors came to Britain (and in so doing, spent £245 million). Tourism is Britain's top dollar earner and the fourth largest source of foreign currency: in short, it is a very important economic activity. It is also one which is increasing in importance: the number of overseas visitors, for instance, doubled during the 'sixties.

Until recently, Government support for this activity has been meagre – unlike the position in many other countries. Indeed, a series of national economic measures (particularly the Selective Employment Tax) has worsened the position of this labour-intensive service industry. In 1967 an experimental Hotel Loans Scheme was set up on a temporary basis to assist hotel developments 'offering prospects of achieving increased earnings from overseas visitors'. Though brought to an end in the following year, the scheme demonstrated that the profitability of investment in new hotels is less than that of comparable investment in manufacturing industries – a conclusion supported by a study of the Hotel and Catering Economic Development Committee published in 1968 under the title *Investment in Hotels and Catering*.[32] Yet the investment allowances, export tax rebates and other benefits allowed to other industries (including shipping and aircraft) have not been made available to hotels. Like other forms of leisure planning, hotels have been poorly treated. This is all the more surprising in view of the clear economic potential – which is much less tangible with public provision such as the national parks.

The growing hotel shortage, the inadequacy of the semi-private British Travel Association and the increasing awareness of the economic importance of the industry have, however, at last resulted in significant Government action and assistance. The Development of Tourism Act, 1969, establishes a new statutory tourist organization and provides for grants and loans to hotels. (It also contains enabling powers for the registration of hotels and other tourist accommodation and for requiring them to display room charges, but these powers are not yet in operation.)

The statutory organization consists of four bodies: the British Tourist Authority, and Tourist Boards for England, Scotland and Wales. Despite the self-denying emphasis which official statements have placed on catering for currency-producing overseas visitors, the Authority and the Boards have a wide-ranging function 'to encourage the provision and improvement of tourist amenities and facilities in Great Britain'.

During the first full year of operation Exchequer aid is expected to amount to about £3½ million for general expenses and probably up to £8 million on grants and loans.

It is, of course, far too early to attempt an assessment of this new legislation. Much will depend on the character and strength of the BTA and the Tourist Boards. It does, however, constitute a force of considerable potential in positive planning for leisure.

In previous editions of this book the discussion of positive planning for leisure dealt mainly with American material and experience; there was little that could be recounted of policies and achievements in Britain. The current position is one of great promise on a wide range of fronts. Perhaps a later edition will be able to recount significant achievements.

REFERENCES AND FURTHER READING

1 Arvill, R., *Man and Environment*, Penguin Books, Revised Edition, 1969.

2 Birmingham University, Physical Education Department, *Inland Waters and Recreation*, Central Council for Physical Recreation, 1964.

3 Board of Trade, *Staggered Holidays*, Cmnd. 2105, HMSO, 1963.

4 Board of Trade, *Hotel Development Incentives*, Cmnd. 3633, HMSO, 1968.

5 British Waterways Board, *Annual Reports*, HMSO.

6 British Waterways Board, *The Future of the Waterways*, HMSO, 1964.

7 British Waterways Board, *The Facts About the Waterways*, HMSO, 1966.

8 British Waterways Board, *Leisure and the Waterways*, HMSO, 1967.

9 Burton, T. L. and Noad, P. A., *Recreation Research Methods: A Review of Recent Studies*, University of Birmingham, Centre for Urban and Regional Studies, Occasional Paper No. 3, 1968 (Distributed by Research Publications Services Ltd.)

10 Burton, T. L. and Wibberley, G. P., *Outdoor Recreation in the British Countryside*, Wye College, University of London, Studies in Rural Land Use, Report No. 5, 1965.

11 Campbell, I., *A Practical Guide to the Law of Footpaths*, Commons, Open Spaces and Footpaths Preservation Society, 1969.

12 Civic Trust, *The Lee Valley Regional Park: An Essay in the Use of Neglected Land for Recreation and Leisure*, 1964.

13 Clawson, M., *The Dynamics of Park Demand*, Regional Plan Association, New York, 1960.

14 Commons, Open Spaces and Footpaths Preservation Society, Special Issue of *Journal* on the Countryside Act 1968, Vol. 18, No. 1, 1968.

15 Council for the Preservation of Rural England, *Annual Reports*, CPRE.

16 Council for Wales and Monmouthshire, *Report on the Welsh Holiday Industry*, Cmnd. 1950, HMSO, 1963.

17 Countryside Commission, *Regional Coastal Reports* (HMSO, 1967–8)

No. 1 *The Coasts of Kent and Sussex*
No. 2 *The Coasts of Hampshire and the Isle of Wight*
No. 3 *The Coasts of South West England*
No. 4 *The Coasts of South Wales and the Severn Estuary*
No. 5 *The Coasts of North Wales*
No. 6 *The Coasts of North West England*
No. 7 *The Coasts of North East England*
No. 8 *The Coasts of Yorkshire and Lincolnshire*
No. 9 *The Coasts of East Anglia*

18 Countryside Commission, *The Coasts of England and Wales: Measurements of Use, Protection and Development*, HMSO, 1968.

19 Countryside Commission, *Coastal Recreation and Holidays* (Special Study Report Vol. 1), HMSO, 1969.

20 Countryside Commission, *Picnic Sites*, HMSO, 1969.

21 Countryside Commission, *Research Register No. 2*, published by the Commission, Spring 1969.

22 Countryside Recreation Research Advisory Group, *Recreation News*, Countryside Commission, 1 Cambridge Gate, London, N.W.1.

23 Douglass, R. W., *Forest Recreation*, Pergamon Press, 1969.

24 Dower, M., *Fourth Wave – The Challenge of Leisure* (A Civic Trust Survey), reprinted from *The Architects Journal*, January 20, 1965, Civic Trust.

25 Eversley, Lord, *Commons, Forests and Footpaths: The Story of the Battle during the last Forty-five Years for Public Rights over the Commons, Forests and Footpaths of England and Wales*, Cassell, 1910.

26 Forestry Commission, *Forestry in the Landscape*, HMSO, 1966.

27 Forestry Commission, *Forestry in the British Scene*, HMSO, 1968.

28 Greater London Council, *Surveys of the Use of Open Space*, GLC, 1968.

29 Greater London Council, *Greater London Development Plan; Report of Studies* (Chapter 5), GLC, 1969.

30 Hampshire County Council, *Open Spaces Open to the Public in Hampshire*, 1966.

31 Hodge, E. W., 'Problems of a National Park', *Town and Country Planning*, December 1958, pp. 488–95.

32 Hotel and Catering Economic Committee, *Investment in Hotels and Catering*, HMSO, 1968.

33 Lee Valley Regional Park Authority, *Lee Valley Regional Park*, 1969 (published by the Authority, Myddleton House, Bulls Cross, Enfield, Middlesex).
34 McKennell, A. C., *Motives in the Timing of Holidays*, Government Social Survey, 1961.
35 Ministry of Agriculture and Fisheries, *Allotments: Report of the Allotments Advisory Committee*, HMSO, 1950.
36 MHLG, *Open Spaces*, Technical Memorandum No 6, MHLG 1956.
37 MHLG, *Leisure in the Countryside*, Cmnd. 2928, HMSO, 1966.
38 MHLG, Circular No. 44/68, *Countryside Act, 1968*, HMSO, 1968.
39 MHLG, *Report of the Footpaths Committee* (Gosling Report), HMSO, 1968.
40 Ministry of Town and Country Planning, *National Parks in England and Wales* (Dower Report), Cmd. 6628, HMSO, 1945.
41 Ministry of Town and Country Planning, *Conservation of Nature in England and Wales* (Huxley Report), Cmd. 7122, HMSO, 1947.
42 Ministry of Town and Country Planning, *Report of the National Parks Committee (England and Wales)* (Hobhouse Report), Cmd. 7121, HMSO, 1947.
43 Ministry of Town and Country Planning, *Footpaths and Access to the Countryside: Report of the Special Committee (England and Wales)*, Cmd. 7207, HMSO, 1947.
44 Ministry of Transport and Civil Aviation, *Report of the Committee of Inquiry into Inland Waterways*, Cmnd. 486, HMSO, 1958.
45 Ministry of Transport, *Transport Policy*, Cmnd. 3057, HMSO, 1966 (Chapter VIII: 'Inland Waterways').
46 Ministry of Transport, *British Waterways: Recreation and Amenity*, Cmnd. 3401, HMSO, 1967.
47 Ministry of Works and Planning, *Report of the Committee on Land Utilisation in Rural Areas* (Scott Report), Cmd. 6378, HMSO, 1942.
48 Mutch, W. E. S., *Public Recreation in National Forests: A Factual Study*, Forestry Commission, HMSO, 1968.
49 National Parks Commission, *Annual Reports*, H. C. Papers, HMSO.

The National Parks Commission has now been replaced by the Countryside Commission. See *Nineteenth Report of the National Parks Commission and First Report of the Countryside Commission for the Year Ended September 30th, 1968*, H.C. Paper 33, HMSO, 1968.

50 National Trust, *Enterprise Neptune: The National Trust Campaign to Save the Coast*, National Trust, 42 Queen Anne's Gate, London, SW.1, 1967.

51 Nature Conservancy, *The Nature Conservancy Handbook 1968*, HMSO, 1968.

52 Nature Conservancy, *The Nature Conservancy: Progress 1964–1968*, HMSO, 1968.

53 North Regional Planning Committee, *Outdoor Leisure Activities in the Northern Region, 1969* (published by the Committee, Civic Centre, Newcastle upon Tyne, 1).

54 Northern Ireland Ministry of Health and Local Government, *Ulster Lakeland; A Tourist Plan for County Fermanagh*, HMSO, Belfast, 1963.

55 Outdoor Recreation Resources Review Commission, *Outdoor Recreation for America*, US Government Printing Office, 1962.

56 Ramblers Association, *Motor Vehicles in National Parks*, 1962.

57 Rodgers, H. B., *The Pilot National Recreation Survey – Report No. 1*, British Travel Association and University of Keele, 1967.

58 *Royal Commission on Common Land: Report*, Cmnd. 462, HMSO, 1958.

59 Select Committee on Estimates, Session 1957–58, *Nature Conservancy*, H.C. Paper 255, HMSO, 1958.

60 Sillitoe, K. K., *Planning for Leisure: An Enquiry into the Present Pattern of Participation in Outdoor and Physical Recreation and the Frequency and Manner of Use of Public Open Spaces, Among People Living in the Urban Areas of England and Wales*, Government Social Survey, HMSO, 1969.

61 Sports Council, *Planning for Sport: Report of a Working Party on Scales of Provision*, Central Council for Physical Recreation, 1968.

62 Sports Council, *The Sports Council: A Review 1966–69* (with bibliography), Central Council for Physical Recreation, 1969.

63 Stamp, D., *Nature Conservation in Britain*, Collins, 1969.

64 Town Planning Institute, *Planning for the Changing Countryside*, 1968.

65 Wolfenden Committee, *Sport and the Community*, Central Council for Physical Recreation, 1960.

Chapter X

NEW AND EXPANDING TOWNS

The most spectacular of post-war planning policies was undoubtedly that of building new towns. The arguments in favour of new towns were simple and overwhelming. The large cities had grown too large: improved housing conditions had been obtained at unwarranted social and economic cost. Yet the need for more houses had not abated and further large-scale peripheral expansion could not be countenanced. The only alternative was long-distance dispersal. Some of this could go to expanded small towns, but the scale of the problem was too great to be dealt with solely by this means. Further, it was obvious that the local government machinery was not suited to undertake building on the scale required. The main solution therefore was taken to be the building of new towns by government-sponsored corporations.

THE NEW TOWNS

Though the new towns policy was conceived largely as a means of dealing with urban congestion (by, to use the planning jargon, 'reception of overspill') it has been applied to other problems.* Even in the London ring of new towns, there is one – Basildon – where a primary object is rural slum clearance. (The area was one of extensive unplanned and largely unserviced shack development.) Peterlee, in County Durham, aims at concentrating in one urban area development which would otherwise have been scattered throughout a number of small mining villages, none of which could provide town facilities and amenities. Cwmbran in South Wales and Corby in Northamptonshire were established to serve adjacent

* A sketch of each of the new towns is given in *Town and Country Planning 1943–51, Progress Report*, Cmd. 8204, 1951, p. 125 ff; L. Rodwin, *The British New Towns Policy*, Harvard University Press, 1956, chapter 7; and F. J. Osborn and A. Whittick, *The New Towns; The Answer to Megalopolis*, Leonard Hill, Revised Edition, 1969.

TABLE X.1

The New Towns 1968[25]

London Ring	*Location* (distance in km.)	*Original*	*Population* *1968*	*Ultimate*
Basildon (1949)	London 48	25,000	77,000	140,000
Bracknell (1949)	London 45	5,000	32,800	60,000
Crawley (1947)	London 48	10,000	67,000	120,000
Harlow (1947)	London 40	4,500	75,000	90,000
Hatfield (1948)	London 33	8,500	25,300	29,000
Hemel Hempstead (1947)	London 47	21,000	68,600	80,000
Stevenage (1956)	London 50	7,000	61,500	105,000
Welwyn GC (1948)	London 35	18,500	42,450	50,000
Total: London Ring		99,500	449,650	674,000
English Provinces;				
Aycliffe (1947)	Durham 19	100	21,180	45,000
Corby (1950)	Leicester 37	15,700	48,150	80,000
Milton Keynes (1967)	London 80	40,000	40,000	250,000
Northampton (1968)	London 106	131,000	131,000	220,000
Peterborough (1967)	London 133	80,500	81,000	175,000
Peterlee (1948)	Durham 16	200	21,600	30,000
Redditch (1964)	Birmingham 22	29,000	33,500	90,000
Runcorn (1964)	Liverpool 22	28,500	31,250	100,000
Skelmersdale (1961)	Liverpool 21	10,000	17,860	80,000
Telford (1963)*	Birmingham 48	70,000	72,000	220,000
Warrington (1968)	Manchester 24	127,000	127,000	205,000
Washington (1964)	Newcastle 9	20,000	23,690	80,000
Total: English Provinces		552,000	648,230	1,575,000
Wales				
Cwmbran (1949)	Cardiff 29	12,000	48,150	55,000
Newton (1967)	Aberystwyth 43	5,000	5,000	13,000
Total: Wales		17,000	53,150	68,000
Scotland				
Cumbernauld (1955)	Glasgow 24	3,000	26,000	70,000
East Kilbride (1947)	Glasgow 14	2,400	61,700	100,000
Glenrothes (1948)	Edinburgh 50	1,000	25,900	95,000
Irvine (1966)	Glasgow 42	36,000	38,650	110,000
Livingston (1962)	Edinburgh 24	2,000	8,600	100,000
Total: Scotland		44,400	160,850	475,000
Total: Great Britain		172,900	1,311,880	2,792,000

* Designated as Dawley in 1963 with ultimate population of 90,000; designated area extended in 1968 and renamed Telford.

The dates in brackets indicate year of designation.

industrial developments. Aycliffe (again in County Durham) was built to take advantage of a large munitions factory which was built during the war, and which would otherwise probably have been abandoned – an unwelcome circumstance in an area so much in need of new industrial development. In Scotland, East Kilbride and Cumbernauld were designed to take overspill from Glasgow, but the third town, Glenrothes, though now fulfilling the same function, was originally intended to provide for miners moving from the worn-out pits of Lanarkshire to the Fifeshire coalfield.

More recent new towns have largely been conceived as part of a policy of regional development or restructuring: Skelmersdale and Runcorn (for Merseyside), Telford and Redditch (for the West Midlands), Washington (for Tyneside), Livingston and Irvine (for central Scotland) and Newtown (in central Wales). These were the 'second generation' of new towns, all designated between 1961 and 1966. Four of them were already established towns of some 20,000 to 30,000 people. Two are planned on a very large scale: Telford (originally designated as a smaller Dawley) is planned to take 100,000 people from the West Midlands conurbation and to grow to about 220,000 by the late 1980s; Milton Keynes is intended to take about 150,000 people, mainly from London, and to grow to around a quarter of a million.

What might be termed a 'third generation' of new towns began to emerge in the mid-'sixties. These are 'partnership towns' of Northampton, Peterborough and Warrington in which the development is to be undertaken jointly by a new-town development corporation and the local authorities. A decision not to go ahead with a similar development at Ipswich was made in 1969, on the grounds that the revised estimates of overspill from London made an additional new town unnecessary 'at present'. At the time of writing a public inquiry had just been held on a proposal for a central Lancashire new town in the Preston-Leyland-Chorley area. This contains about 250,000 people and a growth to 500,000 is envisaged.

As with so many other aspects of town and country planning, new concepts are being embodied in old terms. Just as 'overspill' is being misleadingly applied to the accommodating of a major population increase, so the term, 'new towns' is being used for major regional developments based on old towns.

THE SELECTION OF SITES

The selection of sites for 'new' towns is very difficult in a small country such as Britain. The requirements are numerous: an adequate water supply (but avoiding the sterilization of a material part of the catchment area for the water supplies of the region); good drainage; a reasonably flat site – not too hilly (which would be expensive) nor too flat (which would detract from the interest and potentialities of the site); near main roads and a through railway line (but not too close since this might involve extra costs for bridging, underpasses, relief roads and so on); a reasonable distance from existing large urban developments; not forgetting the avoidance of areas of 'outstanding natural beauty', of great historical interest, of mining subsidence or large surface workings, and of first-class agricultural land. Clearly these ideal requirements can rarely be met: the problem then becomes one of balancing costs and benefits.

Of the ten sites proposed in Abercrombie's Greater London Plan only two – Stevenage and Harlow – were actually designated. Four were rejected on the grounds that they were too close to existing towns and therefore unlikely to survive as separate entities: Redbourn (near Hemel Hempstead, St Albans and Harpenden); Stapleford (near Hertford); Margaretting (near Chelmsford); and Holmwood (near Dorking – and in a particularly beautiful piece of countryside). Ongar was rejected partly because of its inadequate rail service (and the high cost of making it adequate) – a difficulty which applied also to Redbourn. White Waltham was situated in an area of valuable agricultural land and, furthermore, would have put a nearby airfield out of use. Crowhurst was considered unattractive to industry and too near Crawley, which had been proposed to take the place of Holmwood.

In the provinces the problem of the risk of subsidence has been acute. A proposed town at Mobberley in Cheshire, though near to Manchester, was seriously considered but rejected because of liability to subsidence due to salt mining. In South Wales attempts to find a suitable site for a new town which could serve workers on the trading estate at Treforest, near Pontypridd, proved abortive.

There is, additionally, the political context within which decisions on new sites are made: this may exacerbate the physical problems or, alternatively, reduce the importance which is attached to them.*

DESIGNATION

Once a site has been chosen the first formal step is *designation*. This is accomplished by means of a draft order, following which there are consultations with interested parties – particularly the local authorities concerned. If any objections cannot be settled administratively, a public local inquiry must be held. 'The inquiry is not a

* See, for example, Rodwin's comments on Cwmbran and Newton Aycliffe, *op. cit.*, pp. 122–4.

judicial or quasi-judicial one; it is a step in the administrative process by means of which objections are publicly stated and the Minister is made aware of the extent to which his proposals are opposed. . . . Before any case comes to inquiry, the proposed site and possible alternatives have been exhaustively investigated, so that it is unlikely that the inquiry will disclose any major factor of which the Minister is not aware.'[13] Unfortunately, though such an attitude may be realistic, it is not one likely to be welcomed by local opponents: at the very least there is a clear need for an enlightened public relations policy. This was notably lacking in the early days of the new towns programme and considerable opposition – and litigation – resulted.

Objections to earlier new towns generally resulted at most in the exclusion of certain areas of agricultural land from the designated area: 317 acres at Crawley, 394 at Harlow, 770 at Bracknell, 1,050 at Corby and 2,020 at Hemel Hempstead. The designated area can, however, be extended at a later date, in which case – unless there are no objections – a further public inquiry is held. Bracknell, for instance, had its designated area increased by over 1,000 acres in 1961.

THE NEW TOWN DEVELOPMENT CORPORATIONS

The New Towns Act of 1946* provides for the setting up of development corporations to plan and create new towns wherever the Minister is satisfied 'that it is expedient in the national interest' to do so. The corporations have powers 'to acquire, hold, manage and dispose of land and other property, to carry out building and other operations, to provide water, electricity, gas, sewerage and other services, to carry on any business or undertaking in or for the purposes of the new town, and generally to do anything necessary or expedient for the purposes of the new town or for the purposes incidental thereto'.

This followed the recommendations of the Reith Committee[14] that a new and separate agency (with no other responsibilities) should be created for each new town. The justification for this was that the creation of a new town was not simply a matter of erecting buildings: it also involved 'the development of a balanced community enjoying a full social, industrial and commercial life'.

The corporations are not, however, the sole agency in new town development. Despite the apparently all-embracing character of their powers, they are not local authorities: education and local health services, for example, remain the responsibility of the normal

* The New Towns Act of 1946 and later legislation has now been consolidated in the New Towns Act, 1965, and the New Towns (Scotland) Act, 1968.

local government machinery. Water, sewage disposal, gas and electricity, and hospitals are likewise the responsibility of the normal local or public authority. Nevertheless, where the necessary provision is beyond the technical or financial resources of the local authority, the development corporations can assist by undertaking the work themselves or by making a financial contribution: this applies particularly to water, sewerage and sewage disposal facilities. This provides a useful degree of flexibility, though it has often been a source of friction between development corporations and local authorities. Much time and effort has had to be spent on determining the allocation of expenditure between these two types of authority. The problem is aggravated by their very different characters:

'. . . relations between the New Town Corporation and the Urban District (or Borough) Council are likely to require careful handling, even granted that there is goodwill on both sides, and unfortunately goodwill has been the exception rather than the rule. The Councillors are aware that the members of the Corporation devote less of their time to the business of the New Town than do the Councillors; that the members are paid but the Councillors are not; that the members are for the most part "strangers from London" while the Councillors are all local residents; and that the members are nominated by a Minister while the Councillors are elected by the ratepayers. The Councillors would be more than human if they did not on occasion feel some measure of both envy and resentment.'[6]

FINANCE

Development corporations also differ from a local authority in that they are wholly financed from the Exchequer. Advances are made by Government Departments out of issues made to them for this purpose from the Consolidated Fund. The New Towns Act of 1946 authorized issues up to £50 million to cover the needs of the first few years, but this total has been successively increased by later Acts. (The present total, authorized by the New Towns Act of 1969, is £1,100 million.) Exchequer advances are payable over sixty years, with interest at the rate prevailing at the date on which the advance is made. There is no concealed subsidy in the form of a concessionary rate of interest: the loans are made at a rate which reflects the current rate for Government credit. (This has varied between 3 per cent and 8½ per cent.) The Reith Committee had recommended that all finance should be found by the State by way of loan, but in fact the administration of these loans has proved to be very different from the Reith conception. The Reith Committee argued that it was 'most important that the financial autonomy and responsibility of the corporation shall be assured, and that development shall not be delayed or restricted by discussions of policy arising over applications for public advances'. This posited a degree of freedom for the corporations which it would be difficult to reconcile with public accountability. The balance is not easy to achieve, particularly where expenditure is proposed on risky ventures or developments for which there is no financial return. Since it is public money which is being invested, the Treasury have to ensure that each proposal is reasonable. But the Act goes further: it specifically requires that before approval is given to any proposal the Minister must be satisfied that 'having regard to all the circumstances' a reasonable financial return can be expected. This gives the central departments a very large degree of control over the operations of the development corporations. In fact, new towns policy – both generally and in relation to individual towns – is framed by the Ministry, not by the development corporations. Since it is the central government which is providing the capital it is difficult to see how this can be otherwise.

The position may well be different in the newer 'partnership' towns where the local authorities will be playing a major, not a subordinate, role. How this will work out in practice remains to be seen.

EMPLOYMENT

The basic conception underlying the new towns was that they should be 'balanced' communities within which the majority of the inhabitants would both live and work. It follows that (to the extent to which this objective is attained) the rate of development will be determined by the growth of local employment. Industrial location in new towns is subject to the same Board of Trade control as exists over the country generally. The need to steer industry away from the high employment area of the South to the areas of unemployment in the North proved difficult in the early years to reconcile with the need to stimulate industrial development in the London new towns, but once they became established these towns rapidly achieved boom conditions – to such an extent, in fact, that it became difficult to build houses at an adequate rate. Less favoured new towns – particularly Peterlee – have found the attraction of industry to be a longer term difficulty. Generally speaking, however, the new towns have been able to offer sites and an environment which have proved most attractive to industrialists.

Development corporations are free to either build factories

themselves and let them to firms, or lease sites on which the firms can build their own factories. (In a few exceptional cases the Ministry have agreed to the freehold disposal of sites.) It is generally felt that a balance of the two is desirable: letting produces a greater profit to the corporations, but the leasing of sites is thought to provide a welcome degree of stability and insurance against the effect of an economic crisis.

TABLE X.2

New factories built in the New Towns to December 31, 1968[25]

	No. of occupiers	*No. of employees*	*Size* (million square feet)
London Ring			
Basildon	123	20,259	4·8
Bracknell	31	10,832	1·7
Crawley	86	17,223	4·0
Harlow	105	15,688	3·9
Hatfield	18	1,460	0·4
Hemel Hempstead	66	12,615	3·0
Stevenage	44	17,230	3·8
Welwyn GC	21	4,731	1·4
Elsewhere England and Wales			
Corby	26	3,446	0·7
Cwmbran	25	2,645	0·2
Peterlee	30	3,300	0·9
Redditch	21	510	0·1
Runcorn	25	1,040	0·4
Skelmersdale	40	4,649	1·7
Telford	28	477	0·2
Washington	19	625	0·4
Scotland			
Cumbernauld	57	5,086	2·0
East Kilbride	149	13,976	4·1
Glenrothes	33	4,901	1·5
Irvine	17	500	0·2
Livingston	15	1,730	0·8
Total	979	142,923	36·2

By the end of 1968, over 36 million square feet of factory space had been built in twenty-one new towns, of which 23 million were in the London ring, 8½ million in Scotland and 4½ million in eight provincial towns. This, however, takes no account of Aycliffe where the Board of Trade (English Industrial Estates Management Corporation) has a large industrial estate employing nearly 9,000 people.

The figures given in the table refer to manufacturing industries: they exclude service industries which account for between 20 and

40 per cent of total employment. Service employment increases in response to local demands as the new towns grow: though provision can be – and is – made for them, they cannot be stimulated in the same way as can manufacturing industry.

Office employment, however, can be encouraged, particularly as the large school populations enter the juvenile labour market. At the end of 1968, twenty-two towns had nearly 3 million square feet of office space completed and a further 780,000 square feet under construction. Several Government Departments have offices in the new towns – the Stationery Office at Basildon, the Meteorological Office at Bracknell, the Scottish Office of the Land Commission at Cumbernauld, the General Post Office and the Ministry of Transport at Hemel Hempstead, as well as the usual local offices of the Department of Health and Social Security and the Inland Revenue.

HOUSING

Of the total of £658 million spent on capital works by the development corporations, £400 million has been for housing. The corporations have built 155,000 houses and have been the main provider in all the new towns. They are not, however, the only house-building agency: local authorities have provided over 18,000 and private builders 12,800 (for owner-occupation). Increasing emphasis, however, is being placed on owner-occupation, partly because of the rising demand for this form of tenure and partly because of the need to attract more private capital into the new towns.[5] In 1967 the Minister advised development corporations that in new towns started since 1961 the aim should be to achieve 50 per cent owner-occupation by the end of the planned build-up period. In the older new towns the aim is to achieve this proportion in new building.

The overwhelming demand in all the new towns has been for houses with gardens. Development has, therefore, been at low densities. This has led to the criticism that they lack 'urban character' – an aesthetic view which seems at variance with the principle of providing the type of dwellings which people want. In fact, great ingenuity and skill has been shown by the development corporations in planning a wide variety of architectural types, a range of interesting layouts and a generally high standard of landscaping. Of course, by no means all the schemes have been successful (though opinions will differ on which these are), but the general standard of new town housing is undoubtedly superior to the generality of post-war housing.

Unlike local authorities, development corporations have no pool of low-cost pre-war housing nor can they meet any deficiencies on their housing accounts from rate subventions. Their rents thus reflect the high costs and interest rates of the post-war period. There are, however, significant differences between different new towns, and between older and newer (Parker Morris standard) houses within individual towns. In Bracknell, for instance, the net rent of a three-bedroom new house with a garage was (in 1967–8) £4.10.0d a week compared with £2.10.0d in the older areas of the town. Curiously, there is no collation of new town rent figures, but in March 1967 the average rent of three-bedroom houses for selected new towns ranged from 37s. 8d in Hemel Hempstead to 59s. 2d in Skelmersdale.[5]

THE COMMISSION FOR THE NEW TOWNS

The New Towns Act of 1946 envisaged that the new towns would eventually be transferred from the development corporations to local authorities. This was in line with Howard's principle that there should be local control and that profits (particularly those resulting from increases in land values) should accrue to the benefit of the towns themselves. It did, however, depart from the Reith Committee's majority view that it was unwise for the functions of (virtually monopoly) land ownership and local government to be combined in a single body.

In fact, as the time for the transfer approached it became clear – to the Conservative Government, if not to the Opposition – that ownership and management should remain in the hands of a body which was independent of the local authority. The New Towns Act of 1959 set up an *ad hoc* public body for this purpose – the New Towns Commission. This Commission will take over all the assets and liabilities of each of the development corporations. To date Crawley, Hemel Hempstead, Hatfield and Welwyn Garden City have been transferred. The present (Labour) Government is committed to some transfer of assets to local authorities, but the extent and terms of this are not yet known. An independent study of the future ownership and management of *housing* has been published.[5] This is being 'studied'. It may be that a decision will be postponed until the reorganization of local government following the Redcliffe-Maud Report.

The Commission are charged with the duty 'to maintain and enhance the value of the land held by them and the return obtained by them from it' while at the same time having 'regard to the purpose for which the town was developed and to the convenience and welfare of the persons residing, working, or carrying on business there'. They have powers to make contributions towards the cost of providing amenities for the town or of providing water supplies, sewerage or sewage disposal services. They can purchase land by agreement (but not compulsorily) either in or near the towns, and promote or assist business activity. Local committees must be set up in each town to manage residential property.

TABLE X.3

Housing in the New Towns to December 31, 1968[25]

	Houses completed at December 31, 1968		
	Development Corporation	Local Authority	Others
London Ring			
Basildon	16,203	2,191	1,193
Bracknell	7,563	432	343
Crawley	11,954	1,691	2,280
Harlow	19,648	819	747
Hatfield	4,207	1,541	283
Hemel Hempstead	11,717	2,267	2,452
Stevenage	15,160	849	981
Welwyn GC	6,190	1,553	380
Elsewhere in England and Wales			
Aycliffe	5,555	—	—
Corby	6,733	2,220	920
Cwmbran	7,329	1,782	766
Peterlee	6,130	74	90
Redditch	185	145	520
Runcorn	390	56	573
Skelmersdale	1,810	376	270
Telford	1,022	738	55
Washington	216	693	301
Scotland			
Cumbernauld	6,899	108	5
East Kilbride	16,426	48	225
Glenrothes	7,308	333	68
Irvine	—	494	351
Livingston	2,231	—	15
Total	154,876	18,410	12,818

The Commission were established in October 1961 and the assets and liabilities of four new towns have so far been transferred to them. Apart from the local committee (who have full delegated powers for housing management), a Local Executive has been set up in each of the towns. These, in fact, consist almost entirely of officers transferred from the development corporations, and deal with the bulk of the Commission's executive functions. Only a small headquarters staff is maintained in London.

Although the new towns for which the Commission are now responsible have reached the stage at which large-scale planned immigration is being reduced, they have a high rate of natural growth. House-building will, therefore, continue at a high level for some time. Special attention is being given to the needs of second-generation families (the newly-wed children of present tenants) and of old people, of which there is a considerable number wishing to move into the new towns in order to live near to their married children. The housing programme includes both unsubsidized rented dwellings and houses for sale.

The Act requires the Commission to pay any financial surpluses to the Treasury: a provision which will no doubt give rise to some argument as to what should be regarded as surplus and how much the towns need by way of 'amenities'.

EXPANDING TOWNS

The New Towns Act was the first instalment of the 'overspill' plan: the second was to be an Act to facilitate town expansion by local authorities. This, however, was deferred until the immediate post-war housing shortage had been met. It was contrary to the political facts of life to expect local authorities to build houses for families from other areas while they still had severe housing problems of their own. It was, therefore, not until 1952 that the Town Development Act was passed.

The essential difference between the New Towns Act and the Town Development Act is apparent from their full titles. The New Towns Act is 'an Act to provide for the creation of new towns by means of development corporations'; the Town Development Act is 'an Act to encourage town development in county districts for the relief of congestion of overpopulation elsewhere'. The former set up special agencies to deal with a problem which was by implication beyond the competence of local authorities. The latter did precisely the opposite: it provided 'encouragement' to local authorities to meet the overspill problem themselves 'by agreement and co-operation'.* As Mr Macmillan (then Minister of Housing) stressed, 'the purpose of the Bill is that large cities wishing to provide for their surplus population shall do so by orderly and friendly arrangements with neighbouring authorities . . . it is our purpose that all these arrangements should be reached by friendly

* This and the following quotations are from the Second Reading debates in the House of Commons, *H.C. Debates*, vol. 496, col. 725, *et seq.*

negotiation and not imposed by arbitrary power'. Such financial help was to be provided as would be 'necessary to get the job going'. At the present time this consists of a housing subsidy and a 50 per cent grant towards the cost of main sewerage, sewage-works and water-works required for the development. The Act also empowers an exporting authority to make contributions to the 'receiving authority'. In practice, although it is of doubtful equity, exporting authorities wishing to participate in a scheme must make an annual contribution for each family rehoused from their areas.[4]

County Councils have power under the Local Government Act of 1948 to make contributions towards expenses incurred by county districts and, in practice, those which welcome overspill within their administrative area do render substantial financial assistance.

Actual development can be undertaken by the receiving authority itself; or by the exporting authority acting either as an agent for the receiving authority or on its own account; or by the county council in whose area the receiving authority is situated.

Tenants can be selected either from the housing list of the exporting authority or by means of an industrial selection scheme. In the latter case only families who secure employment in the receiving area are eligible for rehousing there.[22]

Town development is very widely defined, as:

'development in a county district (or partly in one such district and partly in another) which will have the effect, and is undertaken primarily for the purpose, of providing accommodation for residential purposes (with or without accommodation for the carrying on of industrial or other activities, and with all appropriate public services, facilities for public worship, recreation and amenity, and other requirements) the provision whereof will relieve congestion or overpopulation elsewhere'.

This description of the Act serves to show how flexible its provisions are.* Since town development is undertaken by local authorities with widely different problems and of varying size and wealth, this flexibility is essential.

A town expansion scheme can operate successfully only if all the local authorities concerned – the 'exporting' authority, the 'reception'

* However, the Act did not provide for the expansion of a county borough, even though this might in some cases have been preferable to expanding a very small town from, say, a population of 5,000 to one of 10,000. The exclusion of county boroughs also resulted in the peculiar situation that the Municipal Boroughs of Swindon (population 80,000) and Luton (120,000) could take advantage of the Act, whereas Canterbury (30,000) and Northampton (100,000) could not. This limitation was removed by section 34 of the Housing Act, 1961.

authority and the county council – are able and willing to co-operate, and if the Board of Trade are likewise able and willing to assist in persuading industry to move into the expanding town. There are big difficulties – technical, administrative, financial, social and political – to be overcome. These constitute a severe strain on the local government machine. However, given a fortuitous combination of circumstances, experience has shown that town expansion schemes can operate to the great benefit of small towns.

TABLE X.4

Town development schemes, 1968

		Dwellings provided by local authorities for town development purposes		*Factories completed at 31.12.1968*	
'Overspill' authority	*No. of schemes*	*Total to be built*	*No. completed at 31.12.1968*	*No. of firms*	*Area (sq. ft.)*
London	31	85,387	35,409	512	18,179,957
Newcastle upon Tyne	2	8,017	1,345	35	1,206,860
Liverpool	4	15,930	4,378	44	1,665,159
Manchester	3	7,950	762	23	500,692
Salford	1	4,505	4,518	—	—
Birmingham	15	20,445	6,508	118	2,790,887
Wolverhampton	4	4,696	4,327	11	67,526
Bristol	4	2,278	2,278	—	—
Total	64	149,208	59,525	743	24,411,081

Source: MHLG, *Handbook of Statistics 1968*, HMSO, 1969, Table 40. (The full table gives figures for each of the sixty-four schemes.)

Haverhill is a case in point: situated in the south-east corner of West Suffolk, this 4,000 population town saw in the Town Development Act a means of arresting its economic decline and obtaining modern urban facilities which it so clearly lacked. Blessed with a local government machine of a calibre hardly to be expected in such an area, a co-operative and forward-looking County Council, and considerable technical and financial assistance from both this county and the exporting authority (the Greater London Council), the town has already provided over 1,700 houses and 480,000 square feet of factory space for thirty-seven firms.

Schemes operated in conjunction with the Greater London Council have the advantage of very favourable financial and technical aid which an authority of this size and wealth can provide. Nevertheless, their contribution to the solution of the London overspill problem has not been impressive. In an attempt to increase the provision, the former London County Council proposed to undertake the building of a new town in Hook, Hampshire.[10] This was strongly opposed by the Hampshire County Council, who proposed as an alternative the expansion of Basingstoke, Andover and Tadley. These alternative proposals were accepted and, since the Hampshire County Council is an active participant in the schemes, hold out a promise of development at a faster speed than is usual with town expansion. They are also on a larger than normal scale: Basingstoke, in particular, is envisaged as expanding from 26,000 to 75,000–80,000.

PROVINCIAL SCHEMES

In the provinces progress has been very slow. Several factors are responsible for this. The exporting authorities have not been so well organized as the Greater London Council to make the Town Development Act work. They have not been so convinced of the necessity of attempting to make it work or, at the least, they have maintained that the scale of their problems requires direct central government action by way of new towns rather than the small-scale assistance to their problems likely to be achieved by 'fiddling around with the Town Development Act'. Then there is the problem of attracting industry to provincial town expansion schemes. For the small number of towns which have welcomed the idea of expansion this has proved the crucial problem.

More frequently, however, there is considerable local opposition to expansion. Apart from the technical and financial difficulties and the strong force of inertia, receiving authorities are generally small, vulnerable and highly disinclined to take risks. There is a fear that expansion will do more harm than good, that it will change the social as well as the physical character of the town – and that it may have unwelcome political consequences. The public inquiry into the proposals for an expansion scheme for Westhoughton was opened with the recorded voice of Vera Lynn singing 'Land of Hope and Glory' as 500 objectors slowly marched in procession to the town hall. Before the inquiry opened prayers were said in local churches against the scheme; 9,000 out of the 11,000 people on the electoral roll had signed a petition; 1,400 objections had been lodged; and two local coach proprietors laid on free day-trips to Bolton, where the inquiry was held.

Though an extreme case, this does illustrate the difficulties facing town expansion proposals. It would be tedious to describe the situation in each of the major congested areas, since the story is so much the same in each. Birmingham's experience may be taken as illustrative. The city has had negotiations with over 100 authorities all over the country, from Exmouth and Barnstaple in the south to Nantwich and Winsford in the north, and from Merioneth and Holyhead in the west to Cromer and Wisbech in the east. Many of the agreements which have been made are unlikely to provide any significant number of houses since the reception authorities are unwilling to build until families are willing to move, and the majority of families are not prepared to move to areas having a restricted range of jobs. Most of the local authorities who have approached Birmingham have done so in the hope that they may secure additional industry, but the City Council, of course, has no powers to direct industry to expansion areas and its attempts to persuade industry to move have met with only limited success. The potential town expansion areas are typically small and isolated and are, therefore, unattractive to industrialists and their workers.

Until recently the official pronouncements of the Government and of the Ministry of Housing on the Town Development Act have been aimed at encouraging local authorities to overcome the inherent difficulties of town expansion policies, rather than providing an objective assessment of the adequacy of the policies. But a revealing comment is to be found in the Ministry's evidence to the Royal Commission on Local Government in Greater London:

'Five or six years' experience of the Town Development Act has shown that these schemes are most difficult to bring to fruition. Small authorities are naturally nervous about the financial and social consequences of embarking on a scheme of which the residual risk falls and is bound to fall on themselves. In addition, there are many ways in which the area may fail to fulfil the tests of a "good" overspill area – for instance, it may be off the main communication routes or be surrounded by first-class agricultural land, or if it is a "good" overspill area, the town may not wish to expand. Generally speaking those towns are most anxious to expand under the Act which have not the attractions to industry and private enterprise which would make expansion natural.' [21]

This is a striking indictment of the framework within which town development has had to operate. It is now accepted that though the Town Development Act provides an opportunity for dealing with the problems of those small towns which are prepared to accept the challenge which it offers (and the difficulties to which it gives rise), it is a weak makeshift. The crux of the matter is that the present structure of local government is quite inadequate to handle problems of overspill and regional restructuring. The reorganization following the Redcliffe-Maud Report will radically change the situation.

REFERENCES AND FURTHER READING

1 Best, R. H., *Land for New Towns*, Town and Country Planning Association, 1964.

2 Central Housing Advisory Committee, *The Needs of New Communities: A Report on Social Provision in New and Expanding Communities*, HMSO, 1967.

3 Commission for the New Towns, *Reports* (annual), HMSO.

4 Cullingworth, J. B., 'Some Administrative Problems of Overspill', *Public Administration*, Vol. 37, No. 4, Winter 1959.

5 Cullingworth, J. B. and Karn, V. A., *The Ownership and Management of Housing in the New Towns*, HMSO, 1968.

6 Duff, A. C., *Britain's New Towns*, Pall Mall Press, 1961.

7 Heraud, B. J., 'The New Towns and London's Housing Problem', *Urban Studies*, Vol. 3, No. 1, 1966, pp. 8–21.

8 Heraud, B. J., 'Social Class and the New Towns', *Urban Studies*, Vol. 5, No. 1, February 1968, pp. 33–58.

9 Karn, V. A., *Social Surveys of Crawley, Stevenage, Aycliffe and East Kilbride*, University of Birmingham, Centre for Urban and Regional Studies, Occasional Papers Nos 8-11, 1970. (Distributed by Research Publications Services Ltd.)

10 London County Council, *The Planning of a New Town*, LCC, 1961.

11 Long, J. R., *The Wythall Inquiry*, Estates Gazette, 1962.

12 MHLG, *Handbook of Statistics 1968*, HMSO, 1969.

13 Ministry of Local Government and Planning, *Town and Country Planning 1943–1951: Progress Report by the Minister of Local Government and Planning on the Work of the Ministry of Town and Country Planning*, Cmd. 8204, HMSO, 1951.

14 Ministry of Town and Country Planning, *New Towns Committee: Interim Report*, Cmd. 6759, 1946; *Second Interim Report*, Cmd. 6794, 1946; *Final Report*, Cmd. 6876, 1946 (Reith Reports).

15 New Town Development Corporations, *Annual Reports*, HMSO.

16 Nicholson, J. H., *New Communities in Britain*, National Council of Social Service, 1961.

17 Ogilvy, A. A., 'The Self-contained New Town', *Town Planning Review*, Vol. 39, No. 1, April 1968.

18 Orlans, H., *Stevenage*, Routledge & Kegan Paul, 1954.

19 Osborn, F. J. and Whittick, A., *The New Towns: The Answer to Megalopolis*, Leonard Hill, Revised Edition, 1969.

20 Rodwin, L., *The British New Towns Policy*, Harvard University Press, 1956.

21 Royal Commission on Local Government in England, *Written Evidence of the Ministry of Housing and Local Government*, HMSO, 1967.

22 Ruddy, S., *Industrial Selection Schemes: An Administrative Study*, University of Birmingham, Centre for Urban and Regional Studies, Occasional Paper No. 5, 1969. (Distributed by Research Publications Services Ltd.)

23 Sharp, E., *The Ministry of Housing and Local Government*, Allen & Unwin, 1969.

24 Thomas, R., *London's New Towns*, PEP Broadsheet No. 510, 1969.

25 *Town and Country Planning:* The first issue of each calendar year is devoted to new towns and includes the most comprehensive set of statistics available. The March issue contains a statistical summary of Town Development schemes. (Tables 1 to 3 in this chapter are taken from this source.)

26 University of Sussex, *Crawley Expansion Study*, West Sussex County Council, 1969.

CONSULTANTS' REPORTS

(all published by HMSO unless otherwise indicated)

Ipswich: A Study in Town Development, 1965. Obtainable only from MHLG.

Northampton, Bedford and North Bucks Study: An Assessment of Inter-related Growth, 1965.

Peterborough: An Expansion Study, 1965. Obtainable only from MHLG.

Worcester Expansion Study, 1965. Obtainable only from MHLG.

A New City: A Study of Urban Development in an area including Newbury, Swindon and Didcot, 1966.

A New Town for Mid-Wales – Consultants' Proposals, 1966.

Dawley: Wellington: Oakengates – Consultants' Proposals for Development, 1966.

Expansion of Ipswich Designation Proposals: Consultants' Study of the Town and its Sub-Region, 1966.

Expansion of Northampton – Consultant's Proposals for Designation, 1966.

Expansion of Peterborough – Consultant's Proposals for Designation, 1966.
Expansion of Warrington – Consultant's Proposals for Designation, 1966.
South Hampshire Study: Report on the Feasibility of Major Urban Growth, 3 vols. 1966.
Ashford Study: Consultants' Proposals for Designation, 1967.
Central Lancashire: Study for a City – Consultants' Proposals for Designation, 1967.
Central Lancashire New Town Proposal: Impact on North East Lancashire, 1968.
Expansion of Ipswich: Comparative Costs – A Supplementary Report, 1968.

Chapter XI

URBAN RENEWAL

The term urban renewal is an Americanism which has only recently found acceptance in this country. The reason for this is not hard to discover. The major part of post-war policy has been directed towards providing extra houses, extra school places, extra open spaces and so on. Redevelopment – the substitution of new social capital for old – only began to get under way in the late 'fifties. The need to plan 'comprehensively' and to improve and preserve as well as to redevelop has become more and more obvious as the inadequacies of small-scale clearance and redevelopment have become apparent. It is increasingly realized that the improvement of urban living conditions requires more than the substitution of new for old buildings, or the clearance of a few industrial eyesores, or the building of by-passes. It requires an approach which is aimed at improving the whole physical fabric of urban life – not merely replacing the threadbare patches. Urban renewal is a convenient shorthand description of this approach. It implies not only redevelopment but also rehabilitation and conservation. It embraces a policy for the improvement of obsolescent structures which cannot yet be demolished, the clean air campaign, a programme for providing twentieth-century amenities in nineteenth-century towns, and an acceptance of the motor car as a major feature of contemporary life.

The field is very large and only a selection of some of the more important issues can be discussed in this chapter. Attention is concentrated on four of these: housing, comprehensive redevelopment, traffic and clean air.

I: HOUSING

Obsolete and obsolescent housing forms the major part of the physical problem of urban renewal – though the fact that so much of this housing is concentrated in the inner areas of large towns provides a real opportunity for dealing with the concurrent problems of obsolete road patterns.

The size of the qualitative housing problem is difficult to measure. Over 6 million – about 38 per cent – of houses date from before the First World War, and of these probably 2 million are over 100 years old. Age, of course, is by no means an infallible guide to condition, but many of these old houses are slums, lack essential amenities or are in a bad state of disrepair. They are socially, if not physically, obsolete, and would be demolished as 'slums' or included in 'clearance areas' or 'comprehensive development areas' on account of their 'bad layout' or 'obsolete development' (to use the statutory phrases) were this economically possible.

Over a third of a million houses were demolished in the slum clearance programme which began in 1930. By 1938 demolitions were running at the rate of 90,000 a year. Had it not been for the war, over a million of these old houses would have been demolished by 1951. The virtual cessation of house-building during the Second World War involved an accumulation of quantitative need which could not be quickly satisfied: slum clearance had to be postponed. The limited house-building programme was almost entirely devoted to providing new houses until 1954. Even repairs were not to be undertaken if they necessitated 'substantial calls' on building resources. In effect, therefore, not only was there a postponement of slum clearance, but also an enforced neglect of existing houses for over fourteen years.

The size of the slum problem is of course essentially related to the standards adopted. A 'slum' is more easily recognized than defined.

Slums

The quality of housing has a number of different dimensions. The Denington Committee drew attention to five:

(i) the structure and condition of housing (stability, damp, natural lighting, etc.);
(ii) the equipment and services built into housing (WC, water supply, drainage, artificial lighting, etc.);
(iii) the quality of the surrounding environment (air pollution, noise, open space, traffic conditions, etc.);
(iv) the space available to individual households (persons per room, bedroom requirements, etc.);
(v) the privacy available in dwellings occupied by more than one household (sharing accommodation and facilities, sound insulation, etc.).

The assessment and quantification of these is no easy matter and there is considerable scope for area variation and personal judgment. This is particularly clear when an overall assessment is required of the need for slum clearance or improvement.

There is no objective criterion of slum conditions. The legislation – which refers to houses 'unfit for human habitation' – certainly does not provide a definition: it merely lists a number of matters which should be *taken into consideration*. Furthermore, a house is deemed unfit only 'if it is so far defective in one or more of the said matters that it is not reasonably suitable for occupation in that condition'. This can only be a matter of judgment.

The 'said matters' are:

repair
stability
freedom from damp
internal arrangement
natural lighting
ventilation
water supply
drainage and sanitary conveniences
facilities for the preparation and cooking of food and for the disposal of waste water.

The official 'slum clearance returns' submitted by local authorities to the Ministry in 1954 gave a total of 853,000 unfit houses of which 378,000 were to be demolished within five years. In 1965 a new series of returns gave a total of 820,000 in spite of the fact that 542,000 had been demolished between 1954 and 1965. Of course, deterioration is a continuing process. Nevertheless, there is more than a suggestion that the official returns do not give a full picture. A study of the published 1954 returns (those for 1965 were not published) fully corroborates this view. Though some local authorities, such as Manchester and Liverpool, included *all* the unfit houses in their estimate, others lowered their sights to what could be dealt with in a given period. To those who know Lancashire there is something odd in the fact that though 43 per cent of the houses in Liverpool were estimated to be unfit, the proportion in Oldham was 26 per cent; in Salford 24 per cent; in Bolton 10 per cent; and in Stretford 0·5 per cent.

In the early 'sixties it came to be recognized, in the Ministry, that adequate policies could not be formulated on the basis of statistics such as these (this applied to the whole range of the Ministry's housing responsibilities). With the very large expansion of the Ministry's statistical services, a national and a series of conurbation house condition surveys were mounted. The national house condition survey carried out in 1967 produced an estimated 1·8 million unfit dwellings, compared with the official 1965 estimate of 820,000.[8] Of these 1·8 million unfit dwellings, 1·1 million were in potential clearance areas and the remaining 700,000 needed to be dealt with individually by repair, closure or demolition. Additionally, some 113,000 dwellings were fit but in or adjoining potential clearance areas. These dwellings would be included with neighbouring unfit housing in clearance area action.

The survey also showed that unfit housing was less concentrated in the conurbations and in the north than had previously been assumed.

Nearly 4 million dwellings (a quarter of the total stock) lacked one of the major amenities and nearly 3 million did not have an internal WC.

Estimates were made of the cost of repairs required for all dwellings in the survey, assuming that they were to be retained in use for at least twenty years. Of the 13·7 million dwellings which were not unfit (and were outside potential clearance areas) some 3·6 (26·5 per cent) needed repairs costing £125 or more and over 400,000 (3 per cent) needed repairs costing £500 or more.

Deferred demolition

These figures amply demonstrate the need both for a continuing slum-clearance programme and an extensive programme of modernization. For the worst houses the 'deferred demolition' procedure can be used. Introduced in 1954, this allows local authorities to acquire houses which can be 'rendered capable of providing accommodation of a standard which is adequate for the time being'. More popularly known as 'patching and propping' – or 'soling and heeling' – these provisions are particularly useful in the older industrial areas where the problems of obsolescence are so markedly concentrated. A total of 88,000 houses for deferred demolition was planned in the first five-year programme and of these 32,000 were in Birmingham, 11,560 in Hull, and 20,000 in Lancashire.* Exchequer grants are available for deferred demolition both for the acquisition of property (equivalent to 50 per cent of the loan charges on the cost of acquisition) and for patching, maintenance and repair (£8 per dwelling per year). These provisions are intended to assist those areas which have a large slum-clearance programme which cannot be rapidly completed. They aim at reducing the hardship experienced by families living in basically unfit houses which, given adequate maintenance, can be improved to provide modern facilities.

Improvement policy

Quite different in concept is that of house 'improvement'. The improvement policy was first introduced in 1949 but it was not until

* No later figures have been published. A large number of the Birmingham houses were purchased under the (now repealed) provisions of the Town and Country Planning Act, 1944.

1954 that it got under way and not until 1969 that the policy shifted effectively from a concentration on individual houses to 'improvement areas'.

TABLE XI.1

House Condition Survey, England and Wales, 1967

Area	*No. of dwellings* *Unfit*	*Fit*	*% Unfit*
Conurbations	600,000	4,717,000	11
Other Urban areas	806,000	6,350,000	11
Rural Districts	430,000	2,797,000	13
England and Wales	1,836,000	13,864,000	12

Fitness	*Number*	*Totals*
Unfit dwellings in potential clearance areas	1,099,000	
Other unfit dwellings	737,000	
Total unfit dwellings		1,836,000
Fit dwellings in or adjoining potential clearance areas	113,000	
Other fit dwellings	13,751,000	
Total fit dwellings		13,864,000
Total dwellings		15,700,000

Age of dwellings	*Total*	*Unfit*	*Fit*
Pre-1919	6,029,000	1,784,000	4,245,000
1919–44	4,255,000	49,000	4,206,000
1944–67	5,416,000	3,000	5,413,000

Amenity lacked	*No. of dwellings*	%
Internal W.C.	2,919,000	19
Fixed bath	2,106,000	13
Wash basin	3,040,000	19
Hot and cold water at three points	3,400,000	22
One or more amenities	3,943,000	25

Repair costs of fit dwellings outside potential clearance areas

Repair costs	*No. of dwellings*	%
Under £125	10,094	73·4
£125–249	2,352	17·1
£250–499	892	6·5
£500–999	350	2·5
£1,000 or more	63	0·5
Total fit dwellings outside potential clearance areas	13,751	100

The policy operated (until the 1969 Housing Act – the impact of which it is much too early to assess) largely by offering grants to owners who wished to improve their property. The objective has been to encourage owners to provide services and amenities in basically sound houses which are lacking the amenities which modern standards and aspirations demand. The justification for the spending of public funds on this is not only that living conditions are thereby improved, but also that unless old houses are modernized they will deteriorate into slums which then need to be cleared and replaced at public expense. The responsibility for making these grants lies with local housing authorities, though three-quarters of the cost is borne by the Exchequer. The grants are given on the basis of one half of the approved cost of the works, subject to a maximum limit.

Improvement areas

By the early 'sixties it came to be accepted that far more emphasis was needed on *areas* as distinct from individual houses. A Ministry circular of 1962[5] asked local authorities to take the initiative in securing the improvement of whole streets or areas. The 1964 Act went further, and gave local authorities powers to declare 'improvement areas' within which a limited degree of compulsion could be used against landlords. By the end of 1968, 421 improvement areas had been declared and work completed on some 4,000 dwellings.

The 1964 provisions were cumbersome in the extreme. This was the result of attempting to provide the maximum safeguards for owners and tenants, and the maximum opportunity for voluntary improvements. The powers were given with reluctance and only because of the urgent need to speed up the rate of improvements and because of the widespread feeling that some element of compulsion was required. But not only were the powers cumbersome: they were also ineffective and did not really enable an authority to secure the improvement of an area as a whole. The provisions related essentially to 'houses in areas' rather than areas which contained houses. The 1969 Housing Act is designed much more with the total environment in view. Local authorities are given power to declare *general improvement areas* within which the aim is to help and persuade owners to improve their houses not only by grants and advice but also by improving the environment. In the words of the White Paper *Old Houses into New Houses*, 'whole areas and streets cannot be brought up to proper standards unless something can be done for the environment as opposed to the interiors of the houses'. The new concept of 'improving the area' encompasses a coherent set of powers, together with an Exchequer grant for such improvements as the provision of children's play spaces and parking spaces, planting trees, and traffic regulation.

At the same time, improvement grants have been substantially increased and improved rent controlled properties are transferred to the 'fair rents' system.

TABLE XI.2

Slum clearance and improvement, England and Wales

	No. of houses demolished or closed	*No. of improvement grants approved*
Up to 1959	303,260	238,865
1960	56,561	130,832
1961	61,969	127,776
1962	62,431	110,506
1963	61,445	119,979
1964	61,215	121,685
1965	60,666	122,993
1966	66,782	107,720
1967	71,152	113,142
1968	71,586	114,216
Total	877,067	1,307,714

Of particular significance is the emphasis in the 1969 Act on voluntary co-operation between those who live in a 'general improvement area' and the local authority. The White Paper emphasizes that 'local authorities must be tireless in explaining their proposals, and in gaining the confidence and approval of those whom they will affect'. But no mention is made of the problems which might arise if the people concerned want something which is opposed to the ideas (and ideals) of the planners.

There has been only limited experience of area improvement, and Ministry guide-lines are necessarily very broad. In selecting areas, emphasis is to be placed on the potential of an area, the basic attractions of the area or its location, the attitudes of its residents and the need for public action. The last point is interesting and is an example of the way in which thinking is developing towards a more sensitive basis for policy. The intention is that public action should be concentrated on sensitive spots where the maximum benefit can be obtained. A Ministry circular talks of avoiding areas which are 'too good' or 'too bad':

'A too good area could be one which is already attracting considerable money into renovation, and where any further encouragement by public funds would not only be unnecessary but might well lead to a drastic change in the social composition of the area. A too bad area is more difficult to define; but it is necessary always to keep in mind that area improvement is not an alternative to slum clearance.'[13]

The importance which is now to be given to improvement is evidenced in another circular which states that 'as from now Ministers will regard the scale and type of work done to improve or repair the existing stock of houses in a local authority's area as an integral part of the authority's housing programme'.[12]

II: COMPREHENSIVE REDEVELOPMENT

Increasing emphasis is now being placed on comprehensive redevelopment. The reasons for this are clear. Redevelopment involves far more than the simple replacement of old buildings by new ones. It has to provide a solution to the problems arising from obsolete road and street patterns and the need to separate traffic and pedestrians. It has to cope with the problems resulting from the increasing land needs of most urban uses – for the movement, parking and garaging of cars, for housing at densities which are acceptable on modern standards, for open space, for educational provision and so on. These needs cannot be satisfactorily met within the physical limitations imposed by out-of-date street patterns and the equally important limitations often created by a multiplicity of ownerships.

Comprehensive development areas

Post-war planning legislation acknowledged the necessity for dealing with these problems on a comprehensive basis: indeed the securing of 'comprehensive redevelopment' was one of the major objectives of the 1947 Act. Local authorities can define as an 'area of comprehensive development':

'any area which in the opinion of the local planning authority should be developed or redeveloped as a whole, for any one or more of the following purposes, that is to say for the purpose of dealing satisfactorily with extensive war damage or conditions of bad layout or obsolete development, or for the purpose of providing for the relocation of population or industry or the replacement of open space in the course of development or redevelopment of any other area or for any other purpose specified in the plan'.

This is a very wide provision which permits the use of comprehensive development area procedures for schemes varying from a small housing project to the 1,300 acre 'new town' for Stepney and Poplar in the East End of London. Though a CDA plan is drawn up by the local planning authority they need not undertake the actual development themselves: much of the office development in, for instance, the City of London and on the South Bank of the Thames has been carried out by private developers within the framework of CDA plans. A large proportion of the central area redevelopment in Coventry, on the other hand, has been carried out by the City Council themselves. Indeed, the machinery was devised within a political context which assumed that local authorities would play the major role in redevelopment:

'Most of the well-known redevelopment schemes since the war have been carried out under the Town and Country Planning Acts of 1944 and 1947. These Acts came into being at a time when it seemed likely that central area redevelopment would for the most part be undertaken comprehensively by local authorities. They were based largely on the premise that land would be acquired by local authorities at existing-use values, and it was contemplated that they would be applied mainly to areas of blitz and blight, where values were unlikely to be high. At that time the private developer had not the opportunity to tackle redevelopment on a large scale. Consequently, central area redevelopments have so far been carried out in circumstances which have necessitated or favoured public ownership and action. The procedure under these Acts was designed to meet that particular set of circumstances, and has owed some of its success to the fact that the local authority concerned has been able to reinforce its planning powers with the wider, more detailed and more adaptable powers attaching to ownership.'[30]

Conditions have, of course, changed radically since the late 'fifties. Controls over private building have been abolished and the backlog of demand for commercial development is now seeking satisfaction. The changed compensation provisions and the increase in land values have combined to discourage local authorities from undertaking development themselves. As another writer has put it, 'the draughtsmen of this Act were thinking more of war damaged areas and slum conditions than of pulsating town centres with high commercial values.... The procedure of the Act is not geared for rapid operation.'[31]

The extensive proposals now being put forward by private developers often cannot be considered in relation to a 'comprehensive' plan for the simple reason that the plans have not yet been prepared. Nor can they be prepared at speed when there are major planning implications involved. The process of statutory and democratic consultation is time-consuming, and the procedure for designating 'comprehensive development areas' is elaborate and cumbersome. The amount of survey work, map-drawing and detailed planning required makes the whole process lengthy.

The basic problem with the CDA procedure is that it 'does not and was not intended to provide a suitable medium for the working out of policies for the town centre as a whole'.[18]

This did not give rise to insurmountable problems when local authorities were the main instigators of redevelopment. Attention was concentrated on particular areas, and private interests were not unduly affected since private land-values had been stabilized. But now that private proposals for redevelopment are being put forward for numerous different areas concurrently, there just is not time to give the necessary consideration to all the relevant long-term issues involved. Private interests cannot be made to wait indefinitely since 'time is money', and, in any case, local authorities are statutorily required to give a decision within two months of the date of application. Where a proposal does not have major planning implications there may be no particular problem, but often this is not the case, and where a developer is not prepared to extend the statutory two months' period, the result may prejudice future socially (and economically) desirable improvements. There has been mounting criticism of this situation: the pressures for development are now too great and too widespread to be coped with solely by the CDA procedure.

The Town Centre Map

An attempt to meet the problem was made by the Ministry in the first of the new series of Planning Bulletins. Local planning authorities were advised to prepare a non-statutory Town Centre Map, showing in broad outline their proposals for the future development of the town centre. The Town Centre Map enables particular proposals to be seen in the context of the town centre as a whole. It aims at assisting in the process of 'Survey–Analysis–Plan' which should underlie any important planning decision or proposal. It is intended 'to provide the public with a clear picture of what is proposed for the town centre and to enable persons interested to express their views on these proposals before the stage of formal submission to the Minister is reached'.

The case for this new planning instrument is outlined in the Planning Bulletin, *Town Centres – Approach to Renewal*:

'What is needed is a means by which the local authority, in conjunction with the local planning authority, can make a broad and relatively quick assessment of the problems and possibilities of the town centre, and which can be developed into a sound basis for more detailed decisions. The aim should be to systematize and simplify the work and discussion which goes into planning for renewal. For this purpose what is wanted is not a plan suitable for statutory submission to the Minister but a map which reflects the process of survey, analysis and policy formation which are behind any planning decision or formal proposal for amendment of the development plan. If such a map is prepared and is used as the basis of planning in the central area and is available for public examination and discussion, the Minister will take full account of it in any matter which comes to him for decision.

'The purpose of introducing such a map is to aid and simplify the job of planning for renewal. It is not intended as an elaborate or highly technical document. It should be a simple statement of major objectives.'

The preparation of such a map, of course, entails a great deal of survey work, though it is stressed that there is no need for policy discussions to be held back until the detailed surveys are complete – 'ideas can be hammered out while the field work proceeds: the one will influence the other'. These surveys should take into account the regional factors affecting the future of the town and particularly of its centre. Important factors here are the competition of other centres (existing and planned); the amount of car-ownership (existing and predicted); the use and potentialities of private and public transport; the limitations of access to the centre imposed by the existing road system; and so on. Within the town centre attention has to be paid to:

Land use – density and amount of floor space.
Property values – with particular attention to the comparative costs of acquisition in different parts of the town centre, and sites where values could be significantly increased by redevelopment or improvement.
Town character – distinguishing features and buildings worth preserving, needing improvement, and ripe for development.
Pedestrian movement – main pedestrian flows and meeting-places within the centre, with reference to congestion, adequacy of pavements, safety and conflict with vehicular traffic.
Vehicular movement – volume and direction of flow at different times, origin and destination; service access; public transport.
Parking – amount, location, duration and trends, related as far as possible to particular parts and functions of the town centre.

The analysis of this survey material needs to be 'directed to the formulation or reappraisal of planning policies and objectives in the town centre'. A recommended 'sequence of survey analysis' would be to determine the prospects for change; the prospects for retaining and improving the features of buildings which bring prosperity and give character to the town centre; the need for change; the opportunities for planned change; the likely rate of implementation; and a broad programme of priority between the various needs revealed by the analysis.

The Town Centre Map itself should reflect the broad land use framework, illustrating a co-ordinated policy of renewal and presenting a guide for public and private redevelopment activities; and a firm road and traffic pattern designed to remove unnecessary traffic from the central area and to facilitate the segregation of vehicles and pedestrians within it.

The concept underlying this 'planning instrument' is that of a partnership between local authorities and private enterprise. The local authority is envisaged as having the role of initiator and overall planner: this should not 'pass by default to individual developers who, however competent their proposals, cannot perform the local authority's functions or absolve them of responsibility for the result'. The local authority's position is considerably strengthened by their powers to achieve land assembly, without which many of the opportunities for other than patch-work redevelopment cannot be implemented. The strength of private enterprise lies in its knowledge of the market, its ability to exploit commercial opportunities and its access to capital.

The situation in relation to comprehensive development areas is now to be considerably affected by the 1968 Planning Act. Under the new system an area requiring comprehensive treatment at an early date will be defined as an 'action area'. This will be subject to ministerial approval (with the usual provisions for objections and a public inquiry, but supplemented by those for public participation).* Should compulsory acquisition be necessary this will follow the normal procedure, again necessitating ministerial approval. In short, there is no longer any need for a formal CDA submission. The powers of compulsory acquisition, however, remain, as do the planning grants for this purpose.

Planning grants

Specific planning grants (except for comprehensive redevelopment of areas of extensive war damage) were abolished in 1959 as part of the reform of local government finance. Between 1959 and 1968 these grants were 'absorbed' (along with many other specific grants) in the *general grant* introduced by the Local Government Act, 1958. The objective was to give local authorities 'a great increase of responsibility in determining the money to be spent on the various services in accordance with local needs'. A further reform, introduced by the Local Government Act, 1966, increased the relative importance of general grants, but brought back the specific planning grants† –

* See Chapter IV, p. 111 *et seq.*

† For a general discussion of the changes in local government finance, see E. Sharp, *The Ministry of Housing and Local Government*, Allen & Unwin, 1969, Chapter VII.

for comprehensive development of 'areas of bad layout or obsolete development', the provision of public open space and the reclamation of derelict land.

Grants are therefore now available for the comprehensive redevelopment of areas of extensive war damage (popularly known as 'blitz') and areas of bad layout or obsolete development ('blight'). These 'blitz and blight' grants amount to 50 per cent of the notional loan charges calculated on the annual loss arising in any particular year. The loss is calculated by taking the capital cost of acquisition, clearing and preliminary development, and subtracting from this the value realized from time to time on disposal of the land by sale, lease or appropriation for other local authority services for new uses after it has been cleared and serviced.

Estimates published in the Ministry's *Handbook of Statistics 1968* forecast total grants amounting to £3·9 million in 1969–70 and £4·6 million in 1970–71.

III: PLANNING FOR TRAFFIC

The necessity for redevelopment to be undertaken on a 'comprehensive' basis stems in large part from the growth in motor traffic. Between 1950 and 1960 the number of vehicles on the roads of Great Britain doubled, to 9½ million. By 1968 the number had increased to 14½ million. The proportion of households with a car rose from 30 per cent in 1961 to 49 per cent in 1968.

This enormous increase in traffic and the resultant urban thrombosis to which it has given rise is too striking and obvious to require detailed documentation. What is less apparent is the even greater rate of increase which may be anticipated in the future. There is a prospect of 18 million vehicles by 1970, 27 million by 1980 and perhaps 40 million by 2010.

Coping with this flood of traffic presents extremely difficult problems. Road 'improvements' can easily destroy the town as a residential environment and, furthermore, be self-defeating. As American experience has shown: 'The greater the expenditures have been, the greater has become the need. With it all, no city can say, regardless of how much it has poured into providing conveniences for its motorists, that it does not have far more congestion and far greater inconvenience today than when it embarked on its costly venture.'[53]

One of the fundamental problems here is that of the location of traffic-generating uses. Until recently, attention was focused (as in the Barlow Report) on the heavy concentration of employment in central areas, the movement of population to outer areas and the

TABLE XI.3

Motor Vehicles licensed, Great Britain, 1904–68

	Private cars and vans	*Motor cycles, scooters and mopeds*	*Public transport vehicles (incl. taxis)*	*Goods vehicles*	*Total (including other categories)*
1904	8,465	—	5,345	4,000	17,810
1920	186,801	287,739	74,608	101,000	650,148
1930	1,056,214	724,319	101,131	351,682	2,272,499
1940	1,423,200	278,300	81,300	446,200	2,325,000
1950	2,257,873	751,738	136,481	899,507	4,409,223
1960	5,525,828	1,861,247	93,265	1,403,311	9,439,196
1965	8,916,600	1,707,300	96,400	1,606,500	12,937,800
1966	9,513,319	1,496,804	93,717	1,574,578	13,286,350
1967	10,302,900	1,442,600	94,100	1,624,500	14,096,000
1968	10,816,100	1,324,400	99,300	1,571,000	14,446,500

Source: Ministry of Transport, *Highway Statistics 1968*, HMSO, 1969.

resultant increase in commuting. The 'overspill' policy was the official answer to this. If jobs could be moved out along with population the traffic pressures on the central areas would be reduced and travel to work journeys reduced. It is coming to be realized that the situation is now much more complex than this. In London, for instance, the tide has turned and the working population of the inner areas is falling. At the same time an increasing complex web of movements (largely made possible by the freedom provided by the motor car) is developing in Greater London and beyond.

TABLE XI.4

*Consumer expenditure on road transport, U.K. 1958–68**

Year	*Expenditure on:* *Buses and coaches*	*Cars and motor cycles*	*Total road transport*	*Expenditure on road transport as percentage of total consumer expenditure*
	£m	£m	£m	%
1958	294	769	1,063	7·0
1962	337	1,180	1,517	8·1
1965	370	1,727	2,097	9·3
1968	396	2,347	2,743	10·3

Source: Ministry of Transport, *Highway Statistics 1968*, based on Central Statistical Office, *National Income and Expenditure* (annual).

* The figures relate to personal expenditure only: they exclude expenditure by businesses, public corporations and public authorities, and expenditure by private persons which is charged to business account.

Policy on this issue is currently in a stage of agonizing reappraisal. There is much talk of 'restructuring' major urban areas, but there is a noticeable note of doubt in the debates. Increasingly emphasis is given to 'flexibility' – an admirable concept, but one which is difficult to reconcile with the fact that roads are far from flexible. They have to be planned ahead and, once built, become a major factor in the situation even if the assumptions on which they were planned are falsified.

The Buchanan Report

A major landmark in the development of thought in this field was the Buchanan Report.[45] This Report is a masterly survey which surmounts the administrative separatism which has until recently prevented the comprehensive co-ordination of the planning and location of buildings on the one hand and the planning and management of traffic on the other. With due acknowledgement of the necessarily crude nature of the methods and assumptions used, the Report proposes as a basic principle the canalization of larger traffic movements on to properly designed networks servicing areas within which environments suitable for a civilized urban life can be developed. The two main ideas here are for 'primary road networks' and 'environmental areas'.

'There must be areas of good environment – urban rooms – where people can live, work, shop, look about and move around on foot in reasonable freedom from the hazards of motor traffic, and there must be a complementary network of roads – urban corridors – for effecting the primary distribution of traffic to the environmental areas'.

This simple concept is not, of course, new, but the urgency of the need for its application on the scale required presents enormous problems. A striking result of the case studies included in the Report is the great scale of the networks and interchanges that are needed. The capital cost of the new primary distribution roads in the Newbury scheme, for example, would be about £4½ million. But, as the accompanying report of the Steering Committee (the Crowther Report) points out, 'This would be once-for-all expenditure. It is estimated that the motor vehicles registered in the Newbury area will pay in 1963 about £770,000 in licence duty and fuel duty. By 1983 it is estimated that the vehicles registered will be paying (assuming unchanged rates) at the rate of £1,560,000. This admittedly crude calculation serves to show "what a fund of future revenue there is available to finance a programme of urban redevelopment".'

But what of the alternatives? Buchanan stressed that the general lesson is unavoidable: 'If the scale of road works and reconstruction seems frightening then a lesser scale will suffice *provided there is less traffic*'. Crowther argues that the scope for deliberate limitations on the use of vehicles in towns would be almost impossible to enforce, even if a car-owning electorate were prepared to accept such limitations in principle. Not all would agree and, as traffic grows, the practical possibilities of the various forms of pricing assume an increased significance. Indeed, it is striking how far opinion on this has changed over the last few years. The White Paper, *Transport in London*, published in 1968,[51] could say quite blandly (as could not have been said a decade earlier):

'The control of traffic must be regarded as a deliberate part of highway and transport planning. In many cases regulation is appropriate. But the price mechanism is often more flexible and more sensitive. It may in time prove possible and worth while to reflect in charging systems the costs which journeys on overcrowded roads impose on other road users. Meanwhile, parking charges and time limits can provide effective control. There will have to be control of all street parking in inner London – with preference being given to short-term callers for whom the use of public transport may well be less convenient than for the regular commuter, and to residents. And there will also have to be control over the amount of privately available off-street parking space in new developments which attract a significant number of workers. (In the past, such space has often encouraged additional car commuting.) The GLC has recently announced new policies along these lines. Finally, there is need to control the ways in which publicly available off-street car parks can be used.'

To return to Buchanan, the great danger in his view lies in the temptation to seek a middle course between a massive investment in replanning and a curtailing of the use of vehicles 'by trying to cope with a steadily increasing volume of traffic by means of minor alterations resulting in the end in the worst of both worlds – poor traffic access and a grievously eroded environment'.

An improvement of public transport is no answer to these problems, though it must be an essential part of an overall plan; indeed, the case studies show that it is quite impossible to dispense with public transport. The implication is that there must be a planned co-ordination between transport systems, particularly with regard to the work journeys in concentrated centres. On this, the Report recommended that 'transportation plans' should be included as part of the statutory development plans.

This has now been accepted and passed into legislation by the 1968 Town and Country Planning Act* (though its implementation

TABLE XI.5

Household car ownership, Great Britain, 1961–68

	Estimated percentages of households with regular use of the following number of cars		
	One or more	*Two or more*	*One only*
1961	30	2	28
1962	32	3	29
1963	34	3	31
1964	37	4	33
1965	41	5	36
1966	45	6	39
1967	47	6	41
1968	49	6	43

Source: Ministry of Transport, *Highway Statistics 1968.*

will take many years). But of equal importance is the momentous Transport Act passed in the same year. Many of the provisions of this lie outside the scope of the present book, though they are by no

TABLE XI.6

Regional differences in car ownership, 1966

	Proportion of households with one or more cars %
England and Wales	46
Scotland	36
Northern Region	37
East Anglia	53
Outer Metropolitan Area	59
Greater London	42
Merseyside Conurbation	34
Central Clydeside Conurbation	27

Source: Sample Census 1966.

means irrelevant to the issues selected for discussion. Attention here is focused on the integration of transport planning with 'town planning' and the establishment of new transport planning authorities in some of the conurbations.

* See p. 59 and p. 111 *et seq.*

Traffic planning machinery

The 1967 White Paper *Public Transport and Traffic*[48] opened on a lyrical note: 'one of the most precious achievements of modern civilization is mobility. It enriches social life and widens experience'. It continued by stressing the implications for planning and transport policy:

'To build mobility into the urban and rural life of this crowded island without destroying the other elements of good living must be one of the major purposes of transport policy. To achieve this, far-reaching changes in attitudes and administration will be necessary. The provision of transport – whether public or private – can no longer be considered in isolation from other developments. It must be built into the whole planning of our community life so that no factory is sited, no housing estate or "overspill" developed, no town re-planned without the implications for the movement of people and goods having been studied and incorporated from the outset.'

This, of course, is the rationale for the new type of development plans which will treat basic transport planning as a part of the general planning of the structure of each locality. But the important point is that 'basic transport planning' means far more than 'road planning', particularly since no conceivable road investment programme could support city structures designed on the basis that nearly all journeys were to be made by private car. (And it must not be forgotten that there will always be a significant proportion of households without cars. Even in the United States this is a fifth.) In short, 'our major towns and cities can only be made to work effectively and to provide a decent environment for living by giving a new dynamic role to public transport as well as expanding facilities for private cars'.

Five 'principles of organisation' flow from this:

1. Since local authorities are responsible for 'planning' they must be the authorities responsible for public transport.
2. All transport matters for which local authorities are to be responsible – the improvement of the local road network, investment in public transport, traffic management measures, the balance between public and private transport – must be focused in an integrated transport plan, which in its turn is related to the general planning for each area.
3. Investment in local public transport must be grant-aided by central government just as investment in the principal road network receives 75 per cent Exchequer grants.

4. The main network of public transport must be publicly owned.
5. The planning and operation of public transport can only be done intelligently over areas which make sense in transport terms. In some of the major urban areas, the traffic situation is so bad and is deteriorating so rapidly that reorganisation cannot await general legislation on local government.

Passenger Transport Authorities

The Transport Act, 1968, gives the Minister power to set up Passenger Transport Authorities where he 'considers it expedient for the purpose of securing the provision of a properly integrated and efficient system of public transport to meet the needs of that area'. The first four areas are Greater Manchester, Merseyside, the West Midlands and Tyneside. (Elsewhere the problems are considered to be less acute and can await the reorganization of local government, though voluntary co-ordinating machinery has been established.) In drawing the boundaries of the PTA areas, the main criterion has been the travel-to-work data from the 1966 census. Account has, however, been taken of major expected developments: thus Redditch (a new town planned to take 33,000 people from Birmingham by the mid-'seventies, many of whom are expected to work in the conurbation) is included even though it currently has relatively insignificant passenger movements to and from the conurbation.

Each PTA consists of two bodies – the Authority which is concerned with policy, and an Executive which is responsible for the implementation of policy and for day-to-day management. A major first task of the Executive is to prepare a plan, for the approval by the Authority, setting out 'proposals for the development of a system of public transport capable of serving the needs of the Area'. The Executive will also 'as an essential first step' take under control all the municipal bus undertakings in the Area. Finally (in this selective summary account) the Executive will have to reach agreement with the Railways Board for the rail services which they require, and will be responsible for providing any new systems of public transport which they (and, of course, the Authority) consider are needed in the Area.

The finance of PTAs

The Executive have a duty at least to break even year by year. (The White Paper states the Government's belief that the new system 'will provide opportunities for a reduction in the costs of providing public transport'.) If the policies of the PTA result in a loss then the Authority must either change its policies or precept on the local authorities in the Area to make good that loss. This is a matter for the Authority to decide.

However, a new system of grants is being introduced to correct the imbalance which has existed in Government financial support for transport in urban areas (with Exchequer grants being available for major road improvements but not for expenditure on public transport). According to the White Paper these amount to 75 per cent (the same rate as for major road investment grants) of the approved cost of projects 'for the provision, improvement or development' of public passenger transport. Eligible projects include:

(*a*) major improvement or extension of railways lines – track, stations, signalling systems, re-equipment with stock special to the project and associated investment for railway services;
(*b*) provision of new fixed track rail and bus systems (e.g. tube railways, monorails, busways);
(*c*) construction or major improvements of:
  (i) bus stations and depots,
  (ii) terminals and vessels for local passenger ferry services,
  (iii) interchanges, including car parks, for people transferring to and from public transport systems.

However, grants will be available only for projects which fit in with plans for the structure of the area, the land use pattern, the road and rail network, the balance between public and private transport – in short, with the basic planning of the locality. Grants are also to be available for the acquisition of new buses (at a normal rate of 25 per cent), for bus fuel (at the rate of 1s.7d a gallon), and for loss-making suburban railway services (initially at a rate of 90 per cent; but tapering off – on the assumption that the PTAs will reorganize the transport services on an overall viable basis).

Transport planning in London

London, characteristically, is different from the other major urban areas of the country. Its problems are so different in intensity and extent that special provisions have had to be made to deal with them. The position is too complex to allow adequate summary within the confines of this book, but some significant features can be indicated. The 1968 White Paper, *Transport in London*,[51] gives a much fuller picture.

Basically, the objective is the same as in the provincial conurbations: to consolidate, as far as possible, transport and traffic planning under the single authority of the Greater London Council which has the responsibility of preparing and implementing comprehensive transport plans. (Internally, the GLC have merged their department of highways and transportation with the planning department to form a new department of planning and transportation.)

Under the provisions of the Transport (London) Act, 1969, the London Transport Board has been abolished and the underground railways and central (red) buses have been transferred to a new London Transport Executive (with effect from January 1, 1970). (The country (green) buses and the Green Line coaches have gone to the National Bus Company.) The Executive is the London equivalent to the provincial PTAs, and like them its members (but not their officers and employees) are appointed by the GLC. All of the London Transport Board's capital debt was written off before the transfer.

British Rail's commuter services (which stretch as far afield as Southend, Ashford, Reading and Bletchley, and are operationally interrelated with long-distance services) do not come directly under GLC control, but provision has been made to allow the Council to bring rail services into a common plan.

IV: CLEAN AIR

It was as early as 1273 that the first action was taken to protect the environment from polluted air: a royal proclamation of that year prohibited the use of coal in London. This was not effective, despite the dire penalties: it is recorded that a man was sent to the scaffold in 1306 for burning coal instead of charcoal. Gentler methods are now preferred, though it was not until the disastrous London smog of 1952 (resulting in 4,000 deaths) that really effective action was taken. The Beaver Report of 1954[61] described the effects of air pollution on health and made comprehensive recommendations on the prevention of pollution by smoke from industry and domestic chimneys, grit and dust, sulphur dioxide, motor vehicle exhausts and smoke from railway locomotives. Particularly telling was the Committee's estimate of the economic cost of pollution: around £250 million a year (in 1954 prices) in terms only of losses that could be given a monetary value. Additionally, between £25 million and £50 million a year was lost through the inefficient burning of fuel.*

In recent years there has been a growing emphasis on reducing air pollution as a part of a more general policy of environmental improvement. The Hunt Committee for instance, in discussing problems of economic growth, argued that 'tackling air pollution, like clearing derelict land, is a necessary part of the environmental rehabilitation which the older industrial areas need'.

* See 'Memorandum by the Economic Sub-Committee' of the Beaver Committee, published as Appendix II of the Beaver Report.[61]

The Clean Air Acts

The Clean Air Acts of 1956 and 1968 prohibit the emission of dark smoke, provide for the control of the emission of grit and dust from furnaces and establish a system for the approval by local authorities of chimney heights. However, the principal source of air pollution is domestic smoke and it is here that powers are the most extensive. Local authorities are empowered to establish *smoke control areas* (subject to approval by the Ministry of Housing) in which the emission of smoke from chimneys constitutes an offence. This involves the conversion of grates to enable smokeless fuels to be burned. Grants are given (normally) equal to seven-tenths of the approved expenditure on the cost of installing smokeless appliances. (Central government reimburses local authorities four-sevenths of their expenditure except where a local authority house is concerned, in which case the proportion is 40 per cent.) The provisions here are flexible. Grant can be made not only on conversion of open grates but also alternatively an equivalent amount can be given towards the cost of installing central heating or electric space heaters.

A *Memorandum* on the 1956 Act[64] stressed the need for detailed surveys of proposed smoke control areas, and the importance of consultation with local fuel producers and distributors, before orders were made defining the areas. Caution was urged: 'The establishment of smoke control areas will necessarily be gradual; it will need to be undertaken in stages, over a period of years in the larger towns. Progress will be governed by the supply of smokeless fuels, the rate at which appliances can be converted or replaced, and the rate at which local authorities are able to formulate and carry through their smoke control plans. Above all, progress – and indeed the whole success of the operation – will depend upon public support; upon people's understanding of the problems involved, and their readiness to co-operate in smoke control measures.'

The heart of the problem lies in the appropriately-termed 'black areas'. These are areas, listed by the Ministry, which in the words of the Beaver Committee 'experience a high frequency of fog in which urban and industrial density produce large amounts of pollution'. By the end of 1968, nearly a half of the premises in these black areas had been included in local programmes, but progress is very uneven over the country. In Greater London nearly 70 per cent of premises are covered by smoke control orders. (As a result there has been a 50 per cent increase in winter sunshine over London.) But there are still twenty-five local authorities in black areas who have not yet made any smoke control orders. One particularly tricky problem here is that of persuading mine workers to give up their concessionary coal in favour of smokeless fuel or cash.

The 1968 Clean Air Act empowers the Minister of Housing to direct a local authority to draw up and carry out a clean air programme for their area. The Hunt Committee, in deploring the shortsightedness of the unenthusiastic local authorities, urged the Minister to use these powers.

Unfortunately, the clean air programme is one which suffers in periods – such as 1968 – when local authorities are being urged to restrain expenditure. Nevertheless, substantial progress has been made since 1956, and attention is now turning to other kinds of pollution, particularly sulphur dioxide and emissions from vehicles.

REFERENCES AND FURTHER READING

Housing

1 Central Housing Advisory Committee, *Our Older Homes: A Call for Action* (Denington Report), HMSO, 1966.
2 Cullingworth, J. B., *Housing in Transition*, Heinemann, 1963.
3 Cullingworth, J. B., *Housing and Local Government*, Allen & Unwin, 1966.
4 Hallmark Securities Ltd., *The Halliwell Report*, published privately, 1966.
5 MHLG, Circular No. 42/62, *Improvement of Houses*, HMSO, 1962.
6 MHLG, *Report of the Committee on Housing in Greater London* (Milner Holland Report), Cmnd. 2605, HMSO, 1965.
7 MHLG, *The Deeplish Study: Improvement Possibilities in a District of Rochdale*, HMSO, 1966.
8 MHLG, 'House Condition Survey, England and Wales, 1967', *Economic Trends* No. 175, May 1968, pp. xxiv-xxxvi.
9 MHLG, *Old Houses into New Homes*, Cmnd. 3602, HMSO, 1968.
10 MHLG, *Barnsbury Environmental Study*, MHLG, 1968.
11 MHLG, Circular No. 63/69, *Housing Act 1969*, HMSO, 1969.
12 MHLG, Circular No. 64/69, *Housing Act 1969: House Improvement and Repair*, HMSO, 1969.
13 MHLG, Circular No. 65/69, *Housing Act 1969: Area Improvement*, HMSO, 1969.
14 MHLG, Circular No. 68/69, *Housing Act 1969: Slum Clearance*, HMSO, 1969.
15 Taylor Woodrow Group, *The Fulham Study*, published privately.
16 Welsh Office, *Welsh House Condition Survey*, HMSO, 1968.

Comprehensive Redevelopment

17 Burns, W., *New Towns for Old*, Leonard Hill, 1963.
18 MHLG, *Town Centres: Approach to Renewal*, Planning Bulletin No. 1, HMSO, 1962.
19 MHLG, *Town Centres: Cost and Control of Redevelopment*, Planning Bulletin No. 3, HMSO, 1963.
20 MHLG, *Parking in Town Centres*, Planning Bulletin No. 7, HMSO, 1965.

21 MHLG, Circular No. 53/67, *Civic Amenities Act 1967*, HMSO, 1967.
22 MHLG, Circular No. 54/67, *Contributions by Developers towards the Cost of Parking Facilities*, HMSO, 1967.
23 MHLG, *Historic Towns; Preservation and Change*, HMSO, 1967.
24 MHLG, Circular No. 12/68, *Local Government Act 1966 – Sections 7 and 8: Grants to Local Authorities in respect of Comprehensive Redevelopment and Public Open Space* (with Annex: *Explanatory Memorandum on Planning Grants*), HMSO, 1968.
25 MHLG, Development Control Policy Note 3, *Industrial and Commercial Development*, HMSO, 1969.
26 MHLG, Development Control Policy Note 5, *Development in Town Centres*, HMSO, 1969.
27 Ministry of Transport, Roads Circular No. 1/68, *Traffic and Transport Plans*, HMSO, 1968.
28 Sharp, E., *The Ministry of Housing and Local Government*, Allen & Unwin, 1969.
29 Tetlow, J. and Goss, A., *Homes, Towns and Traffic*, Faber, Revised Edition, 1968.
30 Town Planning Institute, 'Central Area Development', *Journal of the Town Planning Institute*, Vol. XLVI, No. 7, June 1960.
31 Tweddell, N., 'Partners in Urban Renewal', *The Cubitt Magazine*, Winter 1963/64.
32 Winterbottom, D., *Planned London* (Town Planning Institute Conference Handbook, May 1969), Town Planning Institute, 1969.

Planning for Traffic

33 Bayliss, B. T. and Edwards, S. L., *Transport for Industry (Summary Report)*, Ministry of Transport, HMSO, 1968.
34 Estimates Committee, Sub-Committee E, Session 1968–69, *Motorways and Trunk Roads*, H.C. Paper 102, HMSO, 1969.
35 Gray, P. G., *Private Motoring in England and Wales*, Government Social Survey, HMSO, 1969.
36 Greater London Council, *Kensington Environmental Management Study*, GLC, 1966.
37 Greater London Council, *Generation of Business Traffic in Central London*, GLC Research Paper No. 3, October 1968.
38 Herrmann, P. G., *Forecasts of Vehicle Ownership in Counties and County Boroughs in Great Britain*, Road Research Laboratory (Crowthorne, Berkshire), 1968.

39 *Journal of Transport Economics and Policy*, published three times a year (January, May and September) by London School of Economics.

40 Kirwan, R. M., 'Economics and Methodology in Urban Transport Planning', in Orr, S. C. and Cullingworth, J. B., *Regional and Urban Studies: A Social Science Approach*, Allen & Unwin, 1969.

41 Leeds City Council, Ministry of Transport and Ministry of Housing and Local Government, *Planning and Transport – The Leeds Approach*, HMSO, 1969.

42 London Transport Board, *Annual Reports*, HMSO.

43 Ministry of Transport, *Passenger Transport in Great Britain* (Annual Statistics), HMSO.

44 Ministry of Transport, *Roads in England* (Annual Report), HMSO.

45 Ministry of Transport, *Traffic in Towns* (Buchanan Report), HMSO, 1963.

46 Ministry of Transport, *Road Pricing: The Economic and Technical Possibilities* (Smeed Report), HMSO, 1964.

47 Ministry of Transport, *Transport Policy*, Cmnd. 3057, HMSO, 1966.

48 Ministry of Transport, *Public Transport and Traffic*, Cmnd. 3481, HMSO, 1967.

49 Ministry of Transport, *How Fast? A Paper for Discussion*, HMSO, 1968.

50 Ministry of Transport, Roads Circular No. 1/68, *Traffic and Transport Plans*, HMSO, 1968.

51 Ministry of Transport, *Transport in London*, Cmnd. 3686, HMSO, 1968.

52 Ministry of Transport, *Roads for the Future: A New Inter-Urban Plan*, HMSO, 1969.

53 Political and Economic Planning, *Solving Traffic Problems – I: Lessons from America*, Planning Broadsheet No. 402, 1956.

54 Rhodes, G., *Administrators in Action: British Case Studies, Vol. II* ('The Wentworth By-Pass'), Allen & Unwin, 1965.

55 Tanner, J. C., 'Forecasts of Vehicle Ownership in Great Britain', *Roads and Road Construction*, November and December, 1965.

56 Tanner, J. C., *Revised Forecasts of Vehicles and Traffic in Great Britain*, Road Research Laboratory (Crowthorne, Berkshire), 1967.

57 Tetlow, A. and Goss, A., *Homes, Town and Traffic*, Faber, Revised Edition, 1968.

58 Thomas, J. M., *Some Characteristics of Motorists in Central London*, Greater London Papers, London School of Economics, 1968.

59 Thomas, R., *Journeys to Work*, Political and Economic Planning, 1968.

60 Thomson, J. M., 'An Evaluation of Two Proposals for Traffic Restraint in Central London', *Journal of the Royal Statistical Society*, Series A, Vol. 30, Part 3, 1967.

Clean Air

61 Committee on Air Pollution (Beaver Committee), *Interim Report*, Cmd. 9011, HMSO, 1953; *Report*, Cmd. 9322, HMSO, 1954.

62 *The Intermediate Areas: Report of a Committee under the Chairmanship of Sir Joseph Hunt*, Cmnd. 3998, HMSO, 1969.

63 MHLG, *Clean Air Act 1956: Memorandum on Miscellaneous Provisions*, HMSO, 1956.

64 MHLG, *Clean Air Act 1956: Memorandum on Smoke Control Areas*, HMSO, 1956.

65 MHLG, *Smoke Control (England and Wales)*, Cmnd. 1113, HMSO, 1959.

Chapter XII

REGIONAL PLANNING

REGIONAL THINKING

At present there is no executive machinery for regional physical planning in Britain. There is a large number of agencies undertaking responsibility for particular services and development on a regional scale, but there is no organization responsible for the co-ordinated programming, development and control. Nationalized utilities and hospitals, regional departments of government departments, large private firms, operate on a regional basis*; there is a host of regional advisory and consultative councils, and committees; and there is an increasing number of *ad hoc* and rather loose organizations of local authorities and others dealing with such diverse matters as further education, industrial development and sport. Finally, there is now the regional economic planning (advisory) machinery established under the aegis of the Department of Economic Affairs, and the very new Passenger Transport Authorities established in a number of the major conurbations.†

Thus though there is no regional planning system, there are many regional planning machines. In this chapter attention is focused on regional economic and physical problems and the development of machinery to deal with them.

A number of strands can be identified in the development of thinking on regionalism. Two are of particular relevance in this book – the physical planning and the economic planning strands. Some account of the former from the local end has already been given. It is now necessary to supplement this with an outline of the situation as it has developed at the centre.

At the end of Chapter II some stress was laid on the lack of a

* As does the Water Resources Board. For an account of the development of national and regional planning of water resources see E. Sharp, *The Ministry of Housing and Local Government*, Allen & Unwin, 1969, pp. 105–17, and the Annual Reports of the Water Resources Board.

† On Passenger Transport Authorities, see Chapter XI.

regional tier of planning between local authorities and the central departments. This lack did not seem (and was not) as important in the mid-'forties as it appeared when population growth, economic growth, increased personal mobility, a rising standard of living and a host of other related factors conspired in the 'fifties to increase pressures on land and the machinery of land planning control. In any case it was not possible to go further at the time. For a time the framework of regional advisory plans (particularly in the London Region) had to suffice. They had some impact: they enabled some broad planning objectives to be communicated to and, more important, to be acknowledged by local planning authorities. Informal arrangements, professional contacts and a generally shared planning philosophy also helped.

By the end of the 'fifties, it became clear that something more was needed. Development plans had become hopelessly out of date due to the cumbersome procedure of approval and the great change in the underlying forces with which they were supposed to cope. Furthermore, the disbandment of the regional organization of the Ministry of Housing in 1954 had (according to the former Permanent Secretary to the Ministry) the opposite effect to that intended. 'There was a strong feeling at headquarters that the divisions did not know their regions or their authorities as well as they should; and that it would be better if headquarters staff could be enabled to devote more time to travelling out. It was thought that abolition of the regional organization would improve Whitehall's knowledge of, and contacts with, the north, the midlands, the east and the south-west to the benefit of all; and that officers and representatives of local authorities might be encouraged to come more frequently to Whitehall as they had done in pre-war years. It did not come off.'[28] And so the problems changed in character and increased in complexity at the very time when the central department was in insufficient touch with local government.

REGIONAL STUDIES

The turn of the tide came in the early 'sixties in three areas for three different reasons. In 1962 a Northern Housing Office of the Ministry was opened in Manchester to assist the large programme of slum clearance and redevelopment in the North and North-West. In 1963 another regional office, with both housing and planning functions, was set up in Newcastle in connection with the 'Hailsham Plan' for the North-East, to which there was a clear political commitment. Probably of greater importance was the beginning, in 1961, of a series of regional studies. These resulted from the awareness in the

Ministry of the inadequacy of the development plans and land allocations to meet the rising pressures for development. These studies started, in traditional manner, as 'regional conferences' and 'land studies' undertaken jointly by officers of local authorities and the Ministry. In the South-East and the West Midlands these developed into new-style regional studies covering unprecedentedly large areas.

The South-East Study was published in March 1964 and included regionally-based proposals of a kind and on a scale which had not been seen since the wartime and immediate post-war period of optimistic planning. New cities (*sic*) were suggested in the Southampton-Portsmouth area, the Bletchley area (later to become Milton Keynes) and the Newbury area. New towns were considered for Ashford and Stansted. Large-scale expansions were proposed for Ipswich, Northampton, Peterborough and Swindon. Consultants were appointed to consider, with the local authorities concerned, many of these proposals.

The next clearly identifiable step in this period of intense examination and thinking came with the decision of the Labour Government in 1964 to set up regional economic planning machinery. The trend towards this was already in evidence. Early in 1964 the President of the Board of Trade was made responsible for 'trade, industry and regional development'. The White Paper, *South-East England*, outlining the Government's reaction to the *Study* was published jointly by the Ministry and the Board. Indeed, *The South-East Study* was the only one to bear the imprint of the Ministry of Housing and Local Government. Before the next studies were completed (on the West Midlands and the North-West) the Department of Economic Affairs had been set up (taking over the regional development division of the Board of Trade). Thereafter the DEA assumed responsibility for the direction and publication of regional studies.

It is at this point that the economic and the physical planning strands became intertwined (though not fused). The DEA* is charged with the responsibility of 'framing and supervising the plan for economic development and for the general co-ordination of action to implement the plan, including, in particular, policies for industry, the region, incomes and prices, and economic growth'.

REGIONAL ADVICE

Eight English Regional Economic Planning Councils have been established. (Similar Councils – one in each country – in Scotland

* Now transferred to the Secretary of State for Local Government and Regional Planning; see Appendix to Chapter III.

and Wales are the concern of the respective Secretaries of State.) These Planning Councils are advisory bodies and consist of a Chairman and about twenty-five Members all appointed by the Secretary of State. The Members are appointed as 'individuals having a wide range of knowledge and experience of their regions': they are not delegates or representatives of particular interests. The Councils' main functions are 'to study and advise on the needs and potentialities of their regions and on the development of a long-term planning strategy for their regions, and to advise central government on aspects of national policy which have a bearing on regional development'.

Alongside each Council is a Board consisting of senior civil servants from the main government departments concerned with regional planning. In the English regions, the Chairmen of the Boards are all senior officials of DEA. The functions of the Boards are 'to co-ordinate the regional economic planning work of Departments, and to co-operate with the Economic Planning Councils in developing the long-term planning strategies for the regions'.

The eight English Councils were established between February and August 1965. In each region the regional office houses the regional planning staff of most of the main government offices. The regional organization of DEA itself is, of course, new since the Department itself is new. Most of the other Government Departments already had some regional organization: these have now, as far as possible, been housed in the same offices, thus providing a physical setting for co-ordination. So far as the Ministry of Housing is concerned its regional organization has now been resuscitated (it was largely disbanded in 1956) but on the basis of the new Economic Planning Regions.

The scope of this new regional planning machinery is by no means clear as yet, though DEA have stated that by the end of 1965 the following four tasks had emerged as being the most important ones at that time:

(i) to work out broad objectives for each region and so provide a comprehensive framework within which decisions in particular sectors can be taken;
(ii) to advise on the formulation of national policies where these can significantly affect the regions;
(iii) to advise on the application in the regions of national policy;
(iv) to stimulate interest within each region and build up a common approach within each region to its problems.

To date the work might be described as being 'regional stocktaking'. The primary objective has been to assemble the facts and

TABLE XII.1

English Regional Economic Planning Regions

Region	*Constituent counties*	*Population 1969* (Millions)	*Regional office*
Northern	Cumberland	3·3	Newcastle
	Durham		
	Northumberland		
	Westmorland		
	Yorkshire – North Riding		
Yorkshire and Humberside	Lincolnshire – Lindsey	4·8	Leeds
	Yorkshire – East Riding		
	Yorkshire – West Riding		
East Midlands	Derbyshire (except High Peak District)	3·3	Nottingham
	Leicestershire		
	Lincolnshire – Holland		
	Lincolnshire – Kesteven		
	Northamptonshire		
	Nottinghamshire		
	Rutland		
East Anglia	Cambridgeshire & Isle of Ely	1·7	London
	Huntingdon & Peterborough		
	Norfolk		
	Suffolk, East		
	Suffolk, West		
South-East	Bedfordshire	17·3	London
	Berkshire		
	Buckinghamshire		
	Essex		
	Greater London		
	Hampshire		
	Hertfordshire		
	Isle of Wight		
	Kent		
	Oxfordshire		
	Surrey		
	Sussex, East		
	Sussex, West		
South-West	Cornwall	3·7	Bristol
	Devon		
	Dorset		
	Gloucestershire		
	Somerset		
	Wiltshire		
West Midlands	Herefordshire	5·1	Birmingham
	Shropshire		
	Staffordshire		
	Warwickshire		
	Worcestershire		
North-West	Cheshire	6·8	Manchester
	Lancashire		
	High Peak District of Derbyshire		

figures relating to the regions which can form the basis for an overall assessment and for a broad regional strategy. Attention has been concentrated on preparing 'studies' on the lines of *The South-East Study*. The first two were published in 1965 for the North-West and the West Midlands.* Both of these were undertaken by 'a group of officials from Government Departments concerned with regional planning', and have been 'referred' to the Planning Councils for the respective regions (without any commitment on the part of Government to the studies' findings or to the proposals which might be made by the Councils). Following the establishment of the Regional Councils, further studies have been undertaken and published. Unlike the earlier two, these are reports by the Councils themselves. But they are not 'regional plans'; indeed they specifically disclaim any pretension to be. As the foreword to *The East Midlands Study* puts it, they are attempts 'to present to the public an account of the region as it is, and as it is changing; it draws attention to problems and opportunities, with an indication of what is involved in them. It is hoped that the study will form an adequate basis for the public discussion out of which the main lines of the region's planning will emerge; until adequate opportunity for that discussion has been provided it would be presumptuous to go further.'

This approach stems from two important factors. First, the essential information and research needed for an adequately based system of regional planning is lacking. Secondly (and this would still be of crucial importance if the former inadequacy were rectified), the Regional Councils have no executive powers and no authority over either the central government or local authorities. They 'represent' the regions only in a very indirect way. They have to tread warily between the sensitive toes of Whitehall and the much more sensitive toes of Town Hall. It could hardly be expected that they would rapidly resolve the conflicts between the constituent local authorities (and particularly between town and county) which have for so long frustrated attempts to plan on any scale other than that circumscribed by local authority boundaries. Essentially the Regional Councils constitute an experiment in forging new, and wider, loyalties – loyalties to a region rather than to a locality. The studies and reports are thus not sets of policies agreed by the regions and submitted to the central government for consideration and action; rather are they the interim findings and thoughts of a group of individuals with experience of and interest in the regions, submitted to all concerned (Government at all levels, and public and private bodies) as a first exercise in regional thinking.

What then is the function of the regional studies? Probably the

* A list is given at the end of this chapter.

clearest statement is to be found in the report of the South-West Economic Planning Council, significantly entitled *A Region with a Future: A Draft Strategy for the South-West:*

'It has come to be recognized that it is too soon in the experience of regional planning to aim at achieving a set of Government-approved plans for all regions which will neatly dovetail with each other and which, in numbers of population, distribution of manpower, growth and location of industry, scale and disposition of public investment, etc., will in aggregate coincide with the forecasts, intentions and capabilities envisaged by the Government for the economy as a whole. The immediate aim should be for each Council to provide themselves with a "regional strategy" by which recommendations can be made on decisions affecting their regions which cannot wait, and advice be given immediately on the implications for their regions of national and local policies.'

The truth of the matter, however, is that the present regional machinery is a temporary makeshift which will be superseded when action is taken on the reports of the Royal Commission on Local Government and the Crowther Commission on the Constitution.

Economic and physical planning are still administratively separate, though the distinction is clearer in theory than in practice, as the Economic Planning Councils and Boards well know. The Ministry of Housing, like the Ministry of Transport (which has had an increasing role to play in an increasingly mobile society), now has regional offices and staff for each of the regions. Their role in the preparation and (less effectively) the implementation of regional and sub-regional plans is crucial.

Two important points need to be stressed. First, the Councils have no executive powers whatsoever: they can comment or rant and rage but they can *do* nothing – they are purely advisory bodies. Secondly, the creation of the Boards in no way affects the existing powers and responsibilities of local authorities and central government departments. Advice and co-ordination: these are the essential functions of the Councils and the Boards.

THE DEVELOPMENT OF ECONOMIC PLANNING POLICIES

Employment and economic change lie at the heart of regional planning. This, indeed, was the starting-point for the Barlow inquiry twenty-five years ago. Post-war industrial location policies have been directed towards reducing unemployment in the development areas and restraining new industrial building in 'congested' areas. This has been the interpretation given to the phrase 'a proper distribution of industry'. This has, in the main, been regarded as a *social* policy running alongside, but not supporting economic policies:

'We should start from the assumption that the economic and industrial expansion of the country should proceed freely in response to growing and changing consumer demand, and that it should proceed on the principle of the most effective use of our national resources. . . . This principle of the most effective use of our resources must clearly be mitigated in some cases by Government action to deal with certain social consequences which the nation does not regard as acceptable.'*

During the 'sixties, however, there was an increasing awareness that a maldistribution of employment had serious economic effects on the national economy. The 1963 Report of the National Economic Development Council on *Conditions Favourable to Faster Growth* provides a good illustration of this new thinking:

'The level of employment in different regions of the country varies widely, and high unemployment associated with the lack of employment opportunities in the less prosperous regions is usually thought of as a social problem. Policies aim, therefore, to prevent unemployment rising to politically intolerable levels and expenditure to this end is often considered a necessary burden to the nation, unrelated to any economic gain that might accrue from it. But the relatively low activity rates† in these regions also indicate considerable labour reserves. To draw these reserves into employment would make a substantial contribution to national employment and national growth.'

This argument, it should be noted, was put forward not by town planners but by economists. It differs very markedly from the traditional type of economic argument; and it rejects the idea that the long-term solution to regional economic decline lies in migration to the prosperous areas. Apart from the social cost of large-scale migration that this would involve, there are two other significant objections. First it would add to the problems of congestion in the South-East and the Midlands – problems which are already straining to the

* The President of the Board of Trade (Mr R. Maudling) on the opening of the Second Reading Debates on the Local Employment Bill, *H.C. Debates*, Vol. 613, Col. 32, November 9, 1959. See also Select Committee on Estimates, Session 1955–6, *Development Areas*, House of Commons Paper No. 139, HMSO, 1955.

† An 'activity rate' is defined as the proportion of civilian employees – employed plus registered unemployed – in a given population age-group.

utmost the machinery of town and country planning. Secondly, it would be quite impracticable for these prosperous areas to absorb the required number of migrants. Furthermore, if the less prosperous regions were allowed to run down, their future problem would become even more difficult to solve. The aim should be to employ a regional development policy which would aim at achieving self-sustaining regional growth. It is here that the relationship between economic planning and town and country planning is most clearly seen: potential industrial developers are concerned not only with labour supply and good sites, but also with adequate services, educational provision, and so on. In short, if industrialists are to be attracted to the less prosperous regions then these regions have to be made both economically and socially attractive. In the words of the White Paper on *The North-East*: 'even generous assistance to enterprise may not be fully effective unless it is backed by faster progress in making towns and villages more pleasant, in improving communications, and in removing scars on the industrial countryside.'

The problem can thus be seen as a compound of the economic and the social. The promotion of industrial activity has to be accompanied by a modernization of the general environment. This is not merely a question of providing a 'bait' to industrialists: it is also a matter of economic efficiency – 'to ensure that the scale of the public services and facilities match the needs of a modern society'. The problem is in part one of historical legacies: the regions where economic growth is comparatively slow are the regions where there is a concentration of physical obsolescence. Indeed, some observers have spoken of a geographical division of the country into two nations – separated roughly by the River Trent. The 'Fortunate Regions' of the South have a high level of employment, a large amount of private investment, a high standard of health, a relatively high standard of social service and social amenity. On the other hand, the 'Unfortunate Regions' of the North, of Wales and of Scotland – the boom areas of the coal age – have an enormous legacy of obsolete social capital, a slower rate of economic growth, an accompanying higher rate of unemployment, a poorer standard of health and social service, and a not unrelated outward migration of population.

More detailed studies would show that the image of the two nations is overdrawn and false in many respects, but the essential point is valid: the regions with a slow rate of economic growth have acute environmental problems which are difficult to cope with in the context of their relatively low level of economic activity and which in turn present obstacles to an increased growth rate. It is for this reason that so much emphasis is now being given to improving 'infrastructure'.

Nevertheless, it does not follow that all existing towns and settlements should be modernized. Some areas have lost their economic *raison d'être* and have little or no potentiality for growth. In any case, a policy of promoting growth is most effective when it is applied to carefully selected areas where the potentialities are particularly good. Since 1960, industrial location policy has been mainly aimed at relieving high unemployment in development districts. This was a major departure from the previous policy of promoting growth more generally in regions. The 'selection' of development districts was made, however, on the basis of unemployment rates. The application of the 'growth point' idea, on the other hand, involves selection on the basis of potentialities:

'Better results might be secured for the slowly expanding regions as a whole by identifying their natural growth points and seeking to attract industry to them. Within the bigger areas a wider choice of location than at present would be available to incoming firms. This would increase the likelihood of attracting a larger number and a greater variety of firms, and of stimulating the development of industrial complexes. Firms would then benefit from the presence of kindred industry. These complexes and other places especially attractive to industry could be developed into growth points within the less prosperous regions. It could be expected that the benefit of new growth in any part would repercuss fairly quickly throughout the region.'[19]

The two regional programmes for Scotland and North-East England represented the first essays in comprehensive regional planning by central government. Their importance lies not so much in the actual proposals made, but in the advance in thought and policy which they represent. They (like the Welsh report, *Wales: The Way Ahead*) do, however, differ from succeeding reports – or 'studies' as they are typically called. They involved a degree of Government commitment which is notably absent from their successors, even when they have been prepared by central government. (The 'official' preface to *The South-East Study* underlines that its main purpose is 'to provide a basis for discussion'; the point is rubbed home even more clearly in the preface to *The West Midlands* regional study where it is stated that the Government 'are not in any way committed by the Study Group's findings'.)

The point is, of course, that regional planning is not simply a matter of planning *within* a region. It has to take place within a framework of national policies which can be translated into decisions about the allocation of resources *between* regions. The White Papers on Scotland and the North-East proposed increases in public service investment which would have involved (for 1964–5) Scotland receiving 11 per cent of the Great Britain total (for a country with less than 10 per cent of the population) and the North-East receiving 7 per cent (with 5½ per cent of the population). These proposals were drawn up on the basis of a political assessment of the needs of these regions, but clearly there are problems in continuing with this approach for all regions.

THE 'INTERMEDIATE AREAS'

Indeed, as aid to the development areas has increased, there has been mounting political pressure from 'intermediate areas' (or 'grey areas', to use the more popular term). It was this pressure which led to the setting up of the Hunt Committee, whose report, *The Intermediate Areas*, was published in April 1969. The terms of reference of this committee were 'to examine in relation to the economic welfare of the country as a whole and the needs of the development areas, the situation in other areas where the rate of economic growth gives cause (or may give cause) for concern, and to suggest whether revised policies to influence economic growth in such areas are desirable and, if so, what measures should be adopted'.

The Committee quickly found that it was no easy matter to judge the presence and severity of 'causes for concern'. In the present state of regional knowledge and analysis, political judgment has a very large role to play. Nevertheless, a brave and useful attempt was made. The major 'cause for concern' was 'slow economic growth . . . where it is associated with unused or under-used labour resources, low earnings, a concentration of industries with a declining labour force, poor communications and a run-down physical environment making areas unattractive for new economic growth, and net outward migration'. Their chosen criteria were:

(*a*) Sluggish or falling employment } as the major indicators
(*b*) A slow growth in personal incomes } of slow growth.
(*c*) A slow rate of addition to industrial and commercial premises – as indicating a low level of industrial and commercial investment and a slow rate of economic growth.
(*d*) Significant unemployment – as the most obvious measure of wasted human resources.
(*e*) Low or declining proportions of women at work – as indicating a particular under-use of resources, especially in areas with a tradition of female employment.

(*f*) Low earnings – as throwing some light on the efficiency of the use of labour and as one of the factors relevant to the economic opportunity of individuals.

(*g*) Heavy reliance on industry whose demand for labour was growing slowly or falling and was likely to continue to do so – as an indication of vulnerability to economic change resulting in possible under-utilization of labour resources.

(*h*) Poor communications (*i*) Decayed or inadequate environment, including dereliction	as material to slow growth in the recent past and to the potential for growth.

(*j*) Serious net outward migration – as a pointer to the danger of accelerating decline, and as a summing up of the reactions of individuals to a complex of social and economic factors such as the local range of employment opportunities, educational and social activities and the state of the social and physical environment.

They concluded that the severest problems were undoubtedly in the development areas and that there was not a clear-cut and well-defined category of 'intermediate area'. Rather were there 'symptoms of concern' present to a varying extent and a varying degree in different parts of the country. Nevertheless, they felt that the North-West and Yorkshire & Humberside stood in the greatest need of a new impetus and recommended special assistance for these regions, and more limited assistance to the Notts-Derbyshire coalfield and to North Staffordshire.

In recommending help to such a large area of the country (containing a fifth of the population of Great Britain) there was no suggestion that the 'growth-area' policy should be abandoned. On the contrary, the Committee were simply following the logic which underlay the setting up in 1966 of broad development areas in place of the former narrower and relatively scattered development districts, chosen on the basis of high unemployment:

'As a result of inducements being made available to industry throughout these wider areas, industrialists are not tied to locations of greatest need, which may not be the most viable long-term locations for industry.'

It followed that the recommended aid might go to relatively prosperous parts of an intermediate area, but this is in principle no different from the position in the development areas.

This, however, is to ignore the political difficulties. Any aid to intermediate areas which is effective in increasing new industrial development must (at least in the short run) have an effect on the development areas. As the Hunt Committee ruefully point out at the beginning of their report, 'the supply of mobile industry available to stimulate economic growth is, taken as a whole, insufficient at present to meet the needs of the development areas and overspill towns, let alone areas of slow growth. We recognize that remedial measures for areas of slow growth may hold back progress elsewhere.'

The Government's reaction was that the selection of areas to be given assistance to industry must be governed strictly by 'criteria of need', in particular the level and character of unemployment, the rate of outward migration and the scope for industrial growth. On this basis seven intermediate areas have been defined: North-East Lancashire, Yorkshire coalfield, North Humberside, Notts-Derby coalfield, South-East Wales, Plymouth and Leith.

It is estimated that aid to these areas will cost nearly £20 million a year. This is to be met out of 'the very substantial and growing sums being spent on assistance to industry in the development areas', which are to continue to have priority.

THE REGIONAL POLICY DILEMMA

Throughout this continuing debate on the allocation of resources between regions there has been little attention paid to the impact on planning within regions – except in very broad, generalist terms such as that the movement of industry from London and the West Midlands will 'relieve congestion'. The Hunt Committee, however, did discuss as a 'possible cause for concern' the flow of industry to overspill areas in the South-East, East Anglia and the West Midlands, and in particular the difficulties being experienced by Telford New Town.

The essential argument here is that the high level of development area incentives is jeopardizing the overspill programme for London and the West Midlands and throws into question the viability of the future programmes which are based on the premise that the transfer of employment from the two conurbations will be on a substantially increased scale. The three Economic Planning Councils (South-East, East Anglia and West Midlands) all put up a case for a relaxation of i.d.c. control and additional finance inducements in overspill areas. The Hunt Committee favoured the former but not the latter. Conurbation firms should, in their view, be allowed to move to an overspill location provided that the Board of Trade has advised the firm of the incentives and attractions of the development areas and provided that the movement is within the planned growth programme of the overspill area. Financial inducements, on the other hand, 'might divert a much needed amount of new work away from areas of high unemployment'.

But is it possible to implement current regional physical planning strategies within the context of the present economic policies of giving priority to development areas? If there is not sufficient industry for the areas of high unemployment and for the overspill areas, something has to give way. Nowhere is this clearer than in the West Midlands.

It is here that we see the unresolved dilemma of present regional policies. Regional planning means different things to central and local government. As Senior has put it, 'what *central* government means by "regional planning" is primarily the correction of economic imbalance *between* one "region" and another; and it is only with reluctance that central government is reconciling itself to the fact that this purpose – crucial to its central function in the economic field – necessarily involves the making of investment decisions *within* "regions" on a territorial as well as a functional basis. What *local* government means by "regional planning", on the other hand, is primarily the expression of national policies in terms of a comprehensive long-term strategy for economic and physical development *within* each provincial-scale "region", in the context of which local planning authorities can work out meaningful structure plans for their own areas.'[25]

This gap cannot be bridged until there is a regional planning machine designed for the job. At present central government can channel (or block) resources to regions, but there is no machinery for rationally distributing resources *within* regions on the basis of a comprehensive strategy. The Ministry of Housing and Local Government has a role and powers quite inadequate for this; and in any case, it is not a proper task for central government – it is essentially a regional matter. Any plan involves the submerging of some interests in favour of others. At national level the priority given to development areas is a clear case in point. But at the regional level there is no system for determining priorities. Each local authority has the interests of its ratepayers at heart and development needed for a wider benefit is jeopardized. Thus (for instance), if a conurbation authority sees industrial overspill as having undesirable effects on its rateable value, and a potentially good overspill authority sees development as an intolerable local burden, an overspill policy is killed at birth, even if it is in the wider interests of the region as a whole. To quote Senior again:

'Any plan which seeks to guide development in the interests of the region as a whole must call for the concentration of investment in particular parts of it and the prevention of development in others. But so long as the region is divided between different implementing authorities, one of them is bound to find that it is being called upon to bear more than its share of the cost and get less than its share of the benefit of giving effect to particular provisions of the overall plan: if this were not so there would be no need for such a plan. And it would be not only altruistic, but positively undemocratic, for that authority thus to subordinate its own ratepayers' interests to that of its neighbour's ratepayers. It is quite unreasonable to expect a wrongly organized local government structure to behave as it would automatically tend to do if it were rightly organized, when the wrong organization automatically produces a different incidence of the costs and benefits of acting in the interest of the region as a whole.'[25]

Until the appropriate machinery is devised,* regional planning will remain largely a central government activity concerned with 'balance' and the location of major investments. The library of regional and sub-regional studies will increase, but effective co-ordinated action will be impossible to achieve.

* For a note on recent changes in the machinery of central government, see Appendix to Chapter III.

REFERENCES AND FURTHER READING

1 Board of Trade, *Industrial Development Act 1966: Annual Reports*, HMSO.
2 Board of Trade, *Investment Grants; Annual Reports*, HMSO.
3 Board of Trade, *Local Employment Acts 1960 to 1966: Annual Reports*, HMSO.
4 Central Office of Information, *Regional Development in Britain*, COI Reference Pamphlet No. 80, HMSO, 1968.
5 Central Statistical Office, *Abstract of Regional Statistics*, HMSO (Annual).
6 Council of Europe, *Regional Planning: A European Problem*, 1968.
7 Cullingworth, J. B. and Orr, S.C., *Regional and Urban Studies*, Allen & Unwin, 1969.
8 DEA, *Economic Planning in the Regions*, DEA, 1966.
9 DEA, *Investment Incentives*, Cmnd. 2874, HMSO, 1966.
10 DEA, *The Development Areas: A Proposal for a Regional Employment Premium*, HMSO, 1967.
11 DEA, *The Development Areas: Regional Employment Premium*, Cmnd. 3310, HMSO, 1967.
12 DEA, *Economic Planning in the Regions*, HMSO, 2nd Edition, 1968.
13 DEA, *The Task Ahead: Economic Assessment to 1972*, HMSO, 1969.
14 Hammond, E., *An Analysis of Regional Economic and Social Statistics*, University of Durham, Rowntree Research Unit, 1968.
15 Hemming, M. F. W., 'The Regional Problem', *National Institute Economic Review*, No. 25, August 1963.
16 *The Intermediate Areas* (Hunt Report), Cmnd. 3998, HMSO, 1969.
17 McCrone, G., *Regional Policy in Britain*, Allen & Unwin, 1969.
18 Mackintosh, J. P., *The Devolution of Power*, Penguin Books, 1968.
19 National Economic Development Council, *Conditions Favourable to Faster Growth*, HMSO, 1963.

20 Needleman, L. and Scott, B., 'Regional Problems and the Location of Industry Policy in Britain', *Urban Studies*, Vol. 1, No. 2, November 1964.

21 Needleman, L., 'What are we to do about the Regional Problem?', *Lloyds Bank Review*, January 1965.

22 Richardson, H. W. and West, E. G., 'Must We Always Take Work to the Workers?', *Lloyds Bank Review*, January 1964.

23 *Royal Commission on the Distribution of the Industrial Population: Report* (Barlow Report), Cmd. 6153, HMSO, 1940.

24 Royal Commission on Local Government in England, Vol. 1, *Report* (Redcliffe-Maud Report), Cmnd. 4040, HMSO, 1969.

25 Royal Commission on Local Government in England, Vol. 2, *Memorandum of Dissent by Mr D. Senior*, Cmnd. 4040–I, HMSO, 1969.

26 Royal Commission on Local Government in England, Vol. 3, *Research Appendices*, Cmnd, 4040–II, HMSO, 1969.

27 Select Committee on Estimates, Session 1955–6, *Development Areas*, H.C. Paper 139, HMSO, 1955.

28 Sharp, E., *The Ministry of Housing and Local Government*, Allen & Unwin, 1969.

29 Smith, B. C., *Regionalism in England*, 3 volumes:
Vol. 1: *Regional Institutions: A Guide* (1964)
Vol. 2: *Its Nature and Purpose 1905–1965* (1965)
Vol. 3: *The New Regional Machinery* (1965)
Acton Society Trust.

30 Smith, B. C., *Advising Ministers: A Case Study of the South West Economic Planning Council*, Routledge & Kegan Paul, 1969.

31 Smith, P. M., 'What Kind of Regional Planning? A Review Article', *Urban Studies*, Vol. 3, November 1966, pp. 250–7 (a review of the North-West and the West Midlands regional studies and the 1966 White Paper on the Scottish economy).

32 Water Resources Board, *Fifth Annual Report*, H. C. Paper 3, HMSO, 1968.

OFFICIAL REGIONAL AND SUB-REGIONAL STUDIES AND PLANS

Surveys by Central Government Officials

The South-East Study 1961–1981 (1964)

The West Midlands: A Regional Study (1965)

The North-West: A Regional Study (1965)

The Problems of Merseyside: An Appendix to the North-West Study (1965)

Reports by Economic Planning Councils
Challenge of the Changing North (1966)
A Review of Yorkshire and Humberside (1966)
The East Midlands Study (1966)
A Strategy for the South-East (1967)
A Region with a Future: A Draft Strategy for the South-West (1967)
The West Midlands: Patterns of Growth (1967)
The North-West of the 1970s (1968)
Halifax and the Calder Valley (1968)
Huddersfield and Colne Valley (1969)
Opportunity in the East Midlands (1969)
Doncaster: An Area Study (1969)
The Plymouth Area Study (1969)
South-East Kent Study (1969)

Command Papers
Central Scotland: A Programme for Development and Growth, Cmnd. 2188 (1963)
The North-East: A Programme for Regional Development and Growth, Cmnd. 2206 (1963)
The Scottish Economy 1965–70, Cmnd. 2864 (1966)
Wales: The Way Ahead, Cmnd. 3334 (1969)

Report of the Central Unit for Environmental Planning
Humberside: A Feasibility Study (1969)

Chapter XIII

THE PLANNERS AND THE PUBLIC

PUBLIC ACCEPTANCE, SUPPORT AND PARTICIPATION

Town and country planning, land values, compulsory acquisition and the like present problems which, if they are to be adequately dealt with, demand a high degree of political sophistication and education on the part of the public. Yet to the 'man in the street' town and country planning is largely seen as a system of apparently arbitrary and irksome controls. Of course, this stems in part from the fact that much of contemporary planning is regulative – and there is a natural tendency to forget or to fail to see the real gains that have been made in, for instance, protecting the countryside from unsightly advertisement hoardings.

'The underlying purpose in the control of development (against the background of an approved Development Plan) is to secure that development takes place in the right places at the right time, and to stop it where it would be wrong. The public judge the success, or otherwise, of this control by what they see in town, village or countryside. What they do not see is what has been stopped by wise control of development. These cases are buried deep in the files of planning authorities and of the Minister. They did not materialize in brick and concrete to destroy or debase the urban or rural scene.'[7]

But the issue goes much deeper. It is a sad commentary on our planning system that the plan for 'enlivening' Piccadilly Circus would have materialized had not a premature press conference aroused public opposition. This case is illustrative: planning proposals are generally presented to the public as a *fait accompli*, and only rarely are they given a thorough *public* discussion. There is, of course, the machinery for objections and appeals, but, as will be shown in this chapter, this is a quasi-judicial process which is limited to a restricted range of interested parties. Furthermore, the general attitude to this system is far less favourable than to the normal judicial system. In any case the important point is not that the scope for registering 'objections' is limited, but that planning requires active 'citizen-participation', or at least public support and goodwill. Yet there is a very real divorce between 'the planners' and 'the planned'. There are several factors here. An important one is the effect of planning decisions on land values. Advance knowledge of planning proposals can markedly affect the value of the land concerned. This may lead to land speculation or to premature objections on the part of owners who expect to be adversely affected. As a result a planning department often has to operate under a veil of secrecy. This can only serve to increase public suspicion. Strangely this situation is itself in part the result of previous lack of public support. Though by no means the full explanation, there can be no doubt that the divorce between planners and the public is one of the factors which has led to the curious half-dismantled planning legislation which we now have – what Lord Holford has called 'a set of spare parts'. It must be axiomatic that compensation for acquisition of land or restriction on its use must be at a level which is publicly acceptable. This is so not merely on grounds of equity but also because 'inadequate' compensation will arouse such opposition as to inhibit public authorities from using their powers. This was the position under the 1947 Act. Each amendment of this Act has been designed to remove further injustices. But injustices still remain and will continue to do so until a scheme is devised which will at one and the same time be adequate for achieving planning objectives and prove publicly acceptable.

The point is basically a simple one: the planners cannot effectively move too far ahead of public opinion. This is not merely a matter of 'public relations': it is also one of leadership and community participation. This is to be seen clearly in the field of community improvement. 'Citizen-participation' may not be necessary for the successful development of a central area multi-level shopping precinct, but it is essential for the improvement of a decaying 'twilight' residential area. In view of the enormity of the British problem of rehabilitating sturdy yet obsolescent housing areas it is strange that so little thought has been given to the potentiality which could be realized if the interest and energy of the general public could be enlisted. Comparisons with the United States are striking. In Britain there is a remarkable acceptance of and reliance on Government; the Americans are less trusting and the curious result is a greater degree of 'grass-roots' democracy. This may not be as effective as United States Government hand-outs suggest, but so far as residential renewal is concerned there have been some dramatic successes. The

British approach usually provides a choice only between private profitable redevelopment and subsidized municipal activity, and neither have, until recently, paid much attention to the twilight areas surrounding town centres.

The issue is not, of course, restricted to town and country planning. Similar problems exist in relation to the social services, to the nationalized industries, and indeed to any form of public or private monopoly or near-monopoly. It goes to the root of democratic government in modern industrial society; and it thus leads far from the central questions which form the subject matter of this book. All that can be attempted here is a discussion of a selection of relevant topics.

APPLICATION FOR PLANNING PERMISSION

More than 400,000 applications for planning permission are made each year to local planning authorities in England and Wales, of which about 85 per cent are granted. This enormous spate of applications involves great strains on the local planning machinery which, generally speaking, is not adequately staffed to deal with them and at the same time undertake the necessary work involved in preparing and reviewing development plans. (There are less than 3,000 qualified planners [of whom many do not practise planning directly, or practise overseas]; by contrast there are 20,000 architects and 20,000 surveyors.) Yet full consideration by local planning staffs is needed if planning committees – the elected members who have the responsibility for granting or refusing applications – are to have the requisite information on which to base their decisions. The importance of this is underlined by the fact that planning committees often have remarkably little time during a meeting in which to come to a decision. Agendas for meetings tend to be long: an average of five to six minutes for consideration of each application is nothing unusual, and in some cases the time may be as little as two minutes.[10] It cannot, therefore, be surprising that in a large proportion of cases (in the bigger authorities at least) the recommendations of the planning officer are approved *pro forma*. This may, of course, result in part from the harmonious relationship which commonly exists between local authority representatives and their officers; and, in any case, lay members tend to accept the technical expertise of their officials, while, on the other hand, the officials well know the minds of their political masters. Yet the point remains that both the elected representatives and the planning officials are hard pressed to cope with the constant flood of applications. Several important implications follow from this. First, and most obvious, is the danger that decisions will be given which are 'wrong' – i.e. which do not accord with planning objectives. Secondly, good relationships with the public in general and unsuccessful applicants in particular are difficult to attain: there is simply not sufficient time. Thirdly, this lack of time corroborates the view of many (unsuccessful) applicants that their case has never had adequate consideration: a view which is further supported by the manner in which refusals are commonly worded. Phrases such as 'detrimental to amenity' or 'not in accordance with the development plan', and so on, mean little or nothing to the individual applicant.* He suspects that his case has been considered in general terms rather than in the particular detail which he naturally thinks is important in his case. And he may be right: understaffed and overworked planning departments cannot give each case the individual attention which is desirable.

This, of course, is not the whole picture. For instance, individuals who may wholly agree with a general planning principle will tend to see it in a different light when it is applied to their own applications. 'The man who has his home in one part of a green belt and owns what an estate agent would call "fully ripe building land" in another part, is as vociferous in relying on green belt principles to oppose building near his home as he is in denouncing the extreme and ridiculous lengths to which those principles have been carried when he is refused planning permission on his other land, and frequently he seems to achieve this without any conscious hypocrisy.'[8] This normal human failing is encouraged by the curious compromise situation which currently exists in relation to the control of land. On the one hand it seems to be generally accepted in principle (as it definitely is in law) that no one has a right to develop his land as he wishes unless the development is publicly desirable (as determined by a political instead of a financial decision). On the other hand, though the allocation of land to particular uses is determined by a public decision, the motives for private development are financial – and the financial profits which result from the development constitute private gain (though now subject to capital gains tax and betterment levy). This unhappy circumstance (which is discussed at length in Chapter VI) involves a clash of principles which the unsuccessful applicant

* The Ministry have repeatedly stressed the importance of giving unsuccessful applicants a reasoned explanation for the refusal of planning permission, e.g. 'It is not enough to say that a design will "injure the amenities" or "conflict with adjoining development"; it must be explained why it will do so.' *Selected Planning Appeals*, 2nd Series, Vol. 1, p. 3, HMSO, 1959; 'It is not sufficient to say that the display of an advertisement would be against the interests of amenity, or against the interests of public safety. In the former case it should be explained what is the amenity and how that amenity would be affected, and in the latter case it should be explained in what way safety would be imperilled,' MHLG *Circular* 38/58.

for planning permission experiences in a particularly sharp manner. It follows that local planning officials may have a peculiarly difficult task in explaining to a landowner why, for example, the field which he owns needs to be 'protected from development'.

Nevertheless, the success which attends this unenviable task does differ markedly between different local authorities. The question is not simply one of the great variations in potential land values in different parts of the country or in the relative adequacy of planning staffs. Though these are important factors there remains the less easily documented question of attitudes towards the public. All that can be said is that in some local authorities a great effort is made to assist and explain matters to an applicant, whereas in others the impression one gains is that of a bureaucratic machine which displays little patience and no kindness towards the individual applicant who does not understand 'planning procedures'.

DELEGATION TO OFFICERS

The 1968 Planning Act, which is discussed more fully later in this chapter, makes provision for the delegation to officers of planning decisions. This is in line with the recommendations of the Maud Report on *Management of Local Government*, the Mallaby Report on *Staffing of Local Government*, and the report of the *Management Study on Development Control.*

The background to this is that 70 per cent of all planning applications are of 'a simple nature'. The *Management Study on Development Control* found that a large proportion of these 'simple' applications were determined by a committee or by the council without presentation of details, without discussion and in accordance with the recommendations of the officers. They concluded that very many development control applications are already effectively delegated to officers for decision but are required to go through a formal procedure of ratification by a body of members. This creates unnecessary work for the local authority and unnecessary delay for the applicant.

Consideration was given to the possibility of a system which allowed for *approvals only* to be issued by a planning officer on certain clearly defined classes of application:

(*a*) Construction of one house in a residential area.
(*b*) Construction of blocks of private garages.
(*c*) Changes of use not conflicting with the development plan and not requiring advertising.
(*d*) Erection of temporary buildings and extension of existing temporary permissions.

(*e*) Construction of vehicular access on other than trunk roads.
(*f*) Construction of extensions to existing residential properties.

It was estimated that this would reduce by up to 50 per cent the number of cases needing to go to committee, 'would save committee time for more important work, would save a considerable amount of administrative work and time and would speed up the issue of decision notices to applicants'.

The Mallaby Committee added that greater delegation would provide more attractive and challenging official careers, and thus stimulate recruitment. In this way a better service would be rendered to the public.

The 1968 Act goes further than the proposals of the *Management Study*. It enables local authorities to delegate decisions on all kinds of planning application except those for listed building consent. The power is entirely discretionary: it is for local authorities to decide which officers, if any, should be given delegated powers and for which kinds of application. A decision of an officer exercising delegated powers has the same standing as one given by the Council itself.

This streamlining at the local level reflects the principle underlying the new legislation – that the planning system should be so organized that decisions are taken at the appropriate level. Thus the Ministry is responsible for broad policy issues, the local authority for local plans and officials for detailed administrative issues which do not warrant committee involvement. In this way a real attempt is being made to reduce the bureaucratic, cumbersome and unwieldy system which has been paralysing the machinery. The relationships with, and the service to, the public should improve considerably. But much will depend on the more subtle factors than formal rearrangements of power: an issue to which we return shortly.

MALADMINISTRATION AND THE OMBUDSMAN

Most legislation is based on the assumption that the organs of government will operate efficiently and fairly. This is not always the case, but, even if it were, provision has to be made for the citizen who feels aggrieved by some action (or inaction) to complain, have his complaint investigated and be satisfied that the investigation is impartial. As modern industrial society becomes more complex the pressures for a machinery of protest, appeal and restitution grow – as is evidenced in such widely differing fields as social security, race relations and press publicity.

At the Parliamentary level, the case for an Ombudsman was reluctantly conceded by Government, and a Parliamentary Commissioner for Administration (Sir Edmund Compton) was appointed in 1967. The Commissioner has not so far found a single case of 'bias or perversity' on the part of the civil service and he reports that he is satisfied that the problems which exist concern 'defective administration' rather than 'maladministration'. In 1968 he reported on 374 cases and found 38 cases where there had been elements of maladministration which had led to some measure of injustice.[16]

There is no doubt about the relief experienced at central government level by the innocuousness of the Commissioner's findings. More important, there has resulted a more favourable attitude to the need for an Ombudsman for local government. Indeed, at the time of writing, legislation on this is promised in the 1969–70 Parliamentary Session.

The activities of local government impinge upon the daily life of citizens more frequently and more directly than those of central government. The new local authorities which emerge from the reorganization of local government will undoubtedly (whatever plan is adopted) be larger and more powerful than most existing authorities. They will also inevitably be more remote, especially if, following the trend towards more efficient management, councillors concern themselves more with policy formulation and less with personal cases. This is particularly the case with town and country planning where there are now the powers for the delegation of decisions to officials.

As these trends continue, the character of local government will change and many issues of policy (not only within the field of 'town and country planning') will be seen for what they are: not technical issues to be settled by professionals but political issues to be settled by politicians responding to political processes, albeit with professional advice.

PLANNING APPEALS

An unsuccessful applicant for planning permission can, of course, appeal to the Minister, and as pointed out in Chapter III, a large number do so. Each case is considered by the Ministry on its merits. This allows a great deal of flexibility and permits cases of individual hardship to be sympathetically treated. But at the same time it can make the planning system seem arbitrary – at least to the unsuccessful appellant. Although there has been a recent trend towards the setting out of certain broad policies, the general view in the Ministry is that a reliance on precedent could easily give rise to undesirable rigidities. 'Conditions vary so fundamentally from case to case and from one part of the country to another that it would be impossible, if not wrong, to draft rules that would hold good uniformly. The basic problem is that a variety of factors operate in a planning case; the art of making a decision lies in the striking of a proper balance. Under the circumstances, there is little that the Ministry can do beyond listing those factors which it considers crucial, and expressing rules of thumb which will help select those which should preponderate.'[10]

Other issues relevant to this view are the traditional local-central government relationship (in which local authorities are considered as equal partners in the processes of government) and the particular character of town and country planning in this country. The flexibility of the development plan, the wide area of discretion legally allowed to the planners in the operation of planning controls, and the very restricted jurisdiction of the courts necessitates a judicial function for the Ministry. But this function is only quasi-judicial: decisions are taken not on the basis of legal rules as in a court of law or in accordance with case-law, but on a judgment as to what course of action is, in the particular circumstances and in the context of ministerial policy, desirable, reasonable and equitable. By its very nature this must be elusive, and the unsuccessful appellant may well feel justified in believing that the dice are loaded against him. The very fact that appeals are heard by ministerial 'inspectors' and (probably) in the town hall of the authority against whose decision he is appealing do not make for confidence in a fair and objective hearing. The contrast with the courts is striking:

'The usual complaint of the civil litigant is not that his case is not fairly and impartially heard and determined, but that, owing to the complexity of the system, the delay and expense are excessive. The views of the planning applicant, except when he is successful, are quite different. He rarely complains of the cost (though quite often of the delay) but frequently takes the view that the inquiry or hearing was nothing more than an opportunity for him to "let off steam".'[8]

It is not easy to suggest what can be done to improve this situation. Keeble, in his book *Town Planning at the Crossroads*, has argued that the basic fault lies in the inadequate and sketchy nature of town plans, as a consequence of which a very large proportion of planning applications relate to development which neither complies nor conflicts with the plan (e.g. a small group of shops in a residential area). In his view the preparation and approval of detailed plans would reduce both the work in dealing with applications and the number of appeals – since a far larger proportion of intending developers would know what would be permitted and what would be rejected. This is precisely the opposite view to that expressed so cogently in the Planning Advisory Group's Report on *The Future of Development Plans,* and now embodied in the 1968 Town and Country Planning Act.

Unfortunately the problem is not merely that of the inadequate 'lead' given by development plans: there is the further point that many plans are out of date. Local planning authorities have been so overwhelmed with development control that a great number of them have been unable to devote the necessary time to keeping their plans in line with changing conditions.

But, of course, part of the expressed dissatisfaction comes from those who are compelled to forgo private gain for the sake of communal benefit: the objections are not really against procedures, and they are not likely to be assuaged by administrative reforms or good 'public relations'. They are fundamentally objections against the public control of land use.

PUBLIC INQUIRIES

Public local inquiries figure largely in both the approval of development plans and in development control. It is, however, important to appreciate the nature and purpose of these inquiries.

Essentially all inquiries are held to allow objections to be raised. An inquiry on a development plan does not aim to provide an adequate examination of its merits: it is an inquiry into objections. The inquiry is not a means by which a local authority seeks to enlist public support for its plan: its very character (with its 'objectors' and 'witnesses') makes it inappropriate for this purpose. A good authority will do its utmost to inform the public and to obtain popular support; and it is usual for local authorities to attempt to meet objections – but all this is best done before the inquiry stage.

The nature of the inquiry involves the Ministry in more than merely considering the individual objections, which naturally usually relate to particular details of the plan rather than to its broad provisions. 'The public inquiry, therefore, has to be supplemented by an examination within the Department of such questions as whether the population for which the plan caters is in accord with probable developments; whether the allocation of land for various uses and purposes is sound and well balanced',[2] and so on. It follows that the Ministry can make substantial alterations to a plan. There is no legal requirement for a subsequent inquiry into such 'modifications', though 'where a proposal in a plan seems to the Minister misconceived but an alternative proposal would itself attract opposition, he has not infrequently deleted the proposal in the plan and asked for a new proposal to be submitted to him later, as an amendment of the plan. This enables him to hear objections to the new proposals before coming to a decision on it.' The Franks Committee thought that this was inadequate and maintained that it was desirable to introduce a procedure whereby those affected could express their views on all proposed modifications. This recommendation was accepted by the Government. A list of 'modifications' together with the reasons for proposing them is now sent to the local planning authority. These are then published and twenty-one days allowed for objections. The decision as to whether an inquiry should be held is taken by the Ministry 'on the circumstances of each case'.

Another change made following the Franks Report was the publication of inspectors' reports. This was a matter of considerable discussion during the proceedings of the Committee. One of the main arguments put forward by the Ministry of Housing opposing publication was that this would cause misunderstanding and embarrassment:

'The objection in principle that we would see to publication is that our inspectors really act in a dual capacity. They act first of all as the inspector who goes down to see the site and who, being a technical man, can give us an appreciation of the soundness of the authority's proposal; they hear the arguments and report to the Minister what took place, what impression it made upon them, what view they take of the site and so on. Then they make a recommendation and in that capacity they are acting as officers of the Department because their recommendation is essentially what should be the application of policy to the facts they found. That is why you can have identical facts but different decisions. They have got to be *au fait* with current policy and say what they think that the Minister, his policy being what it is, would wish to do in the particular case as they found it. We think that publication of the recommendation would cause embarrassment.'[2]

This passage clearly illustrates how a public inquiry is different from a judicial review. It is usual to apply the phrase 'quasi-judicial', but this is not very satisfactory, as the Franks Report implied. They saw the problem essentially as one of finding a reasonable balance between conflicting interests:

'On the one hand there are Ministers enjoined by legislation to carry out certain duties. On the other hand there are the rights and feelings of individual citizens who find their possessions or plans interfered with by the administration. There is also the public interest, which requires both that Ministers and other administrative bodies should not be frustrated in carrying out their duties and also that their decisions should be subject to effective checks or controls.'

The Franks Committee argued that inspectors' reports should be published, and this view was accepted by the Government. It is interesting to note that figures released in 1963 show that in the great majority of cases (on planning appeals) the Minister's decision has been 'broadly in line' with the recommendations of the inspector.

This is not the place to discuss all the issues relevant to these procedures: the interested reader is referred to the report of the Franks Committee. The immediate point is simply that neither the statutory provisions, nor the arguments on administrative inquiries, are concerned primarily with the encouragement of public participation in the planning process. To achieve this a local authority has to forge its own procedures. An account of the efforts of one (exceptional) authority is given later in this chapter. First, however, it is necessary to discuss the question of 'third parties'.

'THIRD PARTY' INTERESTS

The rights of 'third parties' – those affected by planning decisions but having no legal 'interest' in the land subject to the decision – were highlighted in the so-called Chalk Pit case.* This, in brief, concerned an application to 'develop' certain land in Essex by digging chalk. On being refused planning permission the applicants appealed to the Minister of Housing, and a local inquiry was held. Among those who appeared as objectors at the inquiry some were substantial landowners, including Major Buxton, whose land was adjacent to the appeal site and was being used for agricultural and residential purposes. The inspector's recommendation was that the appeal should be dismissed, mainly because there was a serious danger of chalk dust being deposited on the land of Major Buxton and others in quantities which would be 'detrimental to the user of the land'; and that there was no present shortage of chalk in the locality. The Minister disagreed with the inspector's recommendations and allowed the appeal. Major Buxton then appealed to the High Court, partly on the ground that in rejecting his inspector's findings of fact, the Minister had relied on certain subsequent advice and information given to him by the Minister of Agriculture

* *Buxton and Others* v. *Minister of Housing and Local Government* (1960), 3 W.L.R. 866. The account given here of this case is based on a summary contained in *Public Law*, Summer 1961, pp. 121–8.

without giving the objectors any opportunity of correcting or commenting upon this advice and information.* But Major Buxton now found that he had no legal right to appeal to the courts†: indeed he apparently had had no legal right to appear at the inquiry. (He only had what the judge thought to be a 'very sensible' administrative privilege.) In short, Major Buxton was a 'third party': he was in no legal sense a 'person aggrieved'. Yet clearly in the wider sense of the phrase Major Buxton was very much aggrieved, and at first sight he had a moral right to object and to have his objection carefully weighed. But should the machinery of town and country planning be used for this purpose by an individual? Before the town and country planning legislation any landowner could develop his land as he liked, provided he did not infringe the common law which was designed more to protect the right to develop rather than to restrain it. The law of nuisance and trespass was not a particularly strong constraint on the freedom to use land. But, as the judge stressed, the planning legislation was designed 'to restrict development for the benefit of the public at large and not to confer new rights on any individual members of the public'.

This, of course, is the essential point. It is the job of the local planning authority to assess the public advantage or disadvantage of a proposed development – subject to a review by the Minister if those having a legal interest in the land in question object. Third parties cannot usurp these Government functions. Nevertheless, it might be generally agreed that those affected by planning decisions should have the right to make representations for consideration by a planning committee.[20] The present position is that third parties have an 'administrative privilege' to appear at a public inquiry, but generally no similar privilege in relation to a planning application.

There is one group of exceptions to this. The Town and Country Planning Act of 1959 introduced a provision designed to give an opportunity for the public ventilation of objections to certain planning proposals of an 'unneighbourly' character. Such developments are advertised and objectors allowed to make written 'representations' to the local planning authority. If the planning application is granted there is no further opportunity for objections – however

* This issue has been the subject of considerable discussion, but cannot be dealt with here. See House of Lords Debates, vol. 230, cols. 740–4, April 20, 1961, Vol. 231, cols. 35–76, May 8, 1961, *Annual Reports of the Council on Tribunals*, 1961 and 1962, HMSO, and *Public Law*, loc. cit.

† Major Buxton later approached the Council on Tribunals. This Council was set up, following the Franks Report, to keep under review and report upon the constitution and working of administrative tribunals and to keep watch upon those administrative procedures which involve or may involve the holding of a statutory inquiry by or on behalf of a Minister of the Crown.

much the objectors may be affected. But, if the application is refused and the applicant appeals, the objectors have the normal privilege of appearing and being heard at the public inquiry. In short, the only new provision here is the requirement for publicity and the formal right to make representations. The types of development covered by these provisions are very limited – public conveniences, refuse disposal and sewerage works, slaughterhouses and theatres, dance halls, skating rinks, etc. It might be possible to extend this list somewhat (to include, for example, fish and chip shops and petrol stations), but to extend it to cover all applications would, quite apart from any objections on principle, lead to the danger of a breakdown in planning procedures. The machinery of planning is already overburdened with development applications and appeals. An extension of the opportunities for representations, objections and appeals would slow down procedures and make them dangerously cumbersome. This is a practical issue of importance, but the fundamental point is that it is the job of local planning authorities to assess what is publicly desirable. Measures designed to make the system open and fair are all to the good. Openness and fairness were two of the principles which the Franks Committee sought to apply to administrative tribunals and inquiries. Their third principle – impartiality – cannot be applied without qualification to planning procedures (as the Committee pointed out). If a local planning authority were merely a judicial body seeking to achieve a fair balance between conflicting private interests, many of the arguments for extending the rights of individuals to be heard and to object, could be accepted. But the local planning authority is not an impartial body: it is an agency of government attempting to secure what it believes to be the best development for its area. In short, it has a fundamentally political responsibility.

THE 1968 ACT AND PUBLIC PARTICIPATION

The 1968 Planning Act is a legislative landmark in the development of a new framework of planning designed to bring about a greater degree of citizen participation. The main stimulus for this has come, not from local authorities, but from the Ministry of Housing and Local Government. Under the old development plan system the Ministry was becoming crippled by what the former Permanent Secretary has called a crushing burden of casework. The concept of ministerial responsibility has been shown to be inapplicable over the total field of development plan approval and appeals against planning decisions. Not only is much of this work inappropriate to a central government department: its sheer weight has prevented the Ministry from fulfilling its essential functions – of establishing major planning policies. Under the new system much of the role of the Minister as the ultimate court of appeal is to be devolved on to local authorities. The Minister's function will be to review and formally approve the broad outlines of local planning policies and, eventually, to consider only those planning appeals which raise issues of ministerial policy.

The new system can be brought into full operation only when local government has been reorganized into units which are appropriate for the exercise of planning functions. But more than a reorganization of boundaries will be needed to make the system work: it demands a major change in the *practice* of local government. Citizen-participation is more than a desirable adjunct: it is an essential basis. If citizen-participation does not work, the system will collapse.

The 1968 Act provides only the barest skeleton of the new system – citizen-participation is much more than adherence to formal procedures. The Act merely provides that, in drawing up a structure plan a local authority must:

(i) give 'adequate publicity' to the report of the survey on which the plan is based, and to the policy which they propose to include in the plan;

(ii) provide publicity for their proposals and 'adequate opportunity' to enable representations to be made by the public;

(iii) take into account these representations in drawing up the structure plan;

(iv) place the plan on deposit for public inspection, together with a statement of the time within which objections may be made to the Minister;

(v) Submit the plan to the Minister, together with a statement of the steps which have been taken to comply with the above requirements, and of consultations which have been carried out with 'other persons'.

A local plan is drawn up within the policy framework of an approved structure plan and does not normally have to be submitted to the Minister for approval (though a copy has to be sent to him and exceptionally he can direct that it 'shall not have effect unless approved by him'). It follows the same procedure as a structure plan, but if there are any objections these are sent to the local authority (not the Minister) and are heard at a public inquiry which is held by an independent inspector who reports to the authority. The Minister will not normally be concerned with local plans (though he will presumably check that they do properly reflect the policy approved in the structure plans).

At first sight it might appear that local authorities are to be judges in their own case, particularly since there is provision for inspectors to be appointed by local authorities. Indeed, much has been made of this 'unfair judicial process'. But the fact is that the process is not a judicial one: it is essentially administrative and political. This is why citizen-participation is so crucial. If local authorities do not succeed in carrying their citizenry with them the new system will fail: public opposition will necessitate a move back to the previous system.

THE SKEFFINGTON REPORT

Concern with – and even interest in – citizen-participation has not been a particularly obvious strength of British local government and it will be even more difficult to achieve with the large authorities which are needed for effective planning. With little experience to build on it was perhaps inevitable that the Government should appoint a committee 'to consult and report on the best methods including publicity, of securing the participation of the public at the formative stage in the making of development plans for their area'. The Committee was set up, under the chairmanship of Mr Arthur Skeffington (Joint Parliamentary Secretary to the Minister of Housing and Local Government), in March 1968 and published its report *People and Planning* in July 1969.

The Skeffington Report made a number of rather obvious recommendations which do not carry us a great deal further, for example:

'people should be kept informed throughout the preparation of a structure or local plan for their area';
'local planning authorities should seek to publicize proposals in a way that informs people living in the area to which the plan relates';
'the public should be told what their representations have achieved or why they have not been accepted';
'people should be encouraged to participate in the preparation of plans by helping with surveys and other activities as well as by making comments'.

The mundane nature of many of the recommendations is testimony to the distance which British local government has to go in making citizen-participation a reality.

Unfortunately, the report does not discuss many of the really crucial issues, though passing references suggest that the Committee were aware of some of them. For instance, it is rightly stated that 'planning' is only one service 'and it would be unreasonable to expect the public to see it as an entity in itself'. The report continues: 'Public participation would be little more than an artificial abstraction if it became identified solely with planning procedures rather than with the broadest interests of people'. This has major implications for the internal organization and management of local authorities. So have the proposals for the appointment of 'community development officers . . . to secure the involvement of those people who do not join organizations' and for 'community forums' which would 'provide local organizations with the opportunity to discuss collectively planning and other issues of importance to the area', and which 'might also have administrative functions, such as receiving and distributing information on planning matters and promoting the formation of neighbourhood groups'.

What is conspicuously lacking in the whole debate on citizen-participation is its political implications. The Skeffington Report noted that it was feared that a community forum might become the centre of political opposition: but the only comment made was 'we hope that that would not happen; it seems unlikely that it would, as most local groups are not party political in their membership'. The issue is not, however, one of *party politics*: it is one of local policies, pressures and interests. Citizen-participation implies a transfer of some power from local councils to groups of electors. It is power which is the crucial issue – not in any sinister sense, but simply in terms of who is to decide local issues. The Ministry does not want to be concerned with these (except where they have ramifications over a larger front: hence central approval of structure plans). This will be a matter of intimate concern for local councillors – and officials as well.

The transfer of considerable statutory powers from central to local government will show only too clearly that planning is essentially a political process – a fact which has been confused by the semi-judicial procedures with which the Ministry has been so preoccupied.

None of this is to argue that the philosophy underlying the new legislation is misplaced: far from it. The intention is to demonstrate that the real problems of citizen-participation and local democratic control go far deeper than issues of formal procedures, of social surveys and public exhibitions. If the new system works it will have a major impact on British political processes; and it will not be confined to 'town and country planning'.

Curiously, it was not the Skeffington Committee but the Seebohm Committee (in their Report on *Local Authority and Allied Personal Social Services*) which highlighted another related issue (and one which the proposed community development officer would particularly face):

'the participants may wish to pursue policies directly at variance with the ideas of the local authorities and there is certainly a difficult link to be forged between the concepts of popular participation and traditional representative democracy. The role of the social worker in this context is likely to give rise to problems of conflicting loyalties. The Council for Training in Social Work suggest in evidence that if community work is to be developed by the local authority, then the authority "will need to recognize the fact that some of its staff may be involved in situations which lead to criticism of their services or with pressure groups about new needs. The workers themselves will need to be clear about their professional role and this will depend upon their training and the organizational structure within which they work". . . . Participation provides a means by which further consumer control can be exercised over professional and bureaucratic power.'

A further problem in citizen-participation is that of determining how representative are the views expressed by participating citizens. As the Skeffington Report implies, the views of 'the non-joiners and inarticulate' are as important as those of 'the actively interested and organized'. And as American experience shows, citizen participation can lead to strong demands to keep an area 'white', to exclude public authority housing, and to safeguard local amenities at a high cost to the larger community. It is not every community which is best placed to assess its needs in relation to a wider area.

Finally, reference needs to be made to the tricky problem of planning blight. The best way of avoiding this is to maintain the utmost secrecy until definite plans can be presented to the public as a *fait accompli*. Obviously this is not easy to reconcile with a greater degree of citizen-participation.

There is no easy answer to this. Indeed, the Skeffington Committee were probably right in saying that 'some increase in planning blight may have to be accepted if there is to be increased participation by the public'. Whether the compensation provisions for planning blight are adequate is another matter.

In the British scene it is likely that citizen-participation will be noteworthy for its gradual growth rather than its excesses. The essential ingredient is a concern on the part of elected members and professional staffs to make participation a reality. Here the experience of Coventry (which is now extensively documented in the Skeffington Report) is useful.

CITIZEN-PARTICIPATION: THE COVENTRY EXPERIENCE

'*Dear Citizen,*

THE PLANNING OF COVENTRY

An important task carried out by Coventry Corporation is town planning. Its aim is to ensure that the city shall have beauty and character, and be a convenient place in which to live and work. A plan was prepared in 1951 but a new plan is now being prepared to take into account changes that have taken place during the last ten years and those which are necessary for the development of Coventry during the next twenty years.

The Corporation is anxious that there should be the widest participation of citizens in the formulation of the new plan.'

So started a letter sent by the Coventry Planning Department to community organizations and head teachers in the City. Public meetings were held in every Ward, and local residents were invited to give their views on what was needed to be done in their localities. These were chaired by local people who were recognized as being independent of local politics. Elected representatives of the Ward, together with members of the Planning Committee and planning officials, attended each meeting. The Committee member explained the objective of the meeting and the official outlined the specific projects scheduled for the area in which the meeting was held. Members of the audience were then invited to ask questions on the plans and to make suggestions. A record was kept of all the items mentioned at each meeting and forwarded to every member of the Council and the chief officers.

These meetings attracted a great deal of public interest. Altogether twenty-eight meetings were held between September 1961 and February 1962 and were attended by about 1,100 people. Support was forthcoming from several organizations in the City, particularly the district Ratepayers' Associations, who themselves promoted discussions on planning problems and public improvements.

The full report of the meetings ran to over 200 foolscap pages. Major proposals were considered for incorporation in the Review of the Development Plan. Minor items were submitted to the appropriate Committee and a sum of £8,000 was earmarked to enable work to be carried out quickly on small schemes.

The type of proposals made is illustrated by the following extracts from the Report:

'Attention was drawn to the considerable amount of kerb-side parking in the Charterhouse area by tradesmen's vans and vehicles by workers in the BTH factory. It was suggested that the Council should provide parking facilities in the area in order to get these vehicles off the road. A large area at the top of Gosford Street was suggested for clearance in order to provide parking facilities.

'It was suggested that Gosford Green should be preserved as an amenity feature in the redevelopment schemes for the area.

'Attention was drawn to the bad state of street lighting in Far Gosford Street and in other small streets in the area. Concern was particularly expressed regarding those streets which carry a substantial volume of traffic.

'Concern was expressed at the number of gable-end type of houses which were being built on the Ernesford Grange Estate. Criticism was made of their boxlike appearance.

'Attention was drawn to the waste land in the vicinity of Churchill Avenue. Residents wanted to know whether the Corporation had any proposals for this, and it was thought that it was suitable for the building of garages.

'A children's playground was very badly needed in the Stoke Aldermoor area. An offer to raise money was made from members of the Stoke Aldermoor Social Club if the City Council would provide the land for the playground.'

In addition to the Ward Meetings, local associations were asked for their observations on, for example, deficiency of public buildings, lack of public services, visual untidiness, vandalism and the reconstruction of the city centre. Head teachers were invited to seek the ideas of school children on the planning of the city – particularly playgrounds, sports facilities, youth clubs and so on.

The annual 'Welcome to Citizenship Exhibition' was supplemented by a letter from the Planning Officer asking for ideas on the future planning of the city. (This exhibition is held for all who reach the age of twenty-one and become eligible for entry on the Electoral Register, and is aimed at explaining and illustrating the work of the various departments of the Corporation.)

Finally, an exhibition of future plans for the city was mounted in the Planning Office and the public were invited to enter an 'Ideas Competition', for which five prizes were awarded.*

The success of this venture would need independent appraisal. There were certainly difficulties. The lessons which the city learnt were†:

* Further details will be found in Appendix 3 to the Skeffington Report.

† I am grateful to Mr Terence Gregory, the City Architect and Planning Officer of Coventry, for the following.

(i) There is a tendency for people to become aligned with protest organizations before they have considered the full implications of a proposal within the totality of the Plan, thus inhibiting rational assessment of policy.

(ii) Modifications to meet objections, or compromises, can create equally important and often greater objections from those subsequently affected by the modification. (The 'sounder' the original proposal the greater are these objections likely to be.)

(iii) The processes of consultation and participation inevitably result in a lengthening of the administrative processes. Decision making is even further removed from the analysis of data. Even a continual review will not eliminate this.

(iv) The complexity of technical evidence (e.g. traffic data, analysis and assignments) presents problems of explanation and communication. There clearly has to be a professional assessment of the relevance and interpretation of complex technical data.

(v) It is essential that pressure groups (e.g. an amenity organization or ratepayers association) are not assumed to be representative of public opinion. Such a pressure group may make representations to expedite action which may be in the interests of one particular locality, or one particular element in environmental planning; but when such action is viewed within a total programme of priorities for the city as a whole, it may be premature or completely unjustified.

(vi) Participation and consultation are essential, but they do not and cannot result in everyone being satisfied, if only because some interests are mutually exclusive.

Finally, and somewhat sadly, though the Coventry venture aroused a great deal of interest it became very clear that 'the majority of the public are largely apathetic towards planning issues or are content to leave matters in the hands of the authority, provided that they themselves are not affected by proposals'.

What is significant in Coventry's approach was that they were not attempting to forestall 'objections' to firm plans, but seeking public participation in the planning process. It is noteworthy that the Coventry planners regard this as a vital and essential part of their work. There are at least three benefits to be gained.[21] First, there is the negative aspect of calming opposition and thus easing the problems of the planners. More important is the question of ascertaining the wishes of the electorate. This is by no means a simple matter. Wishes may cancel each other out, they may be contradictory, impracticable or completely utopian. And, in any case, the local authority must itself act as guardian and interpreter of the common good. Nevertheless, in so doing it should maintain a close relationship with the public it serves. Though ideally it should demonstrate its value of political leadership, it must always ensure that it does not get too far ahead of public opinion. On the other hand, a progressive authority can interpret its role in such a way as to exert a very considerable influence on the formation of public opinion.

Thirdly, an approach to planning which welcomes and encourages citizen-participation is a good thing in itself. In spite of the lip-service which is given to this, it is unfortunately true that citizen-participation is often regarded as a time-consuming and fruitless frill. This is far from being the case: if democratic planning is to cope with the mounting problems of a complex industrial and land-hungry society, it is essential that the public image of the planners should be improved. There is, of course, a definite limit to which 'government by participation' can replace 'government by consent', but an authority which can take the public into its confidence and enlist its support will thereby become a more effective planning agency. This demands a completely different outlook on the part of many planning authorities. To illustrate, at the 1963 conference of the Town and Country Planning Association a vice-chairman of one planning committee argued that though it was possible, it was also extremely difficult to obtain any useful advice from the average citizen group: 'Your local planner needs not to be a sensitive ear listening to the Townswomen's Guild or the Chamber of Commerce and this, that or the other. He needs to be a single-minded steam-roller.' In the final analysis the real problem is to find the balance between the advantages of increased public consultation and participation and the need for a reasonable speed in planning procedures. This might be achieved by defining the occasions on which consultations can produce the maximum benefit. If this is not done, the danger is that the planning machine might become so bogged down with citizen-participation that its effectiveness and efficiency would be seriously harmed.

Citizen-participation cannot be effective unless it is organized. This, of course, is one of the fundamental difficulties. Though a large number of people may feel vaguely disturbed in general about the operation of the planning machine (and particularly upset when they are individually affected), it is only a minority who are prepared to do anything other than grumble. The minority may be growing, and with the general rise in educational levels we can hope that it will continue to do so. It has to be recognized, however, that citizen-participation will, as far as can be seen, always be restricted: 'The activity of responsible social criticism is not congenial to more than a minority. Most of us for most of the time are content to remain complacently acquiescent in our social niche. . . . The activist, the social critic, the reformer will always be a small section of any society. Their activities require not only extra effort which few are willing to expend, but also the ability to criticize and organize which comparatively few possess.'[1]

The minority is, nevertheless, an important one, and as the success of the Consumers' Association and similar bodies has shown, it can be instrumental in activating widespread interest and support (even if this stops short of actual participation). A little official encouragement might have surprisingly widespread effects. At the local level this could be on the lines suggested by the Coventry experiment. At the national level it might take the form of government financial assistance towards the administrative overheads of a central agency – as is done with the Civic Trust and the National Federation of Housing Societies. But the leadership role and concern for wider community interests must always remain the responsibility of the local authority.

IN CONCLUSION

The debate on citizen-participation (like that on local government reorganization and regional devolution) raises the fundamental question of whether the machinery of government is deploying its resources in the most effective way. The issue is important not only in the interests of the mental health of the central administration, but also because their over-commitment with detailed aspects of planning and issues which are of purely local concern means that there are insufficient human resources left for a consideration of the broader planning issues which should be their particular responsibility. Fogarty in his book *Under-Governed and Over-Governed* has put this argument in general terms. Ministers, top managers and trade union leaders, he argues, 'have over-committed themselves to settling detailed problems, and as a result have left themselves with too little time and energy to deal competently with the broader issues of overall government and management. By doing so they have also defeated even their immediate purpose and have made it harder to find sound solutions even to problems of detail.' Town and country planning 'has fiddled with details. But it has succeeded neither in promoting timely action over such major features of regional development as the reshaping of the older conurbations or the building of new motorways, nor in creating a satisfactory urban landscape in newly developing areas, nor in bringing home to people in particular localities what they themselves might do to improve their neighbourhood amenities on the lines of the well-known schemes of the Civic Trust.'

The argument does not have to be accepted in full for its major point to be appreciated. Now that regional planning is beginning to move into the realm of practical politics, it is becoming increasingly important to reduce the amount of effort consumed by details. Broad regional policy-making is a more fitting task for central government then considering appeals on the design of suburban bungalows. It is in this context that the question of public support and citizen-participation needs to be considered. In the long run it may well prove to be a fundamental issue in adapting the planning machine to meet the problem of the second half of the twentieth century. The issue is now recognized at central government level and it is entering the debate on local government reorganization. The 1968 Planning Act represents a bold step towards a realignment of political forces in the field of town and country planning. If it succeeds it will not stop there.

REFERENCES AND FURTHER READING

1 Broady, M., 'Social Change and Town Development', in *Planning for People*, National Council of Social Service, Bedford Square Press, 1968.

2 Committee on Administrative Tribunals and Enquiries (Franks Committee): *Minutes of Evidence and Memoranda Submitted by Government Departments*, Vol. 2, HMSO, 1956.

3 Committee on Local Authority and Allied Personal Services, *Report* (Seebohm Report), Cmnd. 3703, HMSO, 1968.

4 Committee on Public Participation in Planning, *People and Planning* (Skeffington Report), HMSO, 1969.

5 Council on Tribunals, *Annual Reports*, HMSO.

6 Coventry City Council, *First Quinquennial Review of the Development Plan: Report on Ward Meetings*, September 1962.

7 Essex County Planning Department, *Development Control Procedures*, May 1963.

8 Grove, G. A., 'Planning and the Applicant', *Journal of the Town Planning Institute*, Vol. 49, May 1963, p. 130.

9 Keeble, L., *Town Planning at the Crossroads*, Estates Gazette.

10 Mandelker, D. R., *Green Belts and Urban Growth*, University of Wisconsin Press, 1962.

11 MHLG, *The Future of Development Plans*, HMSO, 1965.

12 MHLG, *Management of Local Government* (Maud Report), HMSO, 1967.

13 MHLG, *Management Study on Development Control*, HMSO, 1967.

14 MHLG, *Staffing of Local Government* (Mallaby Report), HMSO, 1967.

15 National Commission on Urban Problems, *Building the American City*, US Government Printing Office, 1969.

16 *Parliamentary Commissioner for Administration, Second Report*, H.C. Paper 129, Session 1968/69, HMSO, 1969.

17 Reynolds, J. P., 'Public Participation in Planning', *Town Planning Review*, Vol. 40, No. 2, July 1969, pp. 131–48.

18 Robson, W. A., *The Governors and the Governed*, Allen & Unwin, 1964.

19 Select Committee on the Parliamentary Commissioner for

Administration, Session 1968–9, *Report*, H.C. Paper 385, HMSO, 1969 (MHLG Evidence, pp. 112–21).

20 Silkin, Lord, 'Third Party Interests in Planning', *Report of the Proceedings of the Town and Country Planning Summer School, 1962*, Town Planning Institute, pp. 40–9.

21 Slayton, W. L. and Dewey, R., 'Urban Redevelopment and the Urbanite', in Woodbury, C. (editor), *The Future of Cities and Urban Redevelopment*, University of Chicago Press, 1953.

Appendix: Some Illustrative Appeal Decisions

ERECTION OF HOUSES ON AN EXISTING ESTATE WHERE FURTHER DEVELOPMENT WAS UNDESIRABLE

'The appellants applied for permission for the erection of ten pairs of semi-detached houses on a site which was situated 1½ miles from a borough in a southern county and which formed part of an existing housing estate erected just before the war.

The estate consisted of some sixty houses which had been built on either side of the one estate road, which jutted straight out into the countryside from a trunk road. Surrounding land to the south, east and west was agricultural. Westwards along the main road there was a small group of houses, a public house and a restaurant. Opposite the junction of the estate road and the main road was a factory, and a little to the east, where the main road crossed a railway, were some six or seven cottages.

The appellants' proposals represented the completion of the estate road in the manner originally permitted by the pre-war planning authority. The Council gave permission for the erection of two of the houses in order to fill undeveloped plots between existing houses, but considered that any extension of the development would be undesirable.

The Council stated that the development was permitted in 1938 as part of the area then zoned for residential development, but that it had since been found advisable to re-plan in order to give effect to the proposals of the Greater London Plan. They contended that the proposal would be harmful to farming interests, since the extension of the estate southwards would sever a considerable area of agricultural land lying to the east and west of it; development would also add to the potential dangers of a very busy trunk road. While the Council considered that the development was unrelated to any existing or proposed development area, the appellants contended that the development, already carried out, together with that to the east, provided a well-sited and suitable community area, and that there was nothing to suggest that the area should not be satisfactorily completed.

The Minister agreed with the Council that the estate was an undesirable type of development, since it was an intrusion of housing into purely agricultural land and some distance from the nearest shops, schools and other necessary services. In those circumstances, he considered that, while infilling could be justified, any extension of the estate should not be permitted and he upheld the Council's decision.'*

DEVELOPMENT IN RESIDENTIAL AREAS†

'(1) The North Birmingham Branch of the British Legion proposed to use for their headquarters, a large three-storey Victorian house at 31 Trinity Road, Birmingham. They said that their present headquarters in a neighbouring street had been compulsorily purchased by the Council and were to be demolished with other adjoining properties to make way for Council flats. The Council would not extend the lease or provide other accommodation, and the branch was faced with extinction after thirty-four years. They had been offered the appeal premises, which were ideal for their purposes, only after countless inquiries. The ground floor would be used for social purposes, the first floor as committee rooms, and the top flat as living accommodation for a caretaker.

The Council acknowledged the good work done by the appellants, but said that the premises were suitable for living accommodation, either for single family occupation or for conversion into three or four flats. There was an acute shortage of houses in the city and the loss of this accommodation was unjustified.

The Minister thought that the house was well suited to the needs of the appellants, and that it would be unfortunate if the branch had to close for lack of premises. Since they had to leave their present building because it was required for redevelopment, he came to the conclusion that they ought to be given permission for the proposed development.

The appeal was allowed.'

'(2) Beginning in 1907, the appellants had developed on garden suburb lines an estate of fifty-four acres at Harborne. The estate contained shops, a club building with the company's office, tennis courts, and a dance hall about 63 feet long by 30 feet wide. The appellants said that they would have liked to retain the hall as a social centre, but its use had declined steadily in recent years. Largely owing to an increase in rates and the opening of another hall with better transport facilities which had taken away business, it was running at a loss, and they therefore sought to change the use of

* Ministry of Housing and Local Government, *Bulletin of Selected Appeal Decisions, No. XI*, September 1952, pp. 4–5.

† These two cases are taken from Ministry of Housing and Local Government, *Selected Planning Appeals, Second Series, Volume 1*, June 1959, pp. 22–3.

their hall to professional offices. There would be no change in the external appearance of the building and the tenant would be carefully selected. There was no question of other applicants as the rest of the estate consisted of small houses. Residents in the vicinity did not object to the proposed change: some of them had complained of the noise when dances were held.

The Council said that this was a pleasant residential area and the intrusion of commercial uses should be resisted for the sake of local amenities. The hall was designed and built for social purposes, and its conversion to an office would mean the loss of a very useful social centre.

The Minister said that he appreciated the difficulties confronting the appellants, but the introduction of the proposed office use into this pleasant residential area would affect amenities, and he considered that he would not be justified in allowing it without considerably more evidence than had yet been offered that the hall could no longer serve a useful social purpose or be run without loss.

The appeal was dismissed.'

INDEX

www.ingramcontent.com/pod-product-compliance
Lightning Source LLC
LaVergne TN
LVHW090804070826
844660LV00022B/1074

* 9 7 8 1 4 4 2 6 3 9 6 0 7 *